Houses that Change the World

The Return of the House Churches

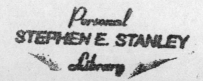

Houses that Change the World

The Return of the House Churches

Wolfgang Simson

OM
publishing

Original title: Häuser, die Welt verändern

Copyright © 1999, C & P Publishing, Emmelsbüll, Germany
www.CundP.de
Printed 2001 by OM Publishing
Reprinted 2001 (twice), 2002
Reprinted 2003 (twice) by Authentic Lifestyle

09 08 07 06 05 04 03   11 10 9 8 7 6

Authentic Lifestyle is an imprint of Authentic Media,
PO Box 300, Carlisle, Cumbria CA3 0QS, UK
and PO Box 1047, Waynesboro, GA 30830-2047, USA
http://www.paternoster-publishing.com

British Library Cataloguing-in-Publication Data
A catalogue record for this book is available from the British Library

ISBN 1–85078–356–X

Cover design by Diane Bainbridge
Typeset by WestKey Ltd, Falmouth, Cornwall
Printed and bound in Great Britain by
Cox & Wyman Ltd, Reading, Berkshire

Contents

Comments

A far more significant book than I expected. It challenges many sacred cows, demonstrates remarkable biblical, theological and strategic insight. The whole church needs to hear what Wolfgang Simson has to say in this seminal work.

Prof. Kenneth B. Mulholland,
Dean, Columbia Bible Seminary

A very important emphasis on ecclesiology, which I believe the Lord is impressing on His church in these days. A remarkable job.

Ernie Addicot, Interdev, UK

I just kept finding myself saying: That's what I believe!
Daniel A. Brown, Senior Pastor,
The Coastlands Aptos Foursquare Church, USA

I read the first pages of the book and my heart was beating so fast I thought I was getting tachycardia.
Dr Dan Trotter, editor of *New Reformation Review*
and Associate Professor of Business Administration,
Hartsville, USA

This is pure gold!
Robert Fitts, author of *The Church in The House*, Hawaii

A monumental and marvelous piece of work! It is going to be a very important contribution to the present situation faced by the church.

Ralph Neighbour, author of
Where do we go from Here?

Really superb, excellent stuff! This book has a phenomenal amount of truth, and has a lot to contribute into the debate concerning the shapes and models of church for the future.

Roger Ellis, Revelation Church,
Chichester, UK

I have actually read this book from cover to cover, something which I haven't done with any Christian book in years except Philip Yancey's What's so amazing about Grace?

Chris Schneider, Servants/Onesimus,
Philippines

Great book! I was a Pastor in the Reformed Church in Switzerland for six years, and can agree with a lot from my own experience.

Matthias Schuurmann,theology teacher,
Windhoek, Namibia

An excellent book, which goes to the heart of the structure problem in our perception of the church. I completely agree with the analysis and much appreciate the book and its message.

Patrick Johnstone, WEC,
London

How this book echoes in my heart!

Tony Black, Reconciliation International,
Scotland

Very challenging and extremely important.

Kai S. Scheunemann, Wiesbaden,
Germany

Hits on a very significant topic sure to be a vital element in the explosion of the church around the world. Tremendous amount of great material. The vision and scholarship of this book are surely the wave of the future. This book is on the cutting edge of things to come. There is no question that if we are going to fill the earth with the knowledge of the glory of the Lord with millions of new congregations we will have to return to the New Testament model presented here.

James Montgomery,
Founder and President,
DAWN Ministries,
Colorado Springs, USA

Comments

The Carmeliters have always known that a group of more than 20 people cannot have real fellowship. You can avoid each other too easily. If church wants to survive, she needs new and effective forms. That is what house churches can provide.

> Jakobus Richter,
> Mühlrad, Germany

Most interesting and very revolutionary. Very worth reading.

> Magde S. Bowes,
> Editor, *The Believer*,
> Vancouver, Canada

A unique study, carefully studying New Testament examples of church-planting.

> Wes Wilson, Vice President,
> Every Home for Christ,
> Colorado Springs, USA

Inspiring! Forced me to rethink some of my convictions.

> Michael Strub, Mission Leader,
> Asia

Ground-breaking! So new and fresh that, to the average reader, it will be quite revolutionary.

> Clive W. Clayton,
> Belgian Evangelical Mission,
> Brussels

I was thoroughly gripped by this book.

> Nic Harding, senior church leader,
> Liverpool, UK

A very good and highly relevant book, excellent work. Written in a challenging style and spirit, but still remains balanced and mature.

> Berthold Becker,
> Intercessors for Germany

Very interesting reading. God is doing something incredibly significant across the world – that's why, in a way, this book comes as no big surprise.

> Andrew Parham, Leadership Team,
> Ichthus Fellowship,
> London, UK

Enjoyed this book heartily. Forthright and passionate, but does not put down those coming from a different position. The analysis of the difference between cell church and house church is the best that I have read.

Dr Robert Banks,
Fuller Theological Seminary,
Pasadena, USA

House churches seem to be tailor-made for today's Generation X.

lrich Salvisberg, former Pastor
and Co-ordinator, Explo 97

Prophetically shocking! An incredible amount of work, hitting on many of the crucial issues facing the church today. A very challenging and stimulating book.

Robert Mountford,
City Vision, UK

Totally agree with the assessment of the Constantinian Church. What also strikes me as absolutely right is the issue of the church having to become more persecution-proof. This is the absolute opposite of the state church that gives you security as long as you are obedient.

Björn Larsson, Priest,
Church of Sweden

Wow! This book challenges our understanding of church and how it's done. I strongly recommend this book to every pastor and church leader.

Eddie Smith, Co-ordinator,
US Prayer Track,
AD2000 & Beyond Movement

This is one of the most significant books that I have seen for a long time.

Peter Brierley,
Christian Research, UK

This book is prophetic and may be too early for many people. It is a must for those involved in leadership, and highly recommended for those involved in frontier missions.

Maarten Bruynes,
Leader of FMC,
YWAM Holland

I am very sure this book will be of great service to the expansion of God's kingdom.

David Lim,
Manila

To be honest, I have given up on all those new church fads and Christian waves. But this thing about house churches excites me deep down. I have hoped for this type of church to become a reality all my Christian life. I can't believe it might come true! I am so excited I could cry.

Computer Programmer,
Switzerland

This might actually work!

Pharmacist,
Switzerland

Something simple, yet dynamic. That is what I have always hoped the church to be.

Medical doctor,
Switzerland

I have been 40 years in ministry. Now, after finding out about house churches, I feel I have climbed the ladder, only to realize that it has been leaning against the wrong wall.

Mission leader,
India

This is exactly the type of church I have seen in action, and what the Holy Spirit has revealed to us, before the missionaries came.

Woman,
Mongolia

I was blessed, edified and excited, as I read this book. It truly grasps the radical essence of New Testament Christianity.

Pastor Barry Kirk,
Tilehurst Free Church (Baptist),
Reading, UK

Preface: A vision too good to be true?

A church that not only has a message, but *is* a message

Being brought up in 'Christian' Germany with churches everywhere, I always felt that there must be something exciting about the community which Jesus started and about which I read in the New Testament – but somehow I could never discover what it was. Together with many friends and colleagues, I dreamed of a community that is as simple as One–Two–Three, yet is dynamic; an explosive thing, able to turn the world and a neighbourhood upside-down. The church as a super-natural invention, endowed with God's gift of immortality; a means to disciple each other, and to make the life of Jesus rub off on each other. An experience of grace and grapes, love and laughter, joy and jellybeans, forgiveness and fun, power and – yes, why not? – paper.

An experience of grace and grapes, love and laughter, joy and jelly-beans, forgiveness and fun, power and – yes, why not? – paper.

A church, which does not need huge amounts of money, or rhetoric, control and manipulation, which can do without powerful and charismatic heroes, which is non-religious at heart, which can thrill people to the core, make them lose their tongues out of sheer joy and astonishment, and simply teach us The Way to live. A church which not only has a message, but is the message. Something which spreads like an unstoppable virus, infects whatever it touches, and ultimately covers the earth with the glory and knowledge of God. A church whose power stems from its inventor, who has equipped it with the most ingenious spiritual genetical code, a sort of heavenly DNA, which allows it to transfer kingdom values from heaven to earth and to reproduce them here. In the process it transforms not only water into wine, but atheists into apostles, policewomen into prophetesses, terrorists into teachers, plumbers into pastors, and dignified village elders into beaming evangelists.

The church I dreamed of is like a spiritual extended family – organic, not organized, relational, not formal. It has a persecution-proof structure. It matures under tears, multiplies under pressure, breathes under water, grows under the carpet; it flourishes in the desert, sees in the dark and thrives in the midst of chaos. A church that can multiply like five loaves and two fish in the hands of Jesus, where the fathers turn their hearts to their sons and the sons their

> *It matures under tears, multiplies under pressure, breathes under water, grows under the carpet; it flourishes in the desert, sees in the dark and thrives in the midst of chaos.*

hearts to their fathers, where its people are its resources, and which has only one name to boast about, the Lamb of God.

God is changing the church, and that, in turn, will change the world. Millions of Christians around the world are aware of an imminent reformation of global proportions. They are saying, in effect: 'Church as we know it is preventing Church as God wants it.' Amazingly, many are hearing God say the very same thing to them. There is a new collective awareness of an age-old revelation, a corporate spiritual echo. In the following 15 theses I will summarize a part of this, and I am convinced that it reflects a part of what the Spirit of God is saying to the church today. For some, it might be the proverbial fist-sized cloud in Elijah's sky. Others already feel the pouring rain.

Fifteen Theses towards a Re-Incarnation of Church

1 Christianity is a way of life, not a series of religious meetings

Before they were called Christians, followers of Christ were called 'The Way'. One of the reasons was that they had literally found the way to live. The nature of church is not reflected in a constant series of religious meetings led by professional clergy in holy places specially reserved to experience Jesus. Rather, it is the prophetic way followers of Christ live their everyday life in spiritual extended families, as a vivid answer to the questions that society asks, and in the place where it counts most – in their homes.

2 Time to change the 'cathegogue system'

The historic Orthodox and Catholic Church after Constantine in the fourth century developed and adopted a religious system based on two elements: a Christian version of the Old Testament temple – the cathedral – and a worship pattern styled after the Jewish synagogue. They thus adopted, as the foundational pattern for the times to follow, a blueprint for Christian meetings and worship which was neither expressly revealed nor ever endorsed by God in New Testament times: the 'cathegogue', linking the house-

The Free Churches freed the system from the State, the Baptists then baptized it, the Quakers dry-cleaned it, the Salvation Army put it in uniform, the Pentecostals anointed it and the Charismatics renewed it, but until today nobody has really changed the system.

of-God mentality and the synagogue. Baptized with Greek pagan philosophy, separating the sacred from the secular, the cathegogue system developed into the Black Hole of Christianity, swallowing most of its society-transforming energies and inducing the church to become absorbed with itself for centuries to come. The Roman Catholic Church went on to canonize the system. Luther reformed the content of the gospel, but left the outer forms of 'church' remarkably untouched. The Free Churches freed the system from the State, the Baptists then baptized it, the Quakers dry-cleaned it, the Salvation Army put it in uniform, the Pentecostals anointed it and the Charismatics renewed it, but until today nobody has really changed the system. The time to do that has now arrived.

3 The third Reformation

In rediscovering the gospel of salvation by faith and grace alone, Luther started to reform the church through a reformation of theology. In the eighteenth century, through movements in the pietistic renewal, there was a recovery of a new intimacy with God, which led to a reformation of spirituality, the Second Reformation. Now God is touching the wineskins themselves, initiating a Third Reformation, a reformation of structure.

4 From church houses to house churches

From the time of the New Testament there has been no such thing as 'a house of God'. At the cost of his life,

Stephen reminded us: God does not live in temples made by human hands. The church is the people of God. The church, therefore, was and is at home where people are at home: in ordinary houses. There the people of God share their lives in the power of the Holy Spirit, have 'meatings', i.e. they eat when they meet; they often do not even hesitate to sell private property and share material and spiritual blessings; they teach each other in real-life situations how to obey God's word – and not with professorial lectures but dynamically, with dialogue and questions and answers. There they pray and prophesy with each other, and baptize one another. There they can let their masks drop and confess their sins, regaining a new corporate identity through love, acceptance and forgiveness.

5 The church has to become small in order to grow large

Most churches of today are simply too big to provide real fellowship. They have too often become 'fellowships without fellowship'. The New Testament church was made up of small groups, typically between 10 and 15 people. It grew not by forming big congregations of 300 people to fill cathedrals and

The traditional congregational church as we know it is, by comparison, a sad compromise: neither big nor beautiful, an overgrown house church and an undergrown celebration, often missing the dynamics of both.

lose fellowship. Instead, it multiplied 'sideways', dividing like organic cells, once these groups reached around 15 to 20 people. This then made it possible for all the Christians to get together into city-wide celebrations, as in Solomon's Temple court in Jerusalem. The traditional congregational church as we know it is, by comparison, a sad compromise: neither big nor beautiful, an overgrown house church and an undergrown celebration, often missing the dynamics of both.

6 No church is led by a pastor alone

The local church is not led by a pastor, but fathered by an elder, a man of wisdom and engaged with reality. The local house churches are then networked into a movement by the combination of elders and members of the so-called fivefold ministries (apostles, prophets, pastors, evangelists and teachers) circulating 'from house to house', like the circulation of the blood. Here there is a special foundational role to play for the apostolic and prophetic ministries (Eph. 2:20; 4:11:12). A pastor (shepherd) is an important member of the whole team, but he cannot fulfil more than a part of the whole task of 'equipping the saints for the ministry', and he has to be complemented synergistically by the other four ministries in order to function properly.

7 The right pieces – fitted together in the wrong way

In the Christian world we have all the right pieces, but we have fitted them together in the wrong way, because of fear, tradition, religious jealousy and a power-and-control mentality.

To do a jigsaw puzzle, we have to put the pieces together according to the original pattern, otherwise the final product, the whole picture, turns out wrong, and the individual pieces do not make any sense. In the Christian world we have all the right pieces, but we have fitted them together in the wrong way, because of fear, tradition, religious jealousy and a power-and-control mentality. Just as water is found in three forms – ice, water and steam – so too the five ministries mentioned in Ephesians 4:11, 12 – the apostles, prophets, pastors, teachers and evangelists – are found today, but not always in the right forms and in the right places. They are often frozen to ice in the rigid system of institutionalized Christianity; they sometimes exist as clear water; or they have vanished like steam into the thin air of free-flying ministries and 'independent' churches, accountable to no one. Just as it is best to water flowers with the fluid version of water, these five equipping ministries will have to be transformed back into new – and at the same time age-old – forms, so that the whole spiritual organism can flourish and the individual 'ministers' can find their proper role and place in the whole. That is one more reason why we need to return to the Maker's original blueprint for the Church.

8 Out of the hands of bureaucratic clergy and on towards the priesthood of all believers

No expression of a New Testament church is ever led by just one professional 'holy man' doing the business of communicating with God and then feeding some relatively passive, religious consumers, Moses-style. Christianity has adopted this method from pagan religions, or at best from the Old Testament.

The heavy professionalization of the church since Constantine has been a pervasive influence long enough, dividing the people of God artificially into an infantilized laity and a professional clergy, and developing power-based mentalities and pyramid structures. According to the New Testament (1 Tim. 2:5), 'there is one God, and one mediator also between God and men, the man Christ Jesus'. God simply does not bless religious professionals to force themselves in between Himself and His people.

The veil is torn, and God is allowing people to access Himself directly through Jesus Christ, the only Way.

To enable the priesthood of all believers, the present system will have to change completely. Bureaucracy is the most dubious of all administrative systems, because it basically asks only two questions: yes or no. There is no room for spontaneity and humanity, no room for real life. This may be all right in politics and business, but not the church. God seems to be in the business of delivering His church from a Babylonian captivity of religious bureaucrats and controlling spirits into the public domain, putting it into the hands of ordinary people whom God has made extraordinary and who, as in the old days, may still smell of fish, perfume or revolution.

9 Return from organized to organic forms of Christianity

What has become a maximum of organization with a minimum of organism, has to be changed into a minimum of organization to allow a maximum of organism.

The 'Body of Christ' is a vivid description of an organic being, not an organized mechanism. Church consists, at the local level, of a multitude of extended spiritual families, which are organically related to each other as a network. The way these communities function together is an integral part of the message of the whole. What has become a maximum of organization with a minimum of organism, has to be changed into a minimum of organization to allow a maximum of organism. Too much organization has, like a straitjacket, often choked the organism for fear that something might go wrong. Fear is the opposite of faith, and not exactly a Christian virtue. Fear wants to control; faith can trust. Control, therefore, may be good, but trust is better. The body of Christ is entrusted by

God into the hands of steward-minded people with a special charismatic gift to believe that God is still in control, even if they are not. Today we need to develop regional and national networks based on trust, not a new arrangement of political ecumenism, for organic forms of Christianity to re-emerge.

10 From worshipping our worship to worshipping God

The image of much contemporary Christianity could be summarized as holy people coming regularly to a holy place on a holy day at a holy hour to participate in a holy ritual led by a holy man dressed in holy clothes for a holy fee. Since this regular performance-oriented enterprise called 'worship service' requires a lot of organizational talent and administrative bureaucracy, formalized and institutionalized patterns developed quickly into rigid traditions. Statistically, a traditional one- or two-hour 'worship service' is very resource-hungry but produces very little fruit in terms of discipling people, i.e. in changing their lives. Economically, it is a 'high input, low output' structure. Traditionally, the desire to worship 'in the right way' has led to much denominationalism, confessionalism and nominalism. This not only ignores the fact that Christians are called to worship 'in spirit and in truth', rather than in cathedrals holding songbooks. It also ignores the fact that most of life is informal, and so too is Christianity as 'the Way of Life'. Do we need to change from being powerful actors and start acting powerfully?

11 Stop bringing people to church, and start bringing the church to the people

The church is changing back from being a Come-structure to being a Go-structure. As a result, the church needs to

stop trying to bring people 'to church', and start bringing
the church to the people. The mission of the church will
never be accomplished just by adding to the existing
structure. It will take nothing less than a mushrooming of
the church through spontaneous multiplication into areas
of the world where Christ is not yet known.

12 Rediscovering the Lord's Supper as a real supper with real food

Church tradition has managed to celebrate the Lord's
Supper in a homeopathic and deeply religious form,
characteristically with a few drops of wine, a tasteless
cookie and a sad face. However, the Lord's Supper was
actually more a substantial supper with a symbolic meaning, than a symbolic supper with a substantial meaning.
God is restoring eating back into our meeting.

13 From denominations to city-wide celebrations

Jesus called a universal movement, and what came was a
series of religious corporations with global chains market-
ing their special brands of Christianity and competing
with each other. Through this branding of Christianity
most of Protestantism has lost its voice in the world and
become politically insignificant, more concerned with
traditional distinctives and religious infighting than with
developing a collective testimony before the world. Jesus
simply never asked people to organize themselves into
factions and denominations, and Paul spoke of it as
'worldly', a sign of baby Christians.

In the early days of the church, Christians had a dual
identity: they were truly His church and vertically converted to God, and they then organized themselves
according to geography, that is, converting also

Fifteen Theses xxiii

horizontally to each other on earth. This means not only Christian neighbours organizing themselves into neighbourhood or house churches, where they share their lives locally, but Christians coming together as a collective identity as much as they can for city-wide or regional celebrations expressing the corporateness of the church of the city or region. Authenticity in the neighbourhoods connected with a regional or city-wide corporate identity will make the church not only politically significant and spiritually convincing, but will allow a return to the biblical model of the city church, the sum total of all born-again Christians of a city or an area.

14 *Developing a persecution-proof spirit*

They crucified Jesus, the leader of all the Christians. Today, His followers are often more into titles, medals and social respectability, or, worst of all, they remain silent and are not worth being noticed at all. 'Blessed are you when you are persecuted,' says Jesus. Biblical Christianity is a healthy threat to pagan godlessness and sinfulness, a world overcome by greed, materialism, jealousy and any amount of demonic standards of ethics, sex, money and power. Contemporary Christianity in many countries is simply too harmless and polite to be worth persecuting. But as Christians again live out New Testament standards of life and, for example, call sin as sin, the natural reaction of the world will be, as it always has been, conversion or persecution. Instead of nesting comfortably in temporary zones of religious liberty, Christians will have to prepare to be again discovered as the main culprits standing in the way of global humanism, the modern slavery of having to have fun and the outright worship of Self, the wrong centre of the universe. That is why Christians will and must feel the 'repressive tolerance' of a world which has lost its absolutes and

therefore refuses to recognize and obey its creator God with
His absolute standards. Coupled with the growing
ideologization, privatization and spiritualization of politics
and economics, Christians will – sooner than most think –
have their chance to stand happily accused in the company
of Jesus. They need to prepare now for the future by developing a persecution-proof spirit and an even more persecution-proof structure.

15 The Church comes home

Where is the easiest place for a person to be spiritual? Is it,
perhaps, hiding behind a big pulpit, dressed up in holy
robes, preaching holy words to a faceless crowd, and then
disappearing into an office? And what is the most difficult
– and therefore most meaningful – place for someone to be
spiritual? At home, in the presence of their spouse and
children, where everything they do and say is automatically put through a spiritual litmus test against reality,
where hypocrisy can be effectively weeded out and
authenticity can grow. Much of Christianity has fled the
family, often as a place of its own spiritual defeat, and then
has organized artificial performances in sacred buildings
far from the atmosphere of real life. As God is in the business of recapturing the homes, the church turns back to its
roots – back to where it came from. It literally comes home,
completing the circle of church history at the end of world
history.

As Christians of all walks of life, from all denominations
and backgrounds, feel a clear echo in their spirit to what
God's Spirit is saying to the church, and start to hear globally in order to act locally, they begin to function again as
one body. They stop asking God to bless what they are
doing – and start doing what God is blessing. They

organize themselves into neighbourhood house churches and meet in regional or city celebrations. You are invited to become part of this movement and make your own contribution. Maybe your home, too, will become a house that changes the world.

Introduction

Why and for whom this book was written

This book is the product of many people in many countries, and draws on the learning experiences of a wide variety of God's servants. I have been writing the notes for it over the past few years in Colombia, the USA, Germany, Switzerland, England, Sudan, Egypt, Cyprus, Saudi Arabia, Dubai, India, Sri Lanka, Bangladesh, South Korea, China and Mongolia, and I have been able to discuss these issues with numerous pastors, missionaries and Christian leaders. Most important of all, I wanted to listen intently to 'ordinary Christians' and find out about their dreams and experiences. I am thankful for all those inspiring visits, listening to stories and holding discussions over cups of tea. I have also been inspired by a host of valuable books and other materials, too numerous to mention. Although German is the language I grew up with, I have attempted to write this book in English – and it shows! I beg that people whose mother-tongue is English will forgive any liberties I may have taken with their language.

Jesus has given us the commission to go and make disciples of all nations. It is the growing conviction of many Christians around the world that this will only ever be achieved by having a church – God's shop window –

within walking distance of every person on the globe. The church – the secret and powerful society of the redeemed – must again become the place where people can literally see the body of Christ, where His glory is revealed in the most practical terms, hands on, down to earth, right next door, unable to be overlooked or ignored, living amongst us every day.

The process of moving towards the goal of whole nations – countries and people groups and regions – being discipled by a mass dispersion of the presence of Christ has come to be known as 'saturation church-planting', the process which God seems to choose in nation after nation to mobilize all His people to work together towards that ultimate goal. The word saturation means to 'fill to the brim', to make full of, to reach a critical mass. God is the God of nations. We can quickly see that planting a few churches here and there is just not enough. What will it take to see the disciplining of whole nations, with their millions of inhabitants and tens of thousands of villages, with longstanding non-christian – or worse, pseudo-christian – traditions and customs and their own formidable spiritual forces, in a world of poverty and urbanization with an inconceivable multitude of opinions, colours, castes and clans, tribes and language groups?

Many have told me, often enough with tears in their eyes, that their nation will not truly change its values and be discipled by anything artificial, by being briefly touched by the abbreviated gospel of a short-lived evangelistic Blitzkrieg, nor even by the type of church that has been there for the last 5, 50 or 500 years. Nothing short of the very presence of the living Christ in every neighbourhood and village of every corner of the nation will do. He has come to live amongst us – and stay on. We therefore need to initiate and promote church-planting movements that initiate and promote other church-planting movements, until there is no space left for anyone to misunderstand, ignore or even escape the presence of Jesus in the form that He has chosen to take on earth – the local church.

This book focuses on the questions: What type of church will it take to do just that? And how do we plant those type of churches? It has three purposes.

1 It is a *vision statement*. It tries to capture and express the visions, hopes and expectations of many Christians around the globe for a New Testament church that will truly *disciple* nations, and not only fill them. This implies a tendency to speak in 'big-picture', broad-stroke language, and I am painfully aware of the attendant danger of oversimplifying life's complexities and sounding almost simplistic at times. I trust God will use others better gifted than myself to fill in the blanks I have to leave.

2 It is a *manifesto*. It declares a threefold conviction: that without a return to the New Testament simplicity of house-churches, the empowering fivefold ministry to spawn a flood of quality house-churches, and the strategic process of saturation church-planting as a united effort of the body of Christ, we will continue to fall short of being obedient to the Great Commission. The number of people alive today – more than six billion – is more than the total of all those who have ever lived before. If ever we needed to recover a New Testament church to disciple the nations, that time is now.

3 It is a *church-planting manual*. It will explain how to plant house-churches. As every business knows, it is best to develop a working prototype of a product first, and then head for mass production. If we know what type of church we want, we will also know how to plant and multiply it.

Why are there no models?

I have tried to resist the temp-
tation of describing a multitude of models that could be
used as blueprints for house-
church planting. Neither
have I set out 'six easy steps
to plant a house-church
movement', because it is
neither easy nor advisable to

*Instead of importing other
people's spiritual success-
stories, I would find it more
natural for us all to search for
the ways which God has
ordained for us to put into
practice.*

take formulae and existing models and try to photocopy
them. For one reason, I simply do not believe in the copy-
cat mentality. It is more important for spiritually significant *principles* to sink in and be grasped, than to take a five-
step outline and copy it. Instead of importing other people's spiritual success-stories, I would find it more natural
for us all to search for the ways which God has ordained
for us to put into practice in our time and place – what we
feel He has revealed to us. I do not want to spare any one of
us this creative tension.

A second reason is that many are looking for a proven
truth, a foolproof method and model, a concept which a
sufficient number of others have already tried and
tested, before they take 'a leap of faith' and go and do
likewise. This play-safe mentality, I suggest, although it
sounds very reasonable, is a spiritual way of hiding
fear: we may leap, but not really out of faith. The core
secret of followers of Christ, men and women alike, in
doing the works of Jesus is not having sufficient
academic and statistical proof before they act, but
having the faithful and obedient desire to follow
Christ's word and do what He said, no matter what,
when, where or who has gone before.

House churches in the West

Some, when they hear the term house church, think of a Chinese church model. Let me therefore make clear for readers in western countries that house churches have never been an exotic foreign model of church, and will not be a strange new foreign import. After all, the first church to be planted in the West was started in the home of Lydia in Philippi, Macedonia. It was a house church.

1 House churches are a good, old European tradition. After the Greek and Roman house churches of the first two centuries and many sporadic 'lay-led' movements after the time of Constantine, it was the Celtic movement that first evangelized Europe, even before Patrick, Columban, Gall or Boniface were alive. The Celts (or *Galli*, as they where known in Latin) were the same race as the Gauls, who invaded Rome around 280 BC, many of whom then settled down in Asia Minor, or 'Galatia', the area to which Paul directed his letter. The holistic concept of the early Celtic Christianity is very close to New Testament (Galatian) house churches as I describe them here. Organic house churches have therefore been an early part of European history and are not at all foreign or new. The fact that between the sixth and ninth centuries the Celtic movement was almost completely assimilated into the Catholic Church – including the structures that go with it – is one of the bigger tragedies of European church history.

2 Almost all contemporary church-plants in the West go through an organic house-church phase in their early days. Many western Christians still look back with fond memories of the spontaneous early months or the 'good old times when we still had our church in homes'. The problem is not so much that there are no house churches

in the West, but that this form of church has neither been consciously acknowledged nor actively sought after.

3 Many church movements, such as some Brethren groups, the Foculare movement and evangelistic movements such as the Alpha courses and Promise Keepers, practise a number of house-church elements, although usually not yet all of them. I believe this is part of their – limited – success. I expect many of them to upgrade towards a more fully developed house-church theology and practice, the result of which will be nothing short of a sensation.

4 An astonishing number of house-church movements have developed in recent years in the West, too numerous to mention. House churches usually do not make much of themselves, and that is part of the reason why few of them are even noticed.

5 There is not a day when I do not hear of new house churches being established in the West. To me it is already now evident that they will very soon play a major role in the process of discipling the western nations.

What about the existing church structure?

Nobody lives in a vacuum, and many of us will have grown up in denominational structures or work in areas with an existing church history. We cannot turn back the wheel of history, but nowhere in the Bible are we told to stoically accept the status quo. Rather, we are to be perfect as God is perfect. This book is not written to suggest that house churches are the only possible way of church. There always will be a mixed forest of denominational and traditional churches, as well as house churches, because each church group can perform particular roles and tasks.

However, this book does suggest that if we want to see whole nations discipled, according to the biblical command of Jesus, we will not be able to accomplish much without either radically returning to New Testament principles and dynamics of church – or making room for others to do so. The focus and perspective of discipling the nations is very different from maintaining a certain church tradition or sitting in the ivory tower of theoretical reflexion. If house churches are a valid expression of the church, as I am advocating here, then we need to embrace it as at least one of many valid forms of church, and see its potential unfold towards discipling the nations.

I believe that God has blessed the world through the existing church structures, and is still doing countless miracles of transforming people's lives, and doing good in ways too numerous to mention. But the church should never settle for less than it has been made for. I believe churches – including house churches – come in all grades and shades of human works coupled with the work of God, an ever-changing mix of spirit and flesh, as long as we will live on earth. But we are all called to lean as much towards the works of the Spirit as possible, and to root out the works of the flesh, if we can. This is humanly impossible, and we need to say it clearly: the church of God is God's invention and humanly not 'doable' or makeable. It cannot be fabricated or manufactured, but will only emerge as we yield ourselves to God and become His very junior partners and stewards in His work of calling His creation back to Himself through His church. But there is hope! God, in His sovereign ways, is able to do the undoable: to make wine out of water, to make donkeys talk, to make water flow from a rock, to part the sea and, most astonishing, even to use ordinary humans for His divine glory.

This book is not advocating that we dream up a perfect, romantic picture of church and admire it from a distance as if it were in a museum, but that we get personally involved as a response to what God is calling

us to do. In this book, I have made plain what I feel God
is calling the church to be, or to become, and I am
willing to be personally involved locally and globally in
that task. I confess that I feel very inadequate at times,
loaded with any amount of my own church traditions
and many inadequacies and biases. This also means
that I am happy to admit that this book is only an
introductory and unfinished statement. But even the
unfinished nature of this book is part of the message:
deus semper major, God is always bigger than we think.
Yes, we have seen something, but yes, it is also only a
part.

Not for pastors in the first instance!

Please understand that this book is very definitely not
written just for pastors. There are several weighty strategic and historic reasons for this, which those of my
collegues who are pastors will surely understand after
reading the book. It is written specifically for four groups
of people, who will, I am convinced, mould the future of
the church.

1 *Women* More than 50 per cent of the church worldwide
   is made up of women, who in traditional Christianity
   have very few opportunities to blossom spiritually or to
   get significantly involved in the ministry. They have
   often been reduced to politely filling quotas in a male-
   dominated and heavily structured world of established
   and free churches, or have stood on the side-lines,
   caring for their children and making sure they 'don't
   disturb church'. I am convinced, however, that women
   need to be right at the centre of the church. If the
   traditional system of church does not allow for that, we
   should not change the women, but change the system.

2 *Family fathers* Young families, and the fathers of these families, are statistically a minority in the organized churches of the last 1,600 years. I am convinced that a lot of eldership potential is lost with uninvolved family fathers, those who cannot cope well and juggle successfully with the three areas of work, family, and church. But what would happen if the centre of church were shifted back into the families? Instead of even more seminary-trained professionals moulding the church, family-and-life-trained fathers would move into the centre of the action. Then, with their fatherly potential, the church would again become part of everyday life, and move away from Sunday-morning Christianity.

3 *The fivefold ministry* Many who feel called by God to a pastoral, apostolic, prophetic, teaching or evangelistic ministry sense themselves to be at odds with the church system. They feel lonely, their potential does not fit in with their current ministries, they suffer from the expectant pressure of church members, or just feel misunderstood. Really, they are searching for a better blueprint, a better overall picture to fit into, where they can live out their gifting and calling in healthy and complementary relationship with others. House-church Christianity, as you will see, will offer just that.

4 *Pastors* But this book is for a special kind of pastor, who is much more interested in furthering the Kingdom of God than looking for one more idea for his own church. If you are a pastor reading this book, you may soon find yourself at a number of crossroads. You may sense that you are working as a pastor, but that you may not really be one. Or you may be convinced that God has called you for a pastoral ministry, but you are still looking for a structure which will allow you to work less but achieve

more, where your pastoral heart can fly free, without constantly being choked by the structures of 'church as we know it'. In that case, house-church Christianity may be exactly what you have been looking for.

Most of all, this book is intended to inspire, encourage and celebrate those Christians who will be God's instruments for gathering the harvest in this last leg of history. As many prophets tell us, it will be a generation of nobodies, without faces and titles, who lead God's movement on earth to fulfil its calling. They will do it under all sorts of conditions: in the midst of persecution or celebrated in talk shows (which is worse?), under unspeakable difficulties or walking on red carpets, despised or adored, ridiculed or consulted, cheated or honoured, scorned or quoted, tortured or pampered, unknown or known, with frequent-flyer cards or walking barefoot. In other words, this is a battle-cry for ordinary followers of Christ, who, through their humble, self-denying and obedient lives, will be made extraordinary in purpose and power to flood this earth with house churches and, through them, the presence, knowledge and glory of Christ, like the waters cover the sea.

Chapter 1

The Reinvention of Church

Bridging the church gap

We read of many people 'coming to Christ' every day. But we usually do not hear much about the silent exodus of people slipping out again, almost unnoticed, through the back doors of churches.

Never in history has there been a phase with more significant and global growth of the Christian church than our own. Current statistics indicate that between 2000 and 3000 churches are planted every week. The worldwide evangelical church has grown from about 150 million in 1974 to about 650 million in 1998, and is today, according to C. Peter Wagner and Ralph Winter, the fastest growing minority on earth.

Yet, at this time of great excitement – and even triumph in some groups – the level of dissatisfaction and frustration with 'church as we know it' has probably also reached global proportions. We read of many people 'coming to Christ' every day, and we rejoice. But we usually do not hear much of those numbers entering membership rolls of local churches, and even less do we hear about the silent exodus of people slipping out again, almost unnoticed, through the back doors of churches. They were attracted, but not included; interested, but not integrated into an enveloping fellowship; harvested and cut, but not gathered into the barn; touched, but not transformed. They turned to look briefly at The Way, then turned away, disappointed with what they saw.

God yes, church no

In a research project in Amsterdam in the early 1990s, young people were asked whether they were interested in God. One hundred per cent of them answered yes. Then they were asked whether they were interested in church: 1 per cent said yes, 99 per cent said no. Most pastors who heard this story made out that something must be seriously wrong with the youth of Amsterdam, since everything is right with the church. How could it possibly be different? Today I reluctantly consider it the other way Around. Maybe the youth of Amsterdam has some lessons to teach the church which we have been unwilling to learn. Maybe we have fallen so much in love with our own traditions that we are almost unable to truly hear and feel the world from our safe and 'holy' distance.

Non-baptized believers

Another piece of research conducted nearly a decade ago by Dr Herbert E. Hoefer, former Director of Gurukul Theological College, in Madras, India, revealed that more than 200,000 of what Hoefer called 'non-baptized believers in Christ' secretly existed in this city of 8 million. This growing number would call themselves Christians but, for a variety of reasons, do not go to church. One reason they state is that they are attracted to Jesus, but not attracted to the church as they have experienced it.

Ask almost anyone who is not yet a Christian what crosses their mind when they hear the word 'evangelical church'. The chances are, you will not like what you hear. It is amazing how well many Christians are able to hide or brush over their own deep frustration with the church. 'Look to Jesus, not to the church,' they say. We know deep down that something is desperately wrong with that statement.

There is a buzzing activity about the church and missions like never before. But, also like never before, pastors are swapping churches, dropping out of ministry or applying for sabbaticals; missionaries are burning out; and many ordinary Christians simply leave their churches and don't go back. Countless Christians have told me that, after trying this model of church, that recipe of revival, riding this wave and catching the spirit that way, attending this 'life-changing seminar' and that 'anointed conference', their lives and their churches are still dreadfully the same: some are prepared to give up, while others, out of groundless hope, or just for want of a better alternative, plough on.

The crisis of missions is a crisis of the church

'I don't like books on missions,' says Stephen Gaukroger, President of the Baptist Union of England and Wales, in the foreword to Patrick Johnstone's book *The Church is Bigger than You Think*: 'They usually tell me what I already know and then make me feel guilty for not doing more about it!' The traditional understanding of missions encourages churches or individuals to 'give money, go to the missions field yourself, or send someone else instead'. But many times this leaves a bad aftertaste, because we never know when we have given, gone, or sent *enough*. Patrick Johnstone puts it this way:

We live in a time when our perception of what constitutes the structures of the church has been moulded by inadequate theology and distorted patterns inherited over the centuries. Few realize the impact of these distortions on congregational life. We soon find out that bashing congregations with a mission challenge or attempting to prick consciences in public meetings bears meagre fruit. We find that the church has inherited a mindset or worldview which has excluded missions altogether.

It is no surprise to me that churches which are not built on apostolic and prophetic foundations (Eph. 2:20) have no apostolic and prophetic mindset. The crisis of traditional missions is a crisis of the church. If mission is the natural heartbeat of an apostolic church, it is an expression of God's grace manifested in apostolic people, not a church trying to fulfil its mission quota. We need to take the legalistic whip out of mission, and I suggest we start at the very heart of missions, with our understanding of the church. For the whip is not only evident in missions: it is at home in the church, as a result of a lack of grace and an overdose of legalism, which often creeps in where the apostolic and prophetic ministries have been replaced by dutiful teachers, beautiful pastors and daring evangelists.

As I shall argue later, when church is reinvented, mission will be completely revived too. 'When the church rejects its mission, the church ceases to be the church,' says Donald Miller. But when the church again becomes the church and accepts its apostolic and prophetic nature, then it can become God's instrument of transforming and discipling neighbourhoods and nations. An individual church can be used by God, in the spirit of global partnership, to pour its oil on other people's fire, so that the light increases and the world can see the one whom it has overlooked for too long: Jesus Christ.

The church gap

Many pastors know and even say: 'the church we preach about is very different from the church we preach to. That's the very reason why we preach.' If even pastors admit that, what about new Christians? English church-planter Terry Virgo wrote:

> In the days of coffee-bar evangelism, there were conferences held on how to bridge the awful gulf between the coffee bar and the church. It was meant for new Christians to help them to cope with dead, irrelevant, formal church services. Once they were told that this cold, unchanging monotony was the people of God enjoying abundant life. Some, therefore, even suggested a half-way house, where people could be prepared for church life.

In the original days of Willow Creek Community Church in Chicago, which has seeker-oriented worship services – worship experiences tailor-made for those seeking God, where not-yet-believers are specifically made welcome and given a comfortable, non-embarrassing and 'safe place for a dangerous message' – they were well aware of the 'church gap', the fascination of people with the person of Jesus, and the dissatisfaction of many with the local church. At that time, however humorously, they suggested a sevenfold strategy of evangelism:

1 Spend quality time with non-Christians.
2 Protect them from the church.
3 Witness to those new friends about Jesus Christ.
4 Protect them from the church.
5 Lead them to Christ.
6 Protect them from the church.

7 When they have matured a bit and are ready for a
  culture shock, introduce them to the church for the first
  time.

Who follows up whom?

A missionary told me about a church of about 200 people
in Europe which wanted to invite non-Christians to a 'spe-
cial-event service'. With the help of a lot of advertising, 50
new people attended this special event. 'Of course, very
few of them actually came back to church. But we are following them up,' he said.

I was amazed. If 50 non-believers attend a church service and are not electrified by the experience, but go away
feeling only indifferent, why is it that the church does not
bear the consequences? Should it not be on its knees trying
to find out what has so obviously and desperately gone
wrong with itself, that so many people can come in contact
with it and yet go away untouched?

Could it be that the church should be following up
itself, rather than bothering unimpressed and indifferent
one-time visitors with spiritual sales techniques? After
1700 years of post-Constantine Christendom, can we
afford still to discuss how to change the world without
being ready to change ourselves? Maybe we all need to
follow the advice of Rick Warren in his book *The Purpose-
driven Church*, to 'stop asking God to bless what we are
doing, and start doing what he is blessing'.

The third Reformation

German church-growth researcher Christian A. Schwarz
suggests that we are in the era of the third Reformation.
The first Reformation took place in the sixteenth century,
when Martin Luther rediscovered the core of the gospel:

salvation by faith, the centrality of grace and of Scripture. It was *a reformation of theology*.

The second Reformation occurred in the eighteenth century when personal intimacy with Christ was rediscovered. It was, says Schwartz, *a reformation of spirituality*, which, born on passionate knees in front of a loving and personal Saviour, gave birth to a new era of enthusiastic missions and evangelism.

All of this, however, was still pouring new wine into old wineskins, sewing new patches onto old cloth. The ecclesiastical system of the Roman Catholic Church was very close to the Old Testament, temple-centred worship patterns, complete with frankincense and priests, sectioned-off areas for the lay people and clerics, and an altar. Luther reformed the content of the gospel, but did not change the basic structure of the 'worship service'. This reformed–Roman-Catholic–Jewish meeting pattern was baptized by Baptists, anointed by Pentecostals, misused by cults, renewed by Charismatic Christians, put into uniform by the Salvation Army, dry-cleaned by Quakers – but was never radically changed. The 'services' were still essentially performances, audience-oriented masses, usually formal and liturgical religious events, where many spectators and consumers observe a few very involved religious specialists performing for them and with them.

The third and last part of the Reformation is, therefore, *a reformation of structure*. It is not a matter of making a few cosmetic changes or alterations here and there, but of building according to fundamental New Testament patterns. If that means that we have to start all over again from the beginning, then so be it: that will be what it will take. Let me offer a few illustrations.

Large cars during the oil crisis

During the oil crisis in the 1970s it was quite difficult to sell large cars because petrol was so expensive. Car manufacturers were scratching their heads, looking at the rows of unsold cars in their yards. Sometimes I think the situation of the churches in a number of nations is the same: the model of church we are offering may simply be too costly, too big. Does the market require another product?

Clogged assembly line

Along similar lines, the church-planting situation in a number of nations is like a clogged assembly line. The product – a new church – seems to be extremely hard to sell and sits on the assembly line, clogging it up for lack of excited customers who want to buy that product. Result: the system shuts down, the work scarcely progresses, people become more and more frustrated. Could it be that we have become specialists in reproducing assembly lines, but have not paid enough attention to examining our prototype product?

Solving the puzzle

Imagine a young boy, unwrapping a new puzzle and immediately trying to put the pieces together. Out of the puzzle box he pulls a picture of a red racing car (he loves red racing cars!) All excited, he tries to assemble the pieces according to the picture. But somehow or other the pieces do not seem to fit as they should. He manages to bend them; he tears off an edge here and there to make them fit with a little brute force; but something seems to be wrong. Finally, his father comes to the rescue. Dad takes the picture of the red racing car – and turns it over. Lo and behold, on the other side is a picture of a beautiful tree, the 'original'. The racing car is only an advertisement for another puzzle made by the same company! The boy sighs with relief, and starts to put the pieces together according to the new original – and within minutes it is done. What was wrong before? He had all the right pieces, but the wrong original. He had unquestionable and honest motives, but quite simply the wrong blueprint.

Spiritual photocopiers

Is this, in short, the situation of a large part of Christendom today? We have all the right pieces: the word of God, people, houses, prayer, motivation, money. But are we putting them all together according to a wrong original? Our very own beloved red racing car? Has the unthinkable happened, that someone sinister has cunningly slipped us an impractical blueprint? And so we stand, transfixed in front of our spiritual photocopiers (Bible colleges, publishing houses, seminaries or leadership programmes), and keep hitting that green button to make copies of what we are convinced is a biblical, canonized, unquestionable, first-hand original, that has been proven by the Bible and history.

I can imagine that Satan, the enemy of the church, has no problem with even the most frantic evangelistic or mission activities and programmes – as long as they are all about making copies of 'red racing cars', our traditional pattern of church which makes no serious threat to his satanic claims on mankind. Maybe the time has come for us to stop scratching the surface of humanity and allow God to recreate church in all of us. It might start with us re-examining our blueprints and turning over our originals.

Our way of church

Most of us will either have grown up in a Christian denomination or have later decided to join one. As a result, we will usually see and interpret Christianity – and even the Bible – through the spectacles of our own familiar tradition, 'our way of belief and practice'. But which tradition is right? As Argentinian evangelist Juan Carlos Ortiz once remarked: 'There are more than 22,000 denominations in the world. How lucky you are that you happen to be in the one that is right!' Since then, not only has the number of denominations risen to between 24,000 and 30,000, but many Christians have begun to understand that most problems of today's churches do not lie outside the system, but inside – inside our inherited, learned and dear patterns of belief and practice, the way we 'do church'.

Who is to blame?

'Our bookshelves are full of Christian books and videos,' says Ted Haggard of New Life Church in Colorado Springs in his book *Primary Purpose – Making it Hard for People to go to Hell from your City*. 'We have churches on every major street, more staff workers than ever before, large Sunday school departments, cell systems, mega- and meta-church seminars. We have Christian bumper stickers, political action groups, huge parachurch ministries – and in the midst of it all, we have lost every major city in North America.' He goes on: 'Rather than rethinking our methods and challenging our own effectiveness, we try to escape responsibility for the eternal damnation of those in our communities by blaming others for our own spiritual ineffectiveness.'

A western model of church for the whole world?

Although there are approximately 240 nations in the world, the last few centuries have seen great activity in just four countries in exporting their models of church into all the world: Germany, the UK, the USA and Italy. Most churches and movements today still have religious headquarters in one of those countries, or at least are strongly connected and influenced from those countries. While I do not at all deny the blessings of this mission era, it has also led to one of the greatest monopolizations of church around the world, where one western model of church has become a standard and dominating practice almost everywhere. American writer Gene Edwards decries this in the title of his disturbing book *The Americanization of the Church*, and we need to remind ourselves of the simple fact that Jesus was not a 'Westerner'. Given the fact that the four main missionary-world powers have been caught up in world wars against each other, killing each other in front of the eyes of the rest of the world, we need to realize that, as 'Christian nations', they lost a large amount of global Christian credibility. The West may have money, materials, rhetoric and even a well-oiled mission machinery, but these cannot replace a genuine calling from God.

Although there are approximately 240 nations in the world, the last few centuries have seen great activity in just four countries in exporting their models of church into all the world: Germany, the UK, the USA and Italy.

I believe we have moved from a colonial era of mission into what I call 'national mission', where each nation is called to develop its own models of church. Often enough this will have to happen through people in every nation praying for themselves, shedding their own tears, incarnating the living Christ afresh within their own time and culture. If the West could then come and, in the spirit of 'crucified colonialism' – the opposite of imperialism and denominationalism – carefully pour some oil on this process, it would be wonderful.

The traditional church – the biggest barrier to belief?

The quickest way to 'church the unchurched' may very well be to 'unchurch the church'.

In a study in Scotland in 1994 under the title *Barriers to Belief*, Revd John Campbell says, 'Many have indicated that one of the greatest barriers to belief in God is the church itself.' If the problem is the system, then even our best solution is part of the problem. That leaves even the most dedicated, visionary, passionate and revived Christians trapped in a system which is sucking their very energy and simply overwhelming them. The way forward, therefore, may not be hidden in slight changes and adaptations to the forms of 'Church as we know it', but in a much more radical rediscovery of the very nature of church itself. The quickest way to 'church the unchurched' may very well be to 'unchurch the church'. Bob Hopkins, one of the initiators of the Anglican Church-Planting Initiative in England, has therefore recommended us to 'stop starting with the church', i.e. to stop taking today's churches and their 'worship patterns' for granted. It seems, after all, that God has been waiting for a long time throughout history, ready to give the right answers to those asking the right questions. House churches, in other words, are the missing link between spirituality and society, between Jesus and his body, between heaven and earth.

A stumbling-block or a treasure?

Jesus compares the Kingdom of God to a man who finds some treasure while ploughing a field (Mt. 13:44) and then goes off to sell all his possessions to buy the field – and the treasure. What first looks like a stumbling-block, a misplaced rock interrupting the daily routine and irritatingly upsetting the fixed agenda of daily ploughing, may turn out to be the greatest find of a person's life. Could it be the same with our liturgical, programme-driven churches? It may happen to you, as God speaks to you about house churches in His own ways. Maybe the answers to the questions of so many of us are hidden, but close by, waiting to be stumbled upon, or locked behind a forbidden door other people do not even think exists. We may find it out of unbearable agony with the status quo which drives us to search and then find, or we may find it quite accidentally. At this point, house churches may still be completely unthinkable, literally unheard of, something which at first may even sound heretical, but as we move on through the fog of tradition and reread our Bibles the matter may become much clearer. However, take some advice from the parable of the hidden treasure. As you discover it, do not go to town and make a big announcement in the market-place. Hide it again in the field, go and sell all that you have, and then go and buy it and do whatever God shows you to do.

The reincarnation of the church

Many churches which are desperate for renewal – or at least for change – tend to overlook the fact that you cannot produce a new quality in the church by changing the structures. As management guru Tom Peters says, renewal and reformation is out, revolution is in; a company does not really need a CEO – a Chief Executive Officer – but a CDO – a Chief Destructive Officer, regularly dismantling obstructive traditions, because it is much easier to rebuild according to a new pattern than to restore and renew an outdated one. Changing a church by changing some outward forms is as futile as trying to change your mentality by changing your clothes or walking backwards in order to stop yourself going to cinemas. Adding a new mission statement or some other cosmetic alteration without a radical genetic reformation of the church will only lead to frustration – like sewing a patch of new cloth onto old cloth, which, says Jesus, is bad advice.

Revival and reformation truly start with a complete rediscovery and reconstruction of the core essence of the church, with New Testament DNA, the genetic code of God, supernaturally empowered with growth potential from within (Mk. 4:26). This spiritual seed material is, like any grain of wheat, equipped and able to develop its own appropriate structures from the inside out, without instruction from outside; it simply unfolds itself according to a creational blueprint within; it unzips. Its soil is the soil of nations and people groups. The result of this incarnation, at least in New Testament times, was a housechurch movement, that swept through the city of Jerusalem like yeast in dough, or like an unstoppable virus, in maybe less than two years.

Biotic principles

Almost all life forms are based on the multiplication of organic cells. Unlimited growth is not a creational principle, but multiplication is. My friend Christian Schwarz has studied what he calls 'biotic' principles, patterns that operate within God's created order of organic life. This led him to develop what he calls 'Natural Church Church Growth'.

Many insights are drawn from agricultural and biological contexts where growth is definitely according to the divine pattern and method, and not like the humanly devised, artificial patterns of mechanical production and growth. These biotic principles stand in stark contrast to the 'technocratic' methods which govern machines. They are as different from each other as a robot is from a human being. One is a machine while the other is an organism. The 'machine' or 'robot' model functions very well in the world of technology but fails in the world of biotic, organic growth.

When we understand that the church is a creation of God, a 'biotic' organism, we must look for God's natural, organic principles to understand how it grows.

When we understand that the church is a creation of God, a 'biotic' organism, we must look for God's natural, organic principles to understand how it grows. Biotic principles utilize the minimum amount of energy to produce the maximum results, and it happens 'all-by-itself'. This prevents the church becoming manufactured, and allows it to be recreated by the Spirit of God according to God's creational patterns. We simply labour in vain if we follow only man-made patterns or formulae, even if they are handed to us in the form of good and cherished traditions. Some biotic principles are as follows:

⟨ *Interdependence* The way the parts of an organism are inter-related is more important than the parts themselves. All organic cells arrange themselves not in a chaos guided by chance, but according to a creational and in-built pattern where each cell or organ is linked with others. In terms of church multiplication this means that no issue or topic or aspect should be seen or even treated in isolation from all the other aspects and parts.

⟨ *Multiplication* Unlimited growth is not the ideal, but multiplication is. The fruit of an apple tree is not an apple, but another apple tree. The fruit of a church is not a convert, but other churches that plant other churches.

⟨ *Energy transformation* This is the principle that observes how existing forces (even contrary ones) can be used positively towards a desired goal. This is also how an organism fights a virus – not in a head-on collision, but using much of the energy of the intruder to defeat the intruder. Through a vaccination process former health-destroying energies are transformed into health-promoting ones. Many churches use the boxer approach to life instead, using energy to reduce an outside 'attack' to zero, and then, in a second strike, deliver its own message.

How to break the '20-barrier'

The book by church-growth researcher Bill M. Sullivan *Ten Steps to Breaking the 200-Barrier* has a very understandable intention which fits ideologically into the mainstream of the Church Growth movement of the 1970s and 1980s: good churches grow big, and very good churches grow very big, so anything that stops a 'healthy' church from growing is a barrier, and those barriers are bad and must therefore go.

The idea of the '200-barrier' is simple. Statistically, most churches stop growing somewhere between 100 and 300 people, on average at about 200. There are good cultural, sociological and even architectural reasons for that. One reason is structural, an in-built problem of the traditional one-pastor church: there are only so many people – in the USA, about 200 – a pastor can personally and effectively care for. He may have a lot of space in his agenda, but a quite limited space in his heart; and people realize that.

As a result, growth grinds to a halt and the church hits an invisible ceiling, the '200-barrier'. I suggest, however, there is a much more important barrier to overcome: the '20-barrier'. How do we break it?

The invisible line: from organic to organizational

As any family get-together will teach us, we can accomplish the goal of fellowship without the need to be heavily structured. Families can get along quite well without a master of ceremonies, a word of introduction, a special song, a sermon by father and a vote of thanks by mother. These things happen at weddings and other festivals, but not in everyday life. Church, however, is not an artificial performance, it is for everyday life, because it is a way of life.

> If we cross the '20-barrier', the group stops being organic, and starts to become formal, and even to feel the need to follow a set agenda.

There is, in each culture, a very important numerical line between the organic and the organized, the informal and the formal, the spontaneous and the liturgical. I call this the 20-barrier, because in many cultures 20 is a maximum number where people still feel 'family', organic and informal, without the need to get formal or organized. Organisms are structured, too, and I am not advocating a total absence of order and structure. But, unlike an organized series of meetings which are typically structured from outside, organisms are usually structured from within. The nature of a meeting defines and therefore limits the size of a meeting. If we cross the '20-barrier', the group stops being organic, and starts to become formal, and even to feel the need to follow a set agenda. Effectiveness in relationship and mutual communication goes down, and the need for someone to coach and lead the meeting goes up. As a result, the house church loses its main original attractions, changes its values, and starts to develop totally different dynamics. It often simply stops functioning by itself, stops being spontaneous and lively, led invisibly and unobtrusively through the in-built family mechanisms of fathering and mothering, and needs to be literally 'run', organized, and visibly led into a new and organized life form – if there is such a thing. The original organism is then a thing of the past, still alive, but trapped into a formal structure that chokes it, conditions it, and ultimately could prevent relational and spontaneous fellowship in the name of organized fellowship.

Biblical *koinonia* means fellowship or sharing, giving generously and participating and sharing something with someone. One of the fatal aspects of this line-crossing is that the original organic form of fellowship usually loses its internal reproduction potential, and can only be cloned and copied, or even manufactured and finally mass-produced with huge effort from outside that ignores and overrules its own in-built explosive growth potential. It is a fact of church history that it has always been a swift step from organized religion to institutionalism and fossilization.

Person no. 21

One of the most important decisions in terms of the structure and future of a church, therefore, is what you do when person no. 21 walks through the door. Structurally, that brings the church into the red phase. You either continue growing upwards and become organized, and lose your house-church dynamics, ultimately even hitting the 200-barrier; or you divide the house church into two or three units and multiply it, thus growing sidewards. This way you may not even notice a 200-barrier.

A wedding a week?

Life in any culture has two aspects, the private and the public, everyday life and the special events – weddings, festivals, funerals and traditional events. Both aspects of life have their own, valid ways of expression. Everyday life is usually expressed in the family, the basic cell unit of every society and culture. Families are usually very organic, informal, relational and consist of whatever it takes to share lives. Weddings and other functions are extraordinary events, for which everyone duly prepares; they are usually formal, need much organization and are often highly structured.

Imagine if you had to attend a wedding every weekend. It follows the same basic pattern, has even the same bridegroom and bride; maybe even the food is the same. After some weeks the excitement would wear down. You would know what to expect, and you would know what's going to happen next. It would still remain a nice thing, a beautiful tradition, but it would feel odd to have the same type of festival every week.

We need to be careful not to do this with church. Jesus has shown us not only a way to celebrate, but a way to live. Both aspects are necessary, both are good. But everyday life is not like a wedding, as any married couple will tell us. If we allow church to take on only 'celebration structures', we will start celebrating 'a wedding a week', and our behaviour will soon be far removed from real life and cease to make sense to ordinary people. It will become an artificial, weekly performance. If church is a God-given way of community life, and if life takes place in the basic unit of a family living in a home, there is nothing more appropriate than for the church to be a house church, to be the church based in simple, ordinary, everyday homes. House churches are not only a way for us humans to express community, they are one of God's means to achieve community.

Small churches may already be far too big

Creation itself teaches us that nothing healthy grows endlessly, but at some point stops growing and starts multiplying. Bigger is not necessarily better or more beautiful. Could it be that, although it is perfectly OK to expect a church to grow, we are generally looking for that growth in in the wrong direction? We are intrigued by those well-publicized and quite exceptional stories of megachurches, and overlook that they are usually extraordinary exceptions, due to extraordinary leaders and circumstances. Perhaps the problem is not so much to break the 200-barrier on the way up, but the 20-barrier on the way down. If real church growth spells m-u-l-t-i-p-l-i-c-a-t-i-o-n, then growth may not be upwards at all, but sidewards. Has all that talk about 'big is beautiful' tricked our thinking? If so, we may have to cut a zero out in our mindset: an average church would then be just 8, 10 or 12 people; a large church, 15, and a 'megachurch' would sport not thousands of attenders, but 21 or 22.

Perhaps, then, the average 'small church' of 25 or 45 people, is not at all too small, but already far too big.

Perhaps, then, the average 'small church' of 25 or 45 people, which is trying to rent a hall or sanction a building fund, which has just bought a pulpit and is still saving for an overhead projector, is not at all too small, but already far too big. They have crossed the organism–organization line long ago, trying to grow up like all those other churches, not realizing that they already have become quite heavy and inflexible, structurally bloated and deformed, only kept going and inching forward by the relentless activities of a busy pastor or leader with his co-workers?

Worldwide, the average size of churches is around 100. Only a very small percentage of churches become bigger than 200, and many are in the 40–60 bracket. The average Sunday morning attendance of the Lutheran churches in Germany, for example, in 1993 was 23.5 people.

Shrink in order to grow

It may require someone with a true apostolic gifting – which is, statistically speaking, fairly rare – to transform any given church into a megachurch. For many churches it could be a liberation to be allowed to become what many of them already are: slightly overgrown house churches struggling with their own size and the unspoken lueprint they are trying to follow. But would it not be much more practical for them to head the other way, and become smaller, to move in the direction of house churches, to 'grow down' rather than keep striving to grow up?

Elton Trueblood once said: 'The church must be smaller before it can be substantially stronger.' I agree. But if we take this one step further, this would also mean that the church of the future will have to become much smaller, before it can become substantially bigger, by becoming much more numerous. Statistically, it will have to shrink in order to grow.

Prophetic voices

A Swiss friend told me recently that God had shown him a prophetic vision of the Thunersee, the Lake Thun near Interlaken. There he observed many small groups of Christians baptizing people. 'The Thunersee will be the biggest baptismal lake in Switzerland,' God told

him. 'But why are those groups so small?' asked my
friend. 'They are house churches,' God told him.
Another friend of mine, a long-serving missionary now
in his 70s, told me of a vision he had, where God had
shown him in prayer that a new form of church will
spread in Switzerland like wildfire: house churches. As
a result of this move of God there will be a large in 2001
gathering of approximately 200,000 Christians near the
city of Lucerne, where those Christians will be united
and speak with one voice to Switzerland as a nation.

Pastor Mike Bickle from Kansas, once shared how, in
Cairo in 1982, God had revealed to him that 'He is going to
change the forms and expressions of church within one
generation to the degree that it will not be recognizable
any more'. The future will tell whether it was God or just a
dream. Rick Joyner, a prophetic teacher from Charlotte,
USA, said something very similar: 'I see such a sweeping
return to biblical Christianity coming that the very understanding of Christianity, by both the world and the
church, will be changed. This does not imply any kind of
doctrinal changes as to what it means to be a Christian, but
a change that causes us to live by the truths we proclaim.
This will be reflected when we truly become known for
our love for one another.'

I respect Amos 3:7–8 and the biblical ministry of prophecy, and I am far from encouraging anyone to pick up
stones of tradition and throw them at prophets. What if
those visions, which are only part of a growing flood of
voices amongst God's people today, are really from God?
What would that mean for us as Christians? For our
churches? Could we simply smile about that nice – but
surely absurd! – thought, turn the page, cut onions, water
the garden, go out in the evening, finally order that overhead projector and carry on with 'church as we know it'?

Cell–congregation–celebration

In Church Growth terminology we differentiate between three levels of church: cell, congregation, and celebration. I would like to explain briefly what these terms mean.

1 The *cell* is typically house-based and sociologically small, between 3 and 20 people. Its purpose is relational fellowship, and its functions are mostly organic, i.e. members are often in direct contact with each other and therefore a natural part of each other's lives.
2 The *congregation* is sociologically of medium size, usually between 20 and 200. It functions more formally, is organized, usually has a pastor, co-workers, a type of worship service and various programmes. It often tries to serve a parish, and functions usually in a 'sanctuary' of some sort, a building specially used for religious purposes. Members do not have direct and natural contacts with each other, because the meeting is too large and not structured to allow for that.
3 The *celebration* is typically a large gathering of 200 or more Christians from an area, expressing their unity in Christ, celebrating what God has done and will do for them, anticipating Christ's return. It is usually led by Christians with apostolic and prophetic ministries. Celebrations can happen in the open air, in stadiums, conference centres or any other large area. People have no way of being in direct contact with all present, and are happily 'lost in the crowd'. In many places in history, the cathedral has tried, and sometimes successfully managed, to fulfil this city-wide function.

The small and the large

> The congregation-type church was introduced, the church became an audience, house churches were marginalized and ultimately forbidden.

In the Bible we find two of these structures or levels, the cell and the celebration. In the New Testament we read of the church regularly meeting in houses, that is in cell-sized units, and meeting in Solomon's Temple court, or in the open air, in large numbers. Of those two, the cell, that is the house-based church, was the natural habitat, the normal and most common form of Christians getting together. Once the Jerusalem Temple was declared out of bounds for followers of The Way, they kept on meeting in homes. When the celebration was not possible, the cell lived on.

The risen Christ strongly identified with the church in the houses, and did not urge them anywhere to form 'Christian synagogues' or to build religious buildings. When Saul was persecuting the churches and broke into homes to drag out the Christians, Jesus asked him in his Damascus encounter: 'Saul, why do you persecute me?'

During the first three centuries after Christ, church historians tell us, the house church remained the normal, natural way of Christians sharing their new lives together. Only after Emperor Constantine in the fourth century was there a radical shift in church structure. The congregation-type church was introduced, the church became an audience, house churches were marginalized and ultimately forbidden. No one could function as Christians privately, without the sanction of the state and its acknowledged and ordained 'orthodox' church. (A more detailed account of the house churches throughout the ages follows in chapter 2.)

The mouse married the elephant

The result of these developments was a structural compromise, a marriage between the mouse (the cell) and the elephant (the celebration), giving birth to a most unusual creation, the congregational-type church. It was, in many ways, a strongly professionalized church, with priests fit for a king. It developed its own specialized buildings for religious purposes, removing church from everyday life into relics from the Old Testament religion, with priests, altars and heavily symbolic rituals, where most visitors could no longer be real participants but only spectators. One of the few exceptions to this was the Orthodox Church, which tried to keep the structure of the extended family as much as possible.

Through this compromise the church lost two of its most powerful dynamics. The congregational church was basically an overgrown house church and an undergrown celebration, and missed out on both very important aspects of the cell and the celebration. The cell provided family dynamics, a private and stable home and organic place of belonging and accountability to Christians. The celebrations were places charged with a somewhat grandiose, truly public atmosphere, where the small house churches reconnected with the big picture and each other, heard apostolic teaching and encountered prophetic vision. This often created a sense of excitement which drew in more people on a public level, and such gatherings could literally shake a city or region, or, for that matter, a village or small town.

Fellowship without fellowship

The congregational-type church with its semi-private atmosphere, its limited fellowship possibilities and its professional clergy was a political solution which suited the state and conveniently fitted into the religious patterns of the world at the same time. It was, in many ways, a triumph of the religious spirit, a return to the law and religious patterns of the Old Testament and even pagan religions, from which Jesus wanted to liberate mankind. The problem, it must be emphasized, is not the Old Testament itself. That is and remains a crucial part of God's revelation to mankind. The problem is carrying over Old Testament principles into New Testament times, ignoring the dynamic development of God's relationship to mankind, where He established the Kingdom of God over and beyond the ethnic focus on the people of Israel.

Since this new congregational structure was powerfully enforced by the state and church laws, it forced its content to adapt to the new structure. In the New Testament, the content defined the form, i.e. the quality defined the structure. Now this process was reversed, and the form moulded the content, the structure defined the quality. One of the results was a hierarchical, power-based structure, with a king-like bishop or pope at the top, and lesser ranks of the Church down to the church warden and the organist.

This also meant that organic and natural Christian fellowship had to be adjusted to fit into a new container, the formal church building, and therefore had to be watered down to fill out the new, bigger structure. Ultimately, fellowship was thinned out to almost homeopathic doses, and started to lose its impact on the Christians themselves as well as on society. The 'fellowship without fellowship' was born.

The end of the Lord's Supper

Another victim of this process was the Lord's Supper. Since it is quite difficult to feed a cathedral full of people with real food, it degenerated into a religious and

symbolic ritual, offering microscopic sips of wine and a
small wafer, often enough only to the 'clergy' while the
masses looked on in pious amazement. This meant that
the Lord's Supper was a supper no more, and lost its powerful meaning, the unprecedented, revolutionary reality,
of a redeemed people, irrespective of classes and caste,
sharing real food with a prophetic meaning, having dinner with God, expecting His physical presence at any time
just like after the resurrection. It thus became 'the Eucharist', a pious and symbolic shell of the original meal of a
tasty lamb that Jesus shared with his disciples. By AD 150
the Eucharist and the love feast were two distinct parts of
the Lord's Supper. As biblical commentator William
Barclay writes: 'The celebration of the Lord's Supper in a
Christian home in the first century and in a cathedral in
the twentieth century cannot be more different, they bear
no relationship to each other whatsoever.'

Did Procrustes work over the church?

It reminds me of the famous giant Procrustes in Greece,
who forced travellers between Athens and Corinth to lie
down on his big bed. If they were found to be too short for
his bed, they were cruelly stretched with ropes to fill the
length of the bed, breaking their bones in the process. If
they ever happened to be too long, they were unceremoni-
ously cut down to fit.

The structural lie

Today, 1700 years after the beginnings of those developments – it did not all happen in the fourth century – we
have become so accustomed to the congregational-type
church that many find it hard even to imagine any other
form of 'real church life' or 'worship services'. Those

*This whole process canon-
ized and institutionalized a
devastating mediocrity, a
middle-of-the road solution
which suited both religious
and political leaders of
the day.*

historical events created a powerful system, a uni-formed pattern, a sanctioned, and later even sanctified, structure, which has mould-ed the experiences and the mindset of people over long centuries, and has created a distorted picture of church that has little in common any more with its original. This whole process canonized and institutionalized a devastating mediocrity, a middle-of-the road solution which suited both religious and political leaders of the day.

The congregational church became a 'structural lie', because it paints the right message in the wrong colours, casts the right material in wrong forms, pours the water of life into contaminated bottles, takes the redeemed sinners and forms them into a harmless species of polite church-goers and programme participants. It makes heavenly promises, but does not deliver them on earth. It forgot to focus on the extended family as the building block of Christianity, and was content to settle into religious tem-ples, more or less heavily ornamented, reciting worship formulae in a small but solid haven of heaven on earth. No wonder that society in general followed the church in this development, and started to lose the family focus, too.

In short, the congregational church became a self-defeating structure, standing in its own way, creating the very problems it wanted to solve, frustrating and breaking the hearts of millions of people who searched for God and found the congregational-type church, a caricature of God's supernatural family on earth. Only true spiritual heroes and outstanding characters were ever able to raise their heads out of this contaminated system and make a difference for some time, as we will see in the next chapter. But whatever they changed, whatever they pleaded for, whatever renewal, revival or reforms they proposed up to this very day, was swallowed up soon enough by the unchanging system of Christendom, by the structure of church they did not dare to touch.

Five elements of a congregational church

In his book *The Second Reformation*, veteran American missionary and author Bill Beckham, describes a congregation – or, as he calls it, a 'cathedral-type' church – like this:

> Since the time of Constantine in the Fourth Century the church has functioned primarily as a 'Cathedral'. At least five important elements are identified with this 'Cathedral' way of being the church:
>
> 1 A Building (a 'Cathedral' or 'Church');
> 2 A special day (Sunday);
> 3 A professional leadership (priest, clergyman, holy man);
> 4 A special service, performed for the people (ceremonies, services, interpretation of dogma, motivation) and
> 5 A way to maintain itself (tithes and offerings).

In spite of different types of church government, different architectural designs of buildings, different titles and clothes for leaders, different worship forms, and different theologies, churches for the most part have functioned through this 'Cathedral' form. Whether Catholic or Baptist, Presbyterian or Pentecostal, 'High Church' or 'Low Church', urban or rural, large or small, rich or poor, Western or Eastern, churches have been 'Cathedral' in nature. This 'Cathedral' system has survived political upheavals, rearrangement of world maps, great social changes, theological heresies, the

Protestant Reformation, and numerous movements. Its adaptability has been nothing short of amazing. Using a combination of the Roman governmental and feudal systems, Emperor Constantine developed a church structure that has lasted for seventeen centuries. The 'Cathedral' structure has had the capacity to absorb all major movements into its structure without changing its own basic form.

As much as I agree with this, it does not take account of the difference between the cathedral and the average congregational parish church. The cathedral basically reflects the temple in the Old Testament, while the congregational church reflects more the pattern of the Jewish synagogue. However, it is true that later on the church tried to squeeze as much as possible of a cathedral-type church into our average parish church, what I have called the congregational model of church.

Principles, not procedures

I am not proposing to revitalize and reinvent the New Testament church straight out of the book of Acts, faithfully copying all its cultural forms and expressions, because we are living in different times and places. Our cities look much more like Corinth than Jerusalem; many countries live in a postmodern and post-Christendom era. However, we can and should learn from New Testament principles, without copying all its time-specific and cultural procedures. We should take the New Testament quality of church very seriously, but develop structures, methodologies and procedures for our own time and cultures and people groups.

From inherited to emerging mode

'The West has compressed celebration into congregation, and forgotten the homes,' says Revd Bob Hopkins of the Anglican Church-Planting Network in England. He goes on to ask: 'Is congregation the concrete in which our cultural understanding of church is set?' And if so, one might add, is this understanding held captive by national pride and church culture? Europe now boasts of a strong residue of Christian history and structures, but the church has largely lost the people. That is why Anglican Robert Warren speaks of the 'inherited mode of church' and an 'emerging mode', a new – or possibly very old – form of church re-emerging according to New Testament patterns.

In order to bring out some of the differences between the congregational churches and the New Testament house churches, here is a selective list of key areas where they differ. The list could be much longer.

	Congregational church	New Testament house church
Place	meets in sanctuaries	moves from house to house
Main functionaries	pastors, teachers, evangelists	apostles, prophets, elders
Finances	tithes and offerings	sharing all they have
Lifestyle	individual	community
Evangelism	outreach, action, programmes, specialists	natural discipling of neighbours; multiplying itself
Battle cry	Getting more people into the church	Getting the church into people's homes
Size	large, impersonal groups	small, intimate groups
Teaching style	static, sermon-centred	kinetic, question and answer style
Most important task of pastor	lead the church programme; preach good sermons; housevisits etc.	equip each believer for doing the ministry themselves
Centre	worship service in a religious building	life in an ordinary house
Keyword	Become a member!	Go and make disciples!
Ministry	performance-oriented	equipping-oriented, empowering others
Mission	sending specialized missionaries	church sends itself as a multipliable unit

Cell church, BEC, house church

Today there are three main movements, each advocating in different ways a return to a cell-based, house-centred church. Most of those movements would say: 'Cell and celebration are important, but the congregation is quite dispensable.' The three different streams are:

1 The classic 'cell church' advocated, for example, by Ralph Neighbour, Bill Beckham, or Yonggi Cho.
2 The Base-Ecclesial Community, mostly within the Roman Catholic Church.
3 The House-Church Movement, maybe best known today from China and Vietnam.

While the cell church looks and sounds almost the same as the house-church movement, it is not. There are very significant and vital differences, which I will point out later. The Base-Ecclesial Community is a long-lasting small group experiment within the Roman Catholic Church, and might very well develop into a cell-church structure within that church. There is not room here, however, to discuss this more deeply, as my main intention is to focus on generic house churches.

Advantages of house churches over traditional churches

I see at least twelve advantages of a cell-based house-church movement over a traditional congregational-style church.

1 Discipled multiplication
House church is a model centred on multiplication and discipleship with huge growth potential, because the 'cell' is the multipliable unit itself. Mentoring,

multiplication and discipleship is the heart of the concept. Congregation is not by definition a discipleship model and structurally tends to prevent mentoring and discipleship. Discipleship never really is only one-to-one: it is a function of community. Next to the Holy Spirit, peer pressure may be the strongest teacher on earth, as any parent of teenagers will agree. The house churches allow for a redeemed use of peer pressure, living out a healthy and loving accountability with each other, learning new kingdom values from each other and, being friends and family with each other, helping each other to live out together the new lifestyle; no one is left to individual and secret struggles, and each therefore quickly matures.

2 Persecution-proof structure
Through their small and flexible way of life and their persecution-proof spirit, house churches can develop into an almost persecution-proof structure – or at least persecution-resistant – as opposed to the very visible and immovable traditional 'church with a cross on its steeple'.

3 Freedom from church growth barriers
Once careful attention is given to prevent house churches from moving from an organic to an organizational mode, house churches can be multiplied through mitosis, an organic cell-reproduction process, and the overall growth of a movement is virtually free from church growth barriers.

4 Involvement of many more people more efficiently
Congregations are often programme-based, where most programmes are organized at the congregational level. They have proved to be quite inefficient and resource

hungry, usually involving 20 per cent of exhausted members of the church doing the work for the other, more passive, 80 per cent. In the house church, almost everyone can be easily and naturally involved, and dead wood is cut out. Since involved people are fulfilled and therefore happy people, the overall quality – and efficiency – of the church grows.

5 Breaking the pastoral care dilemma
The house-church model breaks the pastoral care dilemma, a known and self-defeating problem of the congregational church: as numbers grow, the pastoral quality usually goes down, because the pastor can no longer tend all his sheep.

6 Providing a place of life transformation and accountability
The house church is an ideal setting to change values, transfer life and therefore transform lifestyles. An analysis of the western church shows that the congregational model is almost totally ineffective at changing basic values and lifestyles. Many Christians end up with the same lifestyle of people around them, and therefore become indistinguishable from society and lose their prophetic edge. House churches provide a place of radical transformation of values and reordering of life, offering mutual and organic accountability, where redeemed peer pressure is made to function for good, and not for bad.

7 The house is a most effective place for new Christians
Much has been written about the inward-looking mentality of the congregational church, whereby the church and its programmes are the centre, and everything else rotates around this hub. This structure traditionally resents new people coming in, 'messing up the order and the

situation'. The congregation is, statistically speaking, a most unfriendly zone for new Christians, accounting for unbelievably large drop-out rates of up to 99 per cent in so-called 'evangelistic follow-up programmes'. In contrast, the cell or house church is a most effective, natural and welcoming zone for new people to come and stay in touch with the Christian community. It provides spiritual fathers and mothers, not teachers and paper. It also reverses the general direction of the perspective of Christians: instead of getting people to the church, they are getting the church to the people.

8 Solving the leadership crisis
House churches are led by elders, and they are just that: older than most, without necessarily being 'elderly'. Elders do not have to be skilled Masters of Ceremonies and learned teachers: modest and authentic fathers and mothers with obedient children will do nicely to start with. They are by then already many years into living a maturing life and passing the test of time, not graduates from a seminary able to perform some religious functions. This leadership is easy to find and develop anywhere without time-consuming schools for religious specialists. It depends on initial and ongoing apostolic and prophetic input and support, ministries which in themselves can be multiplied and therefore match and grow exponentially with a multiplying house-church movement. Traditional Sunday Schools, Bible Schools and seminaries are mostly static, addition-based leadership development systems which grow, at best, in a linear and not an exponential way. They are an informational system, not a transformational system, as Beckham rightly points out. Therefore they cannot match a multiplying movement of house churches with an exponentially growing need for elders.

9 *Overcoming the clergy–laity division*

'Nowhere in the New Testament do we find references to a pastor leading a congregation,' says Barney Coombes. The house church does not need a pastor in the traditional sense at all, because elders, functioning together with the corporate giftedness of the house church, maintain and multiply the life of the church. This therefore breaks the curse of the clergy–laity division, which the congregational system reinforces.

10 *It is more biblical*

> *The Bible absolutely does not teach us to say that a holy crowd gathering on a holy day at a holy hour in a holy sanctuary to participate in a holy ritual performed by holy men in holy clothes for a holy fee is a New Testament church.*

We cannot afford to ignore biblical revelation for too long and get away with it. Tradition is a strong teacher, but God's word is more reliable and simply better. Even in an age of Postmodernism and relativity, the Bible still teaches absolutes. The Bible absolutely does not teach us to say that a holy crowd gathering on a holy day at a holy hour in a holy sanctuary to participate in a holy ritual performed by holy men in holy clothes for a holy fee is a New Testament church. God's work done God's way still attracts God's blessing. Even in Moses' time God exhorted him to build 'according to the pattern'. It is worth struggling even with our own trusted tradition for the purpose of regaining biblical truth, because it is not tradition which sets us free, but the truth of God's word.

11 *It is undeniably cheaper*

The congregational church can be defined as 'plot plus building plus priest plus salary plus programmes'. The house church is 'people plus ordinary houses plus faith plus shared life', which is undeniably cheaper. As congregational churches cost enormous sums of money to establish, and more money to maintain and to propagate, the cells and house churches literally make money, because they produce more than they consume. In an age

The congregational church can be defined as 'plot plus building plus priest plus salary plus programmes'. The house church is 'people plus ordinary houses plus faith plus shared life', which is undeniably cheaper.

when there seems to be an endless cry for more money for 'the work of church', we should not overlook alternatives but be good stewards of the financial talents that God gives us.

12 It resurrects the city church

I see the present church organized into 4 levels:

a. the house (where organic fellowship is possible, irrespective of what we call it);
b. the congregational church (the traditional meeting-oriented denominational church);
c. the city or region;
d. the denomination (the network, conference or organisation of denominational churches of an area).

While the traditional church is typically focused on two levels (b and d), the cell church would be focused on a and b. The house church, however, allows us to regain a focus on a and c. The church in the New Testament was named according to its geographical location, not denomination. With a new wave of house churches, this also opens up a way back to the 'city church', literally the church of the city – all Christians of a city or region together, meeting regularly or irregularly in city-wide celebrations, where the city's most gifted Christians and humble servants of the Lamb forget all titles and politics and, in a new maturity, sacrifice their own name, denominationalism, reputation and single-handed success to the single advancement of the King-dom of only one King, the Lamb of God.

Imagine the public tumult when this collective, city-based and authentic leadership regularly provides prophetic vision, teaches apostolic standards, stands united, blesses each other and speaks to the world with one voice. What the devil has tried hard to prevent at any cost will again come true: 'the Romans', 'the Ephesians', 'the Corinthians', 'the church of Jerusalem', Vienna, Singapore, Baghdad, KhartouÙm or Montevideo will reconnect with each other, each forming itself into a supernatural corporate identity and movement under one single Lord and Master, and speaking with a collective and powerful voice to its city and nation.

What happens at the small level of house churches will eventually spill over on a larger, city scale, where the church will 'excel at the small and therefore excel at the large'. Instead of Christians being regularly excited top-down through imported motivators and speakers at artificial conferences based on names and topics, the healthy, authentic and infectious joy and excitement at the house level will bubble up and express itself city-wide, where no one can miss it any more, and people will repeat the statement made first in Jerusalem: 'You have filled our city with your teaching!' And if ever God should choose to repeat instances as at Pentecost, where 120 upper-room Christians suddenly face the challenge of accommodating 3000 converts in one day, they would be prepared, because the flexible structure of multiplying house churches would already be in place.

In many areas of the world, local and regional pastoral fellowships and prayer networks are emerging. I believe this can be the begning of a regional process, a Spirit-led, intuitive and slow convergence of people with like-minded spirits, which creates healthy relationships first, which leads to the formation of a collective spiritual identity, a vessel of unity, into which, at a special *kairos*-point in history, a greater challenge can be placed: collectively to take on the challenge of discipling our city or region – together!

Chapter 2

House Churches in History

Rediscovery through the valley of the Dark Ages

The New Testament church was a growing church, says Dr Alan Kreider, and from history we know that it kept growing for quite some time. According to an epistle to Diognetus written in the late second century, 'Christians, day by day increase more and more.' In the middle of the third century Origen exclaimed: 'Multitudes of people are coming to faith.' Ramsay MacMullen, professor of ancient history at Yale, has estimated that in each generation some 500,000 people were added to the church up until the conversion of Emperor Constantine in AD 312, when the church finally made up between 5 and 8 per cent of the population of the Roman empire.

Multiplying house churches

The Christians in New Testament times and immediately after were meeting literally in house churches, usually in the largest rooms of its members. Church historians agree that they could have rarely been more than 15 or 20 people. Once a house church grew bigger than that, it usually multiplied by simply starting

another house church nearby. If not, this growth immediately caused problems. Origen, preaching in a home
in Caesarea, once complained that 'some have hidden
in remotest corners of the house to occupy themselves
with profane stories'.

Join the candidates for death

Although Christians were not constantly persecuted,
and times of relative freedom were interwoven with
subtle or fierce persecutions, every Christian knew that
persecution could break out at any moment, due to a
local crisis, an imperial edict, or a 'wolf' that had got in
among the sheep as a lying informer like Judas, about to
betray the followers of Christ to the Herods of the day.
This was what Paul calls 'the fellowship of the sufferings of Christ', as he writes from his prison cell to the
Philippians (Phil. 3:10). Tertullian writes: 'We are
besieged and attacked, they kept us prisoners in our
own secret congregations.' Every Christian was, by
definition, a candidate for death. If one wanted a soft
life, or wanted to get ahead in respectable circles, one
simply did not become a Christian. When a Christian,
under pressure or interrogation, simply affirmed, 'I
am a Christian!', it had a powerful ring of authority
to it. The power to face persecution came for many
Christians from a vivid vision of the future, the living
expectation of the imminent return of the Messiah.
People knew that this person was ready to die for
this statement, and that caused awe or consternation.
Persecution was so much part of the lives of the early
Christians, that it moulded their thinking – and their
structure! This is discussed further in chapter 6.

History: more than propaganda written by the victors

There are two ways to read the Bible: we can read our experiences into it, and search for 'confirmations' from the Bible to underline what we already 'knew'; or we can understand the Bible even to contradict our experiences, which can be substantially more painful – but liberating in the process. We can approach history in the same way. Either history will be, as a common communist slogan says, simply 'propaganda written by the victors', an interpretation of history to fit and justify the present rule or status quo; or history becomes the science to truly discover the facts of the past, even if they do not seem to fit the picture we have of our own history. If we now look for reasons for the multiplying and growth of the house-church movements in the New Testament and in the first few centuries AD, we might be surprised not to find what we expect to be there, and startled to find some quite different dynamics.

No evangelism

> *If we are convinced that 'evangelism' is what we all need to do, we will soon start to see evangelism on every page of the Bible, even if it is not there at all.*

A case in point is evangelism. If we are convinced that 'evangelism' is what we all need to do, we will soon start to see evangelism on every page of the Bible, even if it is not there at all. Except for Philip (Acts 9) and the fivefold ministry (Eph. 4:11), there is almost no mention of 'evangelists' or 'evangelism' as we know it in the New Testament and the records of the early church at all. Alan Kreider speaks of a 'telling silence of encouragement to "evangelize".' The New Testament does not speak about evangelizing as a 'plain preaching activity', and Jesus seems to be, in fact, outspoken against going 'door to door' (Lk. 10), a very common 'evangelistic method' in some countries. There is, however, much emphasis on the 'making of disciples'. Arthur Darby Nock says that in the history of the early church 'there was little, if any, direct preaching to the public masses; it was simply too dangerous.' The church not only had a message, it was the message. Because the church in itself was 'good news', there was no

Only when the church as a structure became 'bad news', an ill-matching structure for an explosive message, did the need for special 'good-news' enterprises emerge.

need for proclamation-style evangelism or going door to door. Only when the church as a structure became 'bad news', an ill-matching structure for an explosive message, did the need for special 'good-news' enterprises emerge. Evangelism without a functioning church model is evangelism because of the lack of a working church model, and it provides literally out-of-body experiences and even out-of-body conversions.

Many historians therefore disagree with English writer Michael Green, who states in his otherwise excellent book *Evangelism in the Early Church*: 'There can be no doubt that . . . open-air evangelism continued through the first two centuries.' The pagan Caecilius, a contemporary of the early church, reported that Christians were 'silent in public, but chattering in corners'. This also meant that in times of illness or crisis their neighbours, who had learned to trust them, would feel free to turn to Christians for help.

Baptist mission professor John Mark Terry, in his book *Evangelism, a Concise History*, reflecting the thinking of our present time, sees evangelism as something doable, then reinterprets the Bible and history from that perspective,

saying: 'Wherever Jesus went, he presented the gospel.'
The evangelism worldview Terry describes is full of
'evangelistic keywords' and methodology: touching, wit-
nessing, sharing, ministering, preaching, telling the good
news and doing evangelism. He even goes so far as to say
that 'Jesus was using a number of different evangelistic
methods'. We need to be careful not to reinterpret church
history through the reading glasses of present styles and
methods of 'evangelism'. Jesus, as well as His body, the
church, not only had a message, He *was* the message. He
did not have the gospel: *He was the gospel.*

The gospel is not a set of doctrines, but a redeemed lifestyle reflecting God's qualities. What the early Christians
did was not 'lifestyle evangelism' true to a proven
method. Rather, their normal everyday life had powerful
in-built evangelistic implications, true to a loving and
compassionate God.

No missions

Georg Kretschmar points out, that 'the recruitment to
faith was never institutionalized, there was no organizing
the congregation for missions'. The impact of the church
as an entity was so strong that most early Christians did
not even pray for the conversion of pagans, but, according
to Yves Congar, a Dominican scholar, they prayed for the
prosperity and peace of the people. There is, says Norbert
Brox, an 'astonishing absence of thinking and talking
about missions'. The reason for this 'absence' is the same
as for the 'absence' of evangelism: the church in itself was
the mission. The 'missionary journeys' of Paul and his
companions were not understood as 'missions' as we
know it by Paul himself: the expression only emerged as
the title to hand-drawn maps of the Mediterranean in the
appendix of Bibles centuries later. Paul was simply doing

apostolic and prophetic ministry, and so was the church that had been planted and emerged through these ministries. Since the church was the mission, it did not send out special 'missionaries' as such: it literally sent out itself, in the form of multipliable units, embryonic units of two and three from a local church, which carried within themselves the vision and virus of church, ready to infect whatever they touched.

No attractive worship services

Although the church in Corinth was still open to outsiders, from the mid-first century onwards pagans were usually neither invited nor admitted to Christian meetings. After the persecution under Nero in the middle of the first century, most churches closed their doors to outsiders. One of the functions of the deacons even sees to have been that of an 'ecclesiastical bouncer', the typically heavy-set person who in today's world stands at the door of private clubs and bars to evict, if necessary by force, unwanted elements. They had to screen the wolves from the lambs, as the 'Testament of our Lord', a mid-fourth-century document describing the functions of the deacons, explains. Paul warned the Galatians that 'false brothers had infiltrated our ranks to spy on the freedom we have in Christ Jesus' (Gal. 2:4). The fellowship meetings of the Christians were not at all meant to be attractive for outsiders, because they were not designed for them. Mid-third-century Bishop Cyprian in Carthage compared the church with the 'enclosed garden' of the Song of Solomon (4:12). Even a catechumen, someone in daily Bible training under an instructor was firmly dismissed before the Christians did their secret rites, the prayers, the Holy Kiss, baptisms and the Lord's Supper. The Christians were very much what Celsus, a critic of the early church, called a 'secret society'.

Worship is never mentioned in the New Testament as the reason Christians gather together, and certainly not consisting of singing a number of songs. Worship consists of an obedient and sacrificial lifestyle: this certainly does sometimes involve singing, but only because the whole of

> *Worship consists of an obedient and sacrificial lifestyle: this certainly does sometimes involve singing, but only because the whole of life is living worship.*

life is living worship. Abraham knew this well, and as he went up to Mount Moriah to sacrifice his only son Isaac, he told his waiting servants that he was going up 'to worship' (Gen. 22).

No mainstream

Christians in the early centuries often called themselves *paroikoi* (1. Pet. 2:11), resident aliens, or 'the alien next door'. The understanding they had of themselves was to be not settlers and dutiful citizens with a special religious persuasion, but 'a colony of aliens', at home everywhere, fully at home nowhere. When people became Christians they were 'converted to marginality', as Brazilian Eduardo Eduardo Hoornaert said. Rather than being part of the main social establishment they were part of a counter-culture, an anti-society, secret and mysterious to many, loyal to 'another king', a distinctively different spiritual tribe. Paul describes himself to Felix as 'a follower of the Way, which they call a sect' (Acts 24:14), and was known as the 'ringleader of a sect' and 'a troublemaker' (Acts 24:5).

So how and why did people become Christians?

If it was not through systematic evangelistic programmes, mission outreach and invitations to attractive worship services, how did people become Christians? And if becoming a Christian meant joining an outcast and secretive society, endangering one's social success and potentially ending up as a candidate for death, why did people want to become Christians?

We will look now at some of the historic reasons why large numbers of people decided to join the church. We may find here clues to similar developments now. Again we should not fall into the trap of slavishly copying historic methodologies and procedures from another time and space, but learn from the underlying principles and work these out by creatively and flexibly in today's cultures and people groups.

Beyond the fact that Christians lived in organic and easily multipliable house churches, equipped and guided by the fivefold ministry (Eph. 4:11), some of the main reasons for people becoming Christians in ancient times, according to numerous historic studies done by Alan Kreider and others, are as follows.

1 Curiosity

Many of today's churches try to be attractive to the world, welcome visitors with sweets and visitor cards, display signs at the entrance reading 'Everyone welcome!'. They have outreach campaigns of all shapes and sizes, focused on getting outsiders to come to church, and they are generally trying to be at least seeker-sensitive or even seeker-driven.

The early churches worked on very different dynamics. One of them was people's insatiable curiosity. People are by nature adventurous and curious, seeking 'to go

where no one has gone before'. Many today wonder why
the occult movements and secret societies like the Free-
masons are still flourishing. The answer is: they appeal to
people's basic instinct to be part of an exclusive family,
group and tribe, for which humans are ready to undergo
almost any sort of initiation process.

Jesus knew this, and had something like a dual communication style, one for those 'inside', and another for those
'outside': 'Jesus spoke . . . to the crowd in parables; he did
not say anything to them without using a parable'
(Mt. 13:34). This pattern seems to continue in the church:
preaching was for those outside the church, teaching for
those inside. Jesus was very firm on this dual pattern: 'The
knowledge of the secrets of the kingdom of God has been
given to you, but to others I speak in parables, so that,
"though seeing, they may not see; though hearing, they
may not understand" ' (Lk. 8:10). Even His words about
the 'narrow gate' created a powerful curiosity and an
almost feverish excitement amongst many to know the
mysterious message and
movement of Jesus. Do they
know something we do not
know? Jesus knew that the
'mystery of the gospel' is not
like 'pearls thrown before
swine', but something discovered, sought out, and only
then, by revelation, found.

> *Today we are sometimes in
> danger of pressing home
> answers to people who
> have not even asked the
> right questions, and pre-
> venting people from
> becoming truly curious.*

People were not freely admitted to churches, and this
only sparked and heightened their interest. If I tell my
four-year-old son not to open that drawer under any
circumstance once I leave the room, I prophetically know
to which place he is almost magically and irresistibly
drawn once I go out: the forbidden drawer. Today we are
sometimes in danger of pressing home answers to people

who have not even asked the right questions, and preventing people from becoming truly curious. Jesus described himself as the water of life, and the disciples as the salt of the earth. If people eat salt, it will make them thirsty, even if they have not been thirsty before. If people are not yet thirsty for the water of life, feed them salt. Then they will become thirsty, and then they will drink.

2 Steadfastness in persecution and martyrdom

The first time that many people in the first centuries set eyes on a real, living Christian was when they saw one die. Many Christians were crucified, attacked by wild beasts, roasted on chairs of molten iron, or just burnt. Their humble and patient and, often enough, joyful endurance of those dreadful torments was medically

A Christianity which has something to die for has a powerful attraction for the living

inexplicable; their love for each other, giving each other the kiss of peace, a revolutionary sign of an obvious secret society before they were killed, was transparent. Those who guarded the Christians on their way to their executions often said: 'There is a power among them!' The fact that they were ready to die for their belief made many secretly wish they had something so powerful to believe in. As a result, more people were fascinated, their curiosity level rose even more – and they were attracted to the church. It has often been said, 'The blood of the martyrs is the seed of the church.' A Christianity which has something to die for has a powerful attraction for the living.

3 Exorcism

When Jesus exercised authority over evil spirits and then told his disciples to 'drive out demons' (Mt. 10:8), his early followers listened carefully – and did as they

were told. In the early centuries, described by many as
'an age of bondage, life-disfiguring addictions and
compulsions' – which does not seem much different
from today – the freedom and fulness of life in Christ
could not remain hidden for long. As one spokesman
for many, Irenaeus pointed to the 'evangelistic' function of exorcism: 'Those who have been cleansed often
both believe in Christ and join themselves to the
church.' In an age of competitive miracle working, the
Christian God and this powerful 'spiritual detoxifica-
tion' in the name of Jesus seemed stronger and more
profound than the influence of other gods.

Catechist Justin of Rome, writing about AD 150,
described how Christians helped other people almost
systematically to renounce demons, and saw them
being liberated from spiritual oppression mainly in
four key areas: unlawful sex, the secret and magic arts,
escalating private wealth, and violent xenophobia. The
early Christians would have seen people who practised
illicit sex outside marriage, who accumulated material
wealth for their personal gain, who were involved in
occultism, or who were violent to foreigners and
strangers, as demonically bound people who needed
the help of Jesus to be released from these overpowering spiritual forces which were beyond any known
human control. As the church stopped focusing on
these ministries in later centuries, they left a gaping
vacuum. This might need to be filled again by the only
organism on earth called and gifted to do so, the church.

4 *They had found the Way to live*
Christians believed they were God's instrument for making a new world, and not only had they found the right
reason and way to die, they had also found the right way
to live. Before they were called Christians, they were

called followers of the Way. This was for two reasons: Jesus had said 'I am the Way'; and the Christians had obviously found the way to live. The way they organized and structured their life was called the church. When a Christian whispered to a pagan, 'I have

Not only had they found the right reason and way to die, they had also found the right way to live. The way they organized and structured their life was called the church.

found the way to live!' it was not offensive but intriguing, and quite attractive in an age when people were aware that things were somehow going wrong in their lives.

In addition, Christians had a communal lifestyle, socially inclusive like no other group in ancient history. They shared material blessings with everyone in need out of a common fund. They even used to pick up discarded babies left to die on the local garbage dumps, and raised them as their own; or volunteered to nurse victims of the plague, endangering their own lives, much to the dumbfounding of their contemporaries. In the eyes of a materialistic society, they were either crazy or holy. They were approachable and trusted friends and counsellors for anyone. This was especially true for the women, perhaps because of their ability to listen to people and be attentive to their questions. Augustine wrote quite embarrassed to a group of men: 'Oh you men, you are easily beaten by your women. It is their presence in great numbers that causes the church to grow.'

The Christians were aware that the life of their 'free communities' was remarkable. It is the 'beauty of life that causes strangers to join the ranks,' one of them wrote. They could self-consciously say: 'We do not talk about great things, we live them.' That is also why the early leaders of the churches gave much attention to maintaining the quality of fellowship, love and relationship amongst each other, because they knew that this is one of the main reasons for people being drawn to Christ and being saved.

5 *The teachings and person of Jesus*

A modern-day Christian leader from Africa once exclaimed about the Christian missionaries he knew: 'They came to preach the gospel to us, but they did not show us how to live!' In the words of Alan Kreider, many early Christians were convinced 'that conversion began not so much at the level of belief but at the level of lifestyle'. Only a person who was willing to change his life was ready for the gospel. Thus, one of the most compelling dynamics of people being drawn to the church was the person and teaching of Jesus Himself. His Sermon on the Mount was not so much understood as a sermon or moral dream, but as a set of godly ethics, a heavenly guide to live by. Pagans of all ages were powerfully drawn to Jesus and His sayings. No other teaching of Jesus was more often repeated than the command to love one's enemies. These words, many held, were so wonderful that they made you either laugh or cry. The church did not preach itself, it preached Christ by promoting his teaching and by living his lifestyle.

> *The church did not preach itself, it preached Christ by promoting his teaching and by living his lifestyle.*

The derailing of the church

The New Testament church has been mostly an organic, relational, spiritual family, multiplying itself. But even before His death, Jesus warned His disciples of deception, false prophets, false Christs, who all have one common purpose: to deceive and to derail the elect. It is natural for all of us to think of this deception as a part of a terrible future, which will happen to others, not to us. However, Paul, Peter and Jude all warn of the immediate coming of ungodly men, false teachers and false prophets, disguising themselves as angels from heaven. They did not mince words: they even cursed in advance those who will do this (Gal. 1:8,9; 2 Pet. 2:1–3; Jude 3–6).

I harbour a terrible suspicion that this deception may have already happened in global proportions through what has been coined 'Christendom', the derailed caricature and doomed version of Christianity. Maybe the worst of what Christ predicted is yet to come, and we need to be prepared for a worst possible scenario. But this also means that today we may stand on the apogee of many already derailed and now institutionalized developments. Even if we want to be true children of our mother churches, we will therefore automatically become part of traditional movements which may have departed long ago from other movements that themselves have departed from some derailed movements in the past. If the river has once found its bed, it is very difficult to change its course. However, our first allegiance as Christians is with the God of the future, not with the history of the past. Rick Joyner, a prophetic teacher from the USA, said it this way: many need to realize that they do not need to be born by the mother (church), but truly be born of the Father in heaven Himself.

A silent revolution

'I am the light of the world,' says Jesus. To darken the light of the world means to darken the world. And dark, the world became. They were literally called the Dark Ages. If there really was a derailing of the church, it is worth going back a few steps in history to look at some of these ecclesiological accidents. How could it all happen?

Church historians agree that it may have begun with challenging and changing the apostolic teaching on repentance, holiness and sin, baptisms and the Godhead itself. One of the first attempts at inventing the non-scriptural distinction between 'clergy' and 'laity' was made by the Nicolaitans, a group that emphasized the difference between 'the listening lay people and the ministering brothers'. They go back to Nicolas, who was one of the first seven church deacons (Acts 6:5), later influenced by Greek Dualism, who then goes on to develop the doctrine of 'the Nicolaitans' (Rev. 2:6), which the risen Christ says he 'hates'. Nicolaitan in Greek is composed of two words. *Nikao* means to conquer, to be above others, and *laos* means common people. 'A Nicolaitan is someone conquering the common people, climbing above the laity,' says Watchman Nee in his book *The Orthodoxy of the Church*. 'The conduct of climbing over and above the common believers as a mediatorial class is what the Lord detests and hates.' The concept of a special clergy caste is already evident in the two letters of Clement of Rome (c. AD 100) and the elevation of the bishop to be the autocratic head of the local church in the letters of Ignatius of Antioch in Syria (c. 110–17).

Then there was the reintroduction of two powerful forces to Christianity: moralism and religion. The one introduced a set of behavioural patterns, a group of laws to live by. The other may have started with the crucifix, starting to 'cross oneself' and ward off some evil spirit through this practice, it may have been a few 'harmless' wax-candles here and some burnt incense there. But it is not harmless at all. It drew back Christianity into the religious 'patterns of the world', complete with idols, charms, religious rites and priests.

From then on it was a quick and constant succession of derailments from the original teachings of Jesus and the apostles. Early 'innovations' were the veneration of the, usually martyred, saints, and the separation of the Lord's Supper as a meaningful and prophetic way to eat together in the presence of Christ into a 'love or agape feast' and the Eucharist, a social potluck dinner and a religious and highly symbolic function. According to Peter H. Davis in his article 'The Church in the House', in the second half of the first century documents such as the Didache and the Canon of Hippolytus show that the Lord's Supper was not 'attached' to a meal, *it was a meal*. Very soon, however, the 'love-feast' became purely social and was abandoned, whereby the Eucharist in its symbolic form – without 'real food' – became the accepted way to celebrate the Lord's Supper.

Based on fear, not faith

True stewards and spiritual fathers in the Kingdom of God were and are equipped with the supernatural gift of faith that allows them to truly believe that God is still in control, even if they are not. They are able to live this healthy tension of uncertainty and unpredictability about what will happen next in the relationship of God and His people, because their strength is not in understanding everything, but in their trust in God. Early on, the church started to give in to the pressure for security. Around AD 150, for example, 'scholastic theology' was introduced as a system to interpret Scripture and defend it against heresies such as Gnosticism. Very soon the defensive system became more important than the message it defended.

Early charismatic movements like Montanism created more problems, because some of their adherents were not easy to control and started to build factions in the church and pull people towards individual charismatic leaders. In order to defend the truth and the church against this, the church strongly focused on dogma and creed, and tightly observed who was able and allowed to do ministry, and who not. In short, it tried to exert greater control, in order to avoid more damage. The motivation was good, but the method was not. Control is the natural development of a lack of trust; it comes from fear, the opposite of faith, and leads people to build a system in order to make sure that nothing can go wrong, or at least to minimize danger and apostasy. As a result, the church focuses more on 'safe' rituals, 'right' formulae and 'approved' liturgies, and tries to become watertight as well as foolproof. As a by-product of this, the church quickly fell into the hands of enthusiastic theological watchdogs, police-men of the faith and a new version of 'bishops', king-like figures who were no longer the most humble servants and plain down-to-earth elders, but impres-sive figureheads and religious prime ministers with an aura of awe-inspiring authority to keep the flock together and the problems outside. Again, a human Saul replaced God as the real king of the people of God.

These spiritual 'kings' were able, in the power of the charismatic personality they commanded, to alter doc-trines and introduce any amount of personal and subjec-tive interpretations as a new teaching, a new dogma; and much of the church went with it. As early as AD 220, Origen introduced the doctrine of infant baptism in Alex-andria. Not only did this become compulsory in the west-ern church by AD 416; but it also remained the church's main way of 'evangelism' and of initiating the general population into the church system, a practice that can be likened to selling spiritual insurance for the afterlife to biblically ignorant but religious and pious parents, who feared for their children and simply had to trust the reli-gious specialists of the day.

The professionalizing of the church under Constantine

When Emperor Constantine converted to Christianity in AD 312 and, in his Edict of Milan, made Christianity a state religion, Christians, tired of centuries of persecution, celebrated him as a saviour, they relaxed – and they experienced probably the biggest single derailment in history. In the years after 312 the church became heavily professionalized: priests were approved and 'licensed' to conduct weddings and other functions in a more and more professional public manner, and the church experienced the doubtful blessing of being equipped with a mediatorial caste between itself and God. The church needed to be 'fit for the king' and his company, and that meant cathedrals, not shabby houses. Thus, the great divide between clergy and laity not only emerged, but was sanctioned, institutionalized, sealed and protected by the state, an error that has cost the lives of millions of martyrs right up to the present day, killed by the hand of secular soldiers, at the instigation of 'properly organized and registered' advocates of Christendom.

The church had gladly accepted national graduation from a persecuted cult to a state-prescribed religion, and lost its prophetic power over social, cultural and pagan habits in the process.

The church had gladly accepted national graduation from a persecuted cult to a state-prescribed religion, and lost its prophetic power over social, cultural and pagan habits in the process. Because it was from now on married to the system that granted and protected all of it. The church lost its identity as a prophetic counter-culture, supernaturally different from the patterns of this world, and became a celebrated insider. As a result, both the state and the church were trapped. The state lost its direction because it had swallowed the beacon and the compass, and the church became drunk with political power.

Banning the house church

From now on, to start a house church meant breaking the law and becoming a criminal. A new era began: the persecution of the church in the name of the 'church'.

In all these developments, one particularly stands out: in AD 380 bishops Theodosius and Gratian ordered that there should be only one state-recognized orthodox church, and one set of faith – the orthodox dogma. Each Roman citizen was forced to be a member and was made to believe in the *lex fidei*, the law of faith. Other groups and movements – including those meeting in homes – were forbidden. That meant the legal end of the house church. This law turned the rules upside down. Until the rule of Severus around AD 222–35, church buildings had not even been allowed by the government, and house churches were the only way for Christians to meet. But from now on, to start a house church meant breaking the law and becoming a criminal. A new era began: the persecution of the church in the name of the 'church'.

Reviving synagogue-style worship patterns

Just as the Jewish *Mishnah* allowed ten male Jews to form a synagogue, Christians have inherited their pattern of worship from the Jewish synagogues, not the temple, says Dr Met Castillo. The Jewish teacher Rabinowitz has identified five elements in synagogue worship: invitation to worship with hymns and a formal call to worship; prayers and petitions; Scripture lessons; an address based on the Scripture lessons; conclusion with benedictions. As Christian worship became more and more formal in Christian church houses – rather than house churches – after Constantine, the basic Jewish synagogue pattern was revived and inherited, with the addition of saying the creed. The church thus fell back into legalistic and ritualistic patterns of worship which would remain almost unchanged during the following centuries, and became the agreed, sacrosanct style of meetings for Christians.

The Priscillian movement

Priscillian was a Spanish nobleman in the fourth century, who immediately revolted against the state-ordered priest-religion. This man, on fire for God, began a large lay movement in Spain and France. He was joined by a considerable number of bishops and priests. They met in small fellowships, called 'brotherhoods', in ordinary houses where only converted and baptized Christians could take part. The orthodox church did not like this at all and had Priscillian and six of his friends put to death at Trier. In this they became forerunners of many similar reformation movements such as the Bogomilians, Petrobusians, Patarenians, Waldensians, Lollards and others.

The Celts

No rule is without exception, and even the Dark Ages produced some of the most marvellous theological works and Christian movements of all times. One of the often overlooked facts of history is that it was not really the Roman Catholic Church that converted Europe, but the Celts. They were an originally barbaric and later a Christian people group, related to the Galatians of Asia Minor and the French

Gauls, spreading from the Upper Danube region down to Portugal and then later over to England and Ireland. They not only produced powerful apostles, such as Patrick of Ireland who initiated one of the most strategic, nationwide church-planting movements of all times, but also sent apostles such as Gall to Switzerland and Boniface to Germany. Between the sixth and ninth centuries the Celts were gradually taken over by the papal doctrines and values of the Roman Catholic Church, often enough through political force. Nevertheless, the Celts dug many wells of fresh spiritual waters to nurture the lands of Europe. As Roger Ellis and Chris Seaton, in their book *The New Celts*, suggest, since those wells have become filled with rubbish and the sand of history, it might be worth cleaning them up and redigging them for the future of Europe.

The downward path

These, however, where the exceptions in the first few centuries after the conversion of Constantine: the spiritual standard of the day was less enchanting. Far gone were the days when the train of Christianity was running on safe prophetic and apostolic tracks, with a clear goal in view. From here on the church was wandering in the desert. It was a time which somewhat resembled the spiritual anarchy which prevails in some countries today, where people in practice believe anything, as long as it is not in the Bible.

Forgotten were the words of Jesus, 'Let the dead bury the dead.' Instead, the church proudly established graveyards close by the 'holy' church buildings, where people felt their mortal remains would be safe from the monsters and dragons of the deep. This practice was fed by the naive and deeply religious belief that God dwells in a special way in church buildings. The Council of Ephesus (431) proclaimed the worship of Mary as the mother of God.

Leo the Great pronounced himself Bishop of Rome (440), and Cesar Valentian (445) confirmed his position as the spiritual leader of the whole Western Empire. Around 500 the priesthood started to observe a common dress code. With Justinian (527–65) the church became truly a state-ordained church: all priests became public servants. As early as 607, after the fall of the Roman Empire, Boniface III was the first bishop to adopt the title 'Pope' in the Roman Catholic Church. Previously this title, *Pontifex maximus*, meaning 'big bridgebuilder', had been used by the Roman emperors to describe themselves as high priests and gods of the Roman Empire. Some further steps down into spiritual darkness were:

709   Kissing the Pope's foot introduced
786   Worship of images and relics develops
850   First use of holy water
995   Canonization of dead saints
998   Fasting on Fridays and before Lent introduced
1079 Celibacy of the priesthood instituted
1090 Prayer beads adopted from several pagan religious systems
1184 The Inquisition, the policing of the faith, begins: millions of Jews and witches (and later, after the Reformation, Protestant believers) will die at the hands of the Church of Rome. It is officially established by Pope Innocent IV in 1252. The Reformation churches later joined in the same spirit
1190 The sale of indulgences – relief from punishment of sins in exchange for the payment of money – instituted
1215 Transubstantiation of the wafer and wine declared: these elements supernaturally change into the body and blood of Jesus at the incantation of the priest
1229 Bible declared to be too holy for ordinary people to read and was forbidden to laymen
1414 Communion cup was forbidden to lay people
1439 Doctrine of Purgatory decreed
1439 Dogma of the sacraments affirmed
1545 The traditional teachings of the Roman Catholic Church granted equal authority with the Bible at the Council of Trent

The Inquisition

As a natural but radical consequence of the decision taken under Gratian and Theodosius in AD 380, the Inquisition, a religious–political joint venture in the form of a Christian 'faith police', lifted its bloody head, killing millions of Protestants at the hands of Catholics, just as, a little while later, many so-called 'Anabaptists' would die at the hands of Protestants. After defeating the Islamic Kingdom in Granada in 1492, the Inquisition found yet another group to hunt: the Moriscos, Islamic Moors who had converted to Christianity. Persecuted and killed by almost everyone were the Jews, seen as the 'murderers of God'.

Only as late as 22 January 1998 did the Vatican, under the leadership of German Cardinal Joseph Ratzinger, open its extensive archives on the Inquisition in the Palazzo del Sant'Uffizio in Rome, where the bloody business of systematically persecuting and killing heretics is documented in no fewer than 4500 large volumes. 'We are concerned about the truth, and this is an act of self-cleansing,' said Cardinal Achille Silvestrini. It is believed, however, that those 4500 volumes represent much less than a third of the original material, the rest of which was lost.

In the words of the German magazine, *Der Spiegel* (23/1998), 'The Inquisition sniffed with dedication after anyone who even faintly smelled of heresy.' Any dangerous written material was immediately put on the *Index Additus Librorum Prohibitum*, the black list of forbidden books and, wherever possible, burnt. The Inquisition was especially cruel in Spain where, as late as 1826, 18 years after Joseph Bonaparte, a brother of Napoleon, had declared the Inquisition illegal, the last hanging of a 'heretic' took place in Valencia. This religious persecution went hand in hand with the proverbial witch-hunt, and we can imagine Satan's glee to see biblically converted women and house church leaders being burnt at the stake by the church in the name of witchcraft. Equally cruel and heartless was the Inquisition in Germany. When, for example, Reformer Jan Hus died at the stake in Konstanz in 1415, the 'Fathers of the Council' simply laughed.

The Reformation

Luther, at Worms in 1521, said some unbelievable and unheard-of words for the ears of his contemporaries: 'I do not believe the Pope and the Church Councils. It is a fact that they have often erred. I am a captive of the Word of God.' The monk Martin Luther, more than 1100 years after the first energetic wave of

> *If it was possible for the very essence of the gospel – salvation by faith, justification by grace – to be buried under the sand of history, could we also have erred in other, lesser issues?*

house churches had died down, was able to rediscover the heartbeat of the gospel, salvation by faith and grace, and the centrality of Scripture. His discovery was like a bomb which broke the theological dam, and prepared the way for the subsequent chain-reaction of reformational insights. Other Reformers like Zwingli, Melanchthon, Calvin, John Knox and others, started to encourage the translation of the Bible and its use by the common man, and the Bible was translated from Latin – the language of the professional clergy – into, initially, 14 popular languages, and reached 40 translations by the year 1600. If it was possible for the very essence of the gospel – salvation by faith, justification by grace – to be buried under the sand of history, what about the rest? If we can gravely err in the very key and core issues, could we also have erred in other, lesser issues? The fact that the Bible was again given into the hands of common people

started what I call the history of rediscovery: it was the turning point where the church started to climb again out of
darkness, escape its own structural prison and rediscover,
step by step, long-forgotten truth and long-forgotten practices, including the house church as an organic form of
church.

Martin Luther's 'Third order of service'

In Luther's *Vorrede zur Deutschen Messe* (his preface to the
German Mass and Order of Service) published in 1526, he
distinguishes three 'orders of services': the Latin Mass, a
public meeting for all in Latin, which Luther specially
designed for the young people (Latin was the cosmo-
politan language, the 'English' of that time); the German
Mass, a second public liturgy in German; and a third kind
of worship meeting about which he writes:

> The third kind of service should be a truly evangelical order
> and should not be held in a public place for all sorts of people.
> But those who want to be Christians in earnest and who pro-
> fess the gospel with hand and mouth should sign their names
> and meet alone in a house somewhere to pray, to read, to
> baptize, to receive the sacrament, and to do other Christian
> work.

Luther even saw the need for a celebration-type service,
attracting the masses, like having 'an open-air worship
service amongst pagans and Turks. I am happy if you ring
all the bells, play all the organs and trumpet on anything
which is loud,' he writes.

Luther, sadly, never got round to implement this most
revolutionary restructuring of the church into cell and
celebration. The history of the church includes a long list
of prematurely aborted attempts to restore the house-

church structure. They ran aground at one point or another, as many, who followed Luther's example, discovered for themselves. Luther said about his own failure to implement the house-church structure: 'But as yet, I neither can, nor desire to begin such a congregation . . . for I have not yet the people for it, nor do I see many who want it. But if I should be requested to do it and could not refuse with a good conscience, I should gladly do my part and help as best I can.'

Dr Martin Lloyd-Jones believed that the true course of Luther's hesitation was 'a spirit of caution, political considerations, a lack of faith in the people in his churches and fear of losing the movement to the Anabaptists'. After 1526 Luther changed his mind and turned back to almost Roman Catholic forms of services, yielding to the

> *Luther was, in this way, like Calvin. They reformed the content but not the form of Christianity.*

pressure of the secular authorities. He is even directly responsible for the martyrdom of many thousands of Christians who did not go along with his teachings – Luther's contribution to the spirit of the Inquisition. From 1530 he maintained that all Christians who publicly preached and taught the word of God without being pastors should be put to death, even if they taught correctly. But Luther was not happy with his achievements. At the end of his life he wrote: 'Amongst thousands there hardly is one true Christian. We are almost pagans with Christian names.' Luther was, in this way, like Calvin, who, amongst other innovations, tried to make every citizen of Geneva come to the worship services, or otherwise pay a fine of three Batzen or ultimately face excommunication. They reformed the content but not the form of Christianity. They 'could not decide to break from the sociological forms of church since the time of Constantine,' writes Bible teacher Visser't Hoft.

The apostolic movement of Schwenckfeld

Luther had a very influential disciple and teacher, Caspar Schwenckfeld (1480–1561). Initially, Luther greeted Schwenckfeld, who was a preaching non-theologian, as 'a messenger from God', and was greatly influenced by him. Schwenckfeld, however, had a dramatic 'born again' experience in 1527, and through his subsequent studies of Scripture started to criticize Luther. He pleaded with Luther not to follow through with his sudden new direction after 1530, his almost Roman Catholic ecclesiology and his teaching that a person can be born again by baptism. 'Luther started to persecute Schwenckfeld with bitter hatred, called him a demonized fool and heretic, and refused even to read his writings, sending them back unread' writes French Bible teacher Alfred Kuen. 'The Reformer of Schlesien had to wander around Europe like a hunted deer.' The outlawed Reformer went around and established lively fellowship in many places, which were basically home cells, Bible groups and prayer groups. To avoid further tensions with the established church, Schwenckfeld did not introduce baptism and the Lord's Supper into his groups. When Schwenckfeld died in Ulm in 1561, Lutheran pastors tried to bring his many disciples back into the churches by force, and if they were not willing, had them thrown into jail and their children taken away from them.

The Anabaptists

When Zwingli started the work of the Reformation in Zürich, a group of former friends of Zwingli dared to establish a Christian fellowship in Zollikon near Zürich, without the permission of the government. They were Felix Mantz, a Hebrew scholar; Conrad Grebel, a member of the city council, from a respected Zürich family; and Georg Blaurock, a former monk and excellent evangelist. Grebel, and many others, had started to discover the Bible, as Zwingli encouraged them to do.

In 1524 Grebel had a son, and he refused to have him baptized, because he believed that the Bible teaches that faith comes first, and baptism only follows afterwards. That was a time when many Christians began to read the Bible together, pray and have the Lord's Supper. In 1525 Zwingli summoned the city council and instigated a law that required everyone to bring all non-baptized children for baptism within eight days, otherwise the parents were to be excommunicated. Baptism, until Easter 1525, was still administered according to the Roman Catholic system, complete with incantations, crossing, anointing with oil and spittle.

Grebel, however, was not to be led astray. He baptized Blaurock, who in turn baptized 15 others. Thus was the Baptist movement born – which the Reformers called Anabaptists, the 're-baptizers', claiming that adult baptisms down-played God's grace extended at the time of infant baptism, and were therefore blasphemy. Zwingli agreed to the sentencing of the leaders of the movement. Grebel died in jail; Blaurock was beaten, sent away and burnt at the stake in the Tirol; Mantz was drowned.

The Anabaptist movement grew like wildfire. According to one historian of the sixteenth century, many feared that the majority of the people would fall for this cult.

Heinrich Bullinger, successor to Zwingli, saw many thousands becoming part of this movement, although it meant persecution. Many died for their new convictions. In the Netherlands and Friesland between 1535 and 1546 alone, 30,000 Anabaptists were killed. 'The Reformers called them sects, and therefore inherited a phrase from the Roman Catholic Church, which declared every form of Christian fellowship outside the church to be a cult,' writes theologian Emil Brunner.

Labadie's Conventicle

In 1640, Jean de Labadie, a former Jesuit, had become a pastor in Amiens, France. He had one goal in life: the fellowship of the true believers in small 'brotherhoods'. Soon, however, he was told that his activities were 'endangering the peace of the State', and he had to flee to Geneva, where he went, says Alfred Kuen, 'to wake up the church of Calvin which had fallen asleep'. Sceptical pastors in Geneva quickly arranged for him to pass on to the Netherlands. The main emphasis of Labadie's work was a shift of focus from church buildings to private homes. Labadie wrote the first book on the foundation of 'Conventicles', small fellowships of converted believers. He gave them practical advice on what to do in house meetings: word of introduction, prayer, singing, Bible reading, free prophecy according to 1 Corinthians 14:24–26, or discussing a biblical text together. His work attracted great attention; one of his students was Philipp Jakob Spener. But because of 'his stubborn determination to gather Christians in small groups', Reformed pastors in the Netherlands resisted him. Labadie was finally excommunicated, and died in Altona.

The Huguenots and the 'Church in the Wilderness'

When Claude Brousson, a famous leader of the Huguenots, was publicly executed in 1698 before a crowd of 10,000 people under the bloodthirsty rule of Louis XIV in mostly Roman Catholic France, he sang Psalm 34 just before he died. That psalm and its message reached as far as the shores of England, and was picked up by Daniel Defoe and others, who were part of the Dissenters, those with a 'different sense' or opinion from the established church. The Dissenters were, in some ways, the English version of the Huguenots, a Protestant movement forced underground by extreme persecution from the established Church. They organized themselves into house churches and 'The Church in the Wilderness', as they called it in reference to the Israelites delivered from the Egyptian oppression (Acts 7:38). In addition to the secret meetings in private homes, there were also large gatherings in forest clearings: again they were living out both structures, cells and celebrations. Defoe ultimately was put in jail, where he wrote the famous story of Robinson Crusoe. 'Crusoe's sailing the oceans was a description of the freedom of a person in Christ. His shipwrecking experience reflected Defoe's imprisonment, and the island was a symbol for his cell in jail,' says veteran missionary Ken McVety.

Spener and the church that was not the church

Philipp Jakob Spener (1635–1705), the father of Pietism in Germany, saw that the existing church needed restoration, and that small groups for individual encouragement and discipline were necessary. He began such meetings in 1670 under the name 'pious gatherings' (*collegia pietatis*). Christians met twice a week in houses, sometimes discussing the previous Sunday morning sermon from the

Lutheran Church, to which they belonged, but then they soon became Bible discussion groups.

This resulted in opposition from Lutheran churches, and in his home city, Frankfurt, the city council refused to allow the groups to meet in homes. 'Spener was a victim of an inadequate definition of his own small groups,' writes Bill Beckham. 'Although he obviously believed the small groups to be the church, he did not want to frighten the established churches. He made the small groups an append-age to the established church and doomed the movement.' His *Gemeinschaften* (fellowships) were basically substan-dard or half-churches, not intended to replace the existing church. He therefore forbade sacraments in the home groups. At the end of his life Spener had become cynical and cautious. Once he moved away from Frankfurt, he did not start any other groups.

John Wesley's cells

Many historians of early Methodism agree that the key to the Methodist revival was the accountability of the new believers in small groups, which Wesley called the 'classes'. Howard A. Snyder in his book *The Radical Wesley* says: 'The classes were in effect house churches. In weekly midweek meetings, which lasted an hour or so, each person reported their spiritual progress, shared on particular needs and problems, and most conversions occurred here.'

Methodism was interconnected by a network of soci-eties (classes joined together). In 1768, thirty years after its start, Methodism had 40 'circuits' and 27,341 mem-bers. By the turn of the century, one out of every thirty Englishmen was a Methodists. 'Wesley put about one out of five people, mostly from poor and uneducated folk, labouring men and women with little or no training, but with spiritual gifts and eagerness to serve into significant ministry and leadership. Thus, he made leaders of thousands of them.' He proved what Luther wished for, but did not dare to try: that ordinary people are made extraordinary by God and are well capable, within a house-church structure, of creating a tremendous movement.

Slowly, Methodism began again to emphasise Sunday morning congregational church meetings in buildings according to the Anglican patterns. 'As they de-emphasized the accountable relationships they had in their class meetings, the revival movement began to decline,' notes Larry Kreider in his book *House to House*. Today, as the following story, reported by the news agency Reuters in November 1998, indicates, even denominational Methodism is sometimes used as a banner to persecute house churches:

> Christian Zealots broke into a home-based church in the Solomon Islands, tied up five men, and destroyed the house because a 'non-Methodist' worship service was being held. The Pacific island's constitution guarantees freedom of religion, but traditional customs and values sometimes intrude on freedoms. A number of variations of the Christian faith are practised and some village bylaws require villagers to attend several worship services a week. Methodist chiefs said ancestral customs allow only Methodist worship in some villages. The mayor of Salamumu said the men had been warned not to worship in the village.

During the 200 years between 1760 and 1960 there were simply too many movements and groups rediscovering the significance of small groups to mention in this book. One may quote as an example for many others, the Brethren movement where, particularly during the period 1830–1920, the small-group, or house-church, model achieved rapid multiplication with worldwide consequences.

The House-Church Movement in Britain

The British House-Church Movement renewed the qualitative aspects of the church without touching the structure, and poured new wine into a new set of old wineskins.

During the 1970s Britain saw the birth of what has been called the Restoration or House-Church Movement. One of the battle cries of this movement was that traditional church services and church life were in dire need of 'restoration' through New Testament principles. This movement was largely driven, not by a new way of understanding the church as a house church as opposed to a meeting in a church house, but by a rediscovery of the spiritual gifts and the consequences of using them in traditional churches. As some traditional churches were simply not prepared to give space for the practice of these gifts, groups of people moved out, like Wesley of old simply preaching in the open air when the Anglican pulpits were forbidden to him. They ventured into literally 'bishop-free zones' where they could practise their new-found belief system without interference from traditional church authorities: and what more convenient place to do this than their own homes? Although these new church groupings initially moved into homes for their meetings – from which they got their name – 'the house-church movement was a misnomer,' says Arthur Wallis, 'because there was no sense in which they viewed the home as sacrosanct. As churches grew, there was no problem in moving to more commodious venues, such as schools, community centres, town halls, or even to purchase disused church buildings.' Houses, as a meeting place, were considered a matter of very little relevance. Much of this movement seems to have fallen back quickly into the very same congregational church structures and worship patterns they departed from, except that they place a high value on a breakthrough pastor, powerful worship, spiritual gifts or fervent evangelism. In other words, they renewed the qualitative aspects of the church without touching the structure, and poured new wine into a new set of old wineskins. Even the planting of many new churches did not change much, because it was ultimately still old structures which were planted anew.

One of the early results of the strong leadership these groups required was what has become known as 'heavy shepherding', an excessive heavy-handed approach to counselling and pastoring resulting from simply too much authority in the hands of one key leader. This has instilled a lot of unnecessary fear in those outside the movement, making it appear cultic, but it has almost completely vanished now. After a spectacular phase of initial growth, many original 'house churches' are no longer house churches in the true sense, and may have never been. Many have now settled for a fairly traditional 'family church structure', have brought forth youth churches or become or joined another network or denomination. About one third of today's evangelical churches in England are now part of the 'New Churches', as they are generally known.

Longevity of house churches

Some have feared that house churches could be just another quickly fading fashion, another flash in the pan. I agree, especially if house churches were allowed to become a new wave or the latest 'model' to follow. Congregational

House churches, however, are a living thing in themselves; they are organic. Far from becoming quickly extinct, they have already stood the test of time.

structures need a considerable amount of control, hierarchy, infrastructure, finance, rhetoric, motivation and mobilization to keep the organization – and its spiritual organisms, fellowships and circles – alive. House churches, however, are a living thing in themselves; they are organic. Far from becoming quickly extinct, they have already stood the test of time. Not only did the church survive in house churches during the New Testament time and up until Constantine; my historical observations make me to believe that the body of Christ, the church, actually survived the centuries of the Dark Ages in the congregational church because of the house church. The house church within the congregational church became God's Ark, where fellowship never really died, and the flame of faith was kept alive.

Most spiritual movements, theological renewal movements or so-called lay movements in history created small groups, 'conventicles', bands, cells. Many did not call them 'house churches' as we do today, but it is evident that historical equivalents to house churches have functioned as a kind of spiritual conservatory over the centuries, and in the present day have helped the body of Christ not only to survive but actually to flourish in nations like Russia or China. Sometimes this flame flared up and developed larger movements like the Moravians, or caused whole congregational denominations to be ignited. Usually, however, this was only for a time, until the structure drowned the spirit again in what I call the 'Galatian pattern': 'Are you so foolish? After beginning with the Spirit, are you now trying to attain your goal by human effort?' (Gal. 3:3).

This pattern seems to have been repeated countless

times in history. No matter how spiritedly a new church or movement began, it always tended to fall asleep sooner or later, usually through being excited about itself and relishing and recounting its own past achievements. As a result, it fell into a congregational mode. This is one of the tragic developments of the church in India, as Donald McGavran in his book *The Founders of the Indian Church* points out. This pattern seems to be found in almost every nation: almost all indigenous churches started in homes; most of them ended up in cathedrals, or the local equivalent.

Apostolic-prophetic reformation

According to Ephesians 2:20 the apostolic and prophetic ministry is not only essential for laying the foundations of the church: apostles and prophets are the very building material of the foundations of a church. Although the Bible reminds us to 'test the apostles' and 'weigh the prophets', it seems clear that the apostolic role is more foundational, and that it is healthy for prophets to submit to apostolic authority as well as to the authority of a local church. I assume that also includes the planting of churches, in the past, present and future.

Dispensational theology neatly divided the history of redemption into segments or 'dispensations', and claimed that the apostolic and prophetic ministry are not needed any more, because we now have the Bible. This led to a dangerous biblicism, where God's word literally became a subject to be studied and scientifically investigated, and almost replaced God Himself as the object of worship, with a subsequent proliferation of 'Bible study groups'.(The other effect was that, from the ranks of the fivefold ministry mentioned in Ephesians 4:11, this left only three ministries: the pastor, the evangelist and the teacher.

Developing churches with only those ministries, without the anointing and gifts of the prophetic and apostolic ministries, has created pastoral and evangelistic models of church, or churches which were built around the ministry of the teacher. These teaching-oriented, pastoral and evangelistic models of church, although they have filled whole countries, have not truly discipled them.

Can evangelists become false prophets?

In many ways, evangelists and their organizations and plans have been and still are received by the wider church today as if they were God's prophets. However, an evangelist is a true evangelist when he does the work of an evangelist. If he starts to act like a prophet, he begins to walk outside of his spiritual jurisdiction, crosses a line, assumes a ministry for which he has no anointing and is in danger of becoming 'a false prophet', side-tracking the body of Christ with a good heart and healthy intentions, but trapped into a wrong understanding of himself and the nature of the task of the church. If we treat evangelists as therophets of today, the true prophets will be looked upon as naive fools. The result is that the church will hesitate to follow prophetic and apostolic direction, because it has already bought into an evangelistic spirit and mentality, and has therefore become less than God wanted it to be.

Many Christians understand that we are seeing today a major resurrection of the apostolic and prophetic ministries on a global scale. This will change the church inside out. We can be sure it will lead to the resurrection of apostolic–prophetic patterns and structures of church. I am convinced the house church is exactly such a pattern.

Getting close: the talk that never happened

One can an imagine a conversation carried on over the centuries between Jesus and the church, His bride on earth. The topic of the conversation: 'House churches through the ages.'

'You may remember that I said, I will build my Church,' Jesus said. 'And because I promised to be always with you until the end of the age, I also wanted the church to be part of your everyday life, in the places where you live, in your houses.'

There was a murmur of astonishment amongst the disciples.

'Oh,' said Pachomius, the founder of the monastic movement. 'What you meant to say was that you wanted us to be part of monastic orders and cells of monks, didn't you?'

'Not exactly,' said Jesus.

'*Ecclesiolae in ecclesia*? – little churches within the real, big church?' asked Luther.

'Close!' said Christ, 'But still not quite yet what I mean.'

'*Collegiae pietatis* – pious Bible-reading groups in homes?' asked Philipp Jakob Spener.

'Prayer groups, or at least community-type fellowships?' asked the Moravians in Herrenhut. 'We could also call them *Gemeinschaften*!' they added.

'No, I intend house churches,' Jesus answered.

'Now we know what you mean. Bible-study groups, right?!'

'Well, how about evangelistic Bible-study groups? Or how do you feel about LEGS, Lay Evangelistic Group Studies,' asked a movement in the Philippines in the 1970s.

In the latter part of the twentieth century, many voices shouted for attention, almost all at the same time.

'Is it youth groups?' they probed. 'Care groups?

Sunday school groups? Small groups? Home groups? House groups? Life groups? Or maybe New Life groups? Follow-up groups? Discovery groups? Discipleship groups? Ministry groups? Oikos groups? Serendipity groups?

'Well, He does not like the word "groups",' someone suggested helpfully. 'Let's try it with cell!'

'Well, how about House Cells, then? Or at least Home Cells? Care Cells? Life Cells? Or just plain Cells?'

No answer.

'Alpha! What He means is Alpha groups!' exclaimed someone. 'He will like the name, and we like the food – and the fact that it is only community for a short time. Just what our short-term society is looking for.'

'Base Ecclesial Communities?' asked a movement in the Roman Catholic Church.

'Is it TLC?'

'What is that?' asked Jesus.

'Well, Tiny Little Churches, of course,' was the answer.

'I do not understand the first two words in that slogan. What is so tiny and little about me?' asked Jesus.

'Well, then, we have found it! Cell church, complete with Assistant Subdivisional Zonal Pastor, Type B Evangelism harvest events and a long list of proven conversation-ice-breaker questions,' exclaimed somebody.

'Well,' said Jesus, 'what I really mean is just house churches, simple unsophisticated house churches, the church as they meet in ordinary homes. Why is that so difficult for you to understand?'

Chapter 3

The Nature of House Churches

What they are, what they do, and how they function

What they are

The house church is a way of living the Christian life communally in ordinary homes through supernatural power. It is the way redeemed people live locally. It is the organic way disciples follow Jesus together in everyday life. Since the redeemed no longer belong to themselves, they adopt a mainly communal, rather than purely private and individualistic, lifestyle. House churches emerge when truly converted people stop living their own life for their own ends, start living a community life according to the values of the Kingdom of God, and start to share their life and resources with those Christians and not-yet-Christians around themselves.

It is the result of the conviction that we do not only experience Jesus Christ and His Spirit in sacred rooms dedicated for that express purpose, but in the midst of life. In that sense, the organic house church is the death bed of egoism, and therefore the birthplace of the church. True community starts, where individualism ends. Art Katz, a Messianic Jew who lived in community much of his life, says:

Community life pulverizes your old ego in the power of the Spirit of God, and rescues you from just living a miserable private life, where after loving each other during a one-hour worship service a week we rush home to water our flowers, sit on our porch, eat our individual meals and wash our car. Our! We need to start to function as part of the fellowship of the redeemed. As the redeemed, we do not go home after a service, we are at home with each other.

House-church Christianity is the body of Christ in an ordinary house, the society of the 'three-times converted': those who are vertically converted to God, horizontally converted to each other, and therefore able to be converted to serve the world in love, compassion and power.

For its everyday life a house church does not need a higher level of organization, bureaucracy and ceremonies than any ordinary large family.

In many ways a house church is like a spiritual extended family, relational, spontaneous and organic. For its everyday life a house church does not need a higher level of organization, bureaucracy and ceremonies than any ordinary large family. In fact, house churches reflect very much the way relatives behave with each other. Because the house church is a supernatural creation, invented and endowed by God, it has, more than just a clan of nice relatives, certain capabilities. One is to form its own support structure from within, namely the fivefold ministry, which functions like the support structure a human body develops, the lymphatic and nerve systems, blood vessels and bone structures. People will do almost anything in order to earn the love, respect or appreciation of the people around them. The house church provides a healthy, non-competitive way for that. It is, after all, a way to love, forgive each other and live together.

How they are

The house church reflects God's qualities and character. This community lifestyle is moulded in the spirit of love, truth, forgiveness, faith and grace. House churches are the way we love each other, forgive each other, mourn with those who mourn and laugh with those who laugh, extend and receive grace and constantly remain in touch with God's truth and forgiveness. It is a place where all masks can fall, and we can be open to each other and still keep loving each other.

What they do

As we are always in danger of taking blueprints and simply copying the 'action part', I want to remind you again that I am not recommending anyone to try to make exact copies of a New Testament church. Rather I want us but to take the New Testament principles and values seriously, as God-given essentials, and only then to create a house-church movement in our time, local soil, specific culture – even our tribe. This is much more a process of incarnation than contextualization, of God becoming flesh again in your context, rather than making cheap photocopies of existing models somewhere else. The people whom God typically and scripturally uses to unfold and incarnate the church in a given situation are apostolic and prophetically gifted Christians.

From studying the New Testament and the early church as well as contemporary house churches, four elements stand out. They seem to be like the basic skeleton of house churches of almost all times.

1 'Meating'

They meet to eat. When Jesus taught people, it usually involved meeting them in their homes, eating and drinking whatever they offered. Typically, the teaching of Jesus was right at the table, over a meal, not just after a meal, surrounded by children and visitors, not in an artificial seminary set-up, but in a real-life situation. The house church, similarly, is a table community, sharing real food. The Lord's Supper was a substantial supper with a symbolic meaning, not a symbolic supper with a substantial meaning. As they were simply eating a lamb together, it dawned on them what this was all about: humans having dinner with God. The Hebrew tradition of eating was to break bread first to start the meal, then have the main course, and then have a toast of wine to end the meal. It had three courses – starter, main course and dessert.

The New Testament reports of the early Christians: 'They ate together with glad and sincere hearts' (Acts 2:46). This was quite possibly a daily experience. Eating was a main purpose of them meeting: 'When you come together *in order to eat*, wait for each other,' says Paul (1 Cor. 11:33). Eating is central to the extension of the Kingdom. When Jesus sent his disciples two by two (Lk. 10:1–8), he advised them to find a man of peace, and 'eat and drink what they give you'. As disciples admitted their own elementary need and accepted food from their hosts, they shared life at a very intimate and basic level, prophetically admitting they were all dependent on God who gives all mankind their daily bread, whether they know it or not. That, in turn, opened their hosts to the bread of life that the disciples had to offer.

The question of who you eat with is central to each person's social identity. In most cultures we usually eat regularly only with those with whom we share the same blood, our family members. This is precisely part of the message of the house church as a 'table fellowship'. In God's household God is the father (Mt. 23:9), Jesus is the master of the house, and the disciples are the children (Mt. 10:25). We are made one family by the blood of Jesus, so we are spiritual blood-relations; and people who previously would have had nothing to do with one another are now close family members and, therefore, even eat together, which, previously, would have been unthinkable. Sharing one of the most basic of human needs, ordinary food, was and still is a sign of deep and revolutionary fellowship, cutting through all previous national, caste, clan and tribal affiliations. In some nations, eating together is one form of sealing a legal contract, or making peace with each other. People of the most diverse backgrounds eating together delivered a strong and powerful message to the world: 'We are now one family. See, we even eat together!'

2 *Teaching each other how to obey*

In Hebrew culture, the traditional teacher was the father teaching his family in his house, usually at meal-times. Teaching traditionally is geared to show somebody how to do something, and to explain why things are the way they are. The goal of the teaching is not increasing knowledge, but helping people to obey and serve God and His purposes (Rom. 1:5). The elders of house churches assume exactly the same house-father role, together with charismatically gifted teachers, either residential or visiting, or visiting apostles teaching from 'house to house' (Acts 20:20). Although the early church grew and multiplied greatly without a written New Testament, the word of God 'spread' (Acts 6:7), 'continued to increase and spread' (12:24), 'spread widely and grew in power' (19:20).

The subject of teaching is 'the word', God's story, the Bible, what God has chosen to reveal to us about Himself, ourselves, the history of the world, and the way to live (1 Thess. 4:1), so we can fit our story into His-story. The

goal of the teaching is that humans, through joyful
obedience liberated from the power of Self through a
bonding relationship to Christ, can better fit in according
to God's created patterns of life and become mature and
normal – according to the norm of God – and therefore be
transformed into the image of Christ. This is systematic
teaching at its best, not geared to deliver a complete A–Z
set of doctrine to students of Christianity on their own.
The original teaching 'system' was relational, geared to
present a disciple mature in Christ through a spirit of
quick obedience and a developed, gift-oriented ministry.

*Learning is not only
hearing, but seeing
how it is done, then
doing it, and finally
teaching it yourself to
others.*

The teaching style can be a
very short talk – not a sermon! –
an illustration, parables and
stories, usually accompanied and
punctuated by 'nods and grunts
of approval', or healthily interrupted by questions and requests
for more tea or another sweet.
This is followed by a question-
and-answer time which is interactive and dynamic, and
allows everyone to participate and get the explanation
he or she needs. 'Questions often reveal what a person
is thinking and can help to remove mental blocks if we
deal with them rightly, and therefore encourage
spiritual growth', says Met Castillo. If there is any kind
of exam to pass in this style of teaching, it is twofold: to
obey the teaching, demonstrating it by a changed life,
and to start teaching others too. Jesus said: 'Teach them
to obey everything I have commanded you' (Mt. 28:20).
Learning is not only hearing, but seeing how it is done,
then doing it, and finally teaching it yourself to others.
The Greek word often translated 'preaching' in the
New Testament is *dialogizomai*, which means to have a
dialogue between people. When Paul 'preached for a

long time' in Ephesus (Acts 20:7) and young Eutychus fell to his short-lived death, Paul did not 'preach' at all in the sense of having an endless monologue; he was having a dialogue, a time of questions and answers. This way the participants have a chance to drive the teaching by their own questions, and that keeps them interested and their learning curve steep.

This is very different from a western concept of teaching, which is often geared to allow people to gain intellectual control over things and then manipulate them according to their desire, and where the teaching style is usually an address, a professorial monologue geared at students in an academic set-up, removed from real life. In technical terms, the eastern teaching style is kinetic: the topic of discussion literally moves around the table from person to person, and everyone is involved. After such deliberation, a consensus is built, a collective opinion emerges, and corporate action can follow. In the West the style is often static, the classroom approach, the teacher indoctrinating a passive crowd, trying to put across his or her points, true to a Greek and Roman concept of scholasticism and intellectualism, where the goal is handing down knowledge through the ages to individuals.

Communication theory has proved that the confrontational and static style is a most ineffective teaching tool. The participatory and kinetic model is most effective in changing opinions and values and therefore in changing people. Some of the reasons for this are that it is simply more humane; it is part of real life, not in an artificial environment; it is driven by real people with real and existential questions, not according to some theoretical textbook and an agenda printed far away.

This teaching style is geared to help people become 'doers of the word', teaching them to obey everything Jesus has taught us (Mt. 28:20). Scientists tell us we remember 10 per cent of what we read; 20 per cent of what we hear; 30 per cent of what we see; 50 per cent of what we hear and see; 70 per cent of what we say ourselves; 90 per cent of what we do ourselves. It is simply good scientific practice, as well as good stewardship with the time and people available, to help and develop others to express themselves, getting them involved, teaching them to teach others how practically to obey Christ in real life. Is there a better and more effective way to teach than by living the truth and the teaching about the truth with others, teaching by example, and, as this New Testament lifestyle is surely highly questionable, being ready to answer any pertinent questions?

A seven-year-old girl might raise her hand and say: 'My dog has been run over by a horse-cart today and died. Do dogs go to heaven?' This would provide a perfect opportunity to teach from the Bible into a real-life experience about heaven and earth, and yes, about the place of dogs in creation. This teaching style speaks straight into the life of people, because life itself asked the question, and the living God, the father of the *oikonomia*, the 'household of God', answered it.

3 Sharing material and spiritual blessings
What the rich young ruler, to whom Jesus said 'Sell everything you have and give to the poor, and . . . come, follow me' (Lk. 18:22) did not do, the church did: 'All the believers were together and had everything in common. Selling their possessions and goods, they gave to anyone as he had need' (Acts 2:44,45). As the company of the redeemed, we do not belong to ourselves any more; we belong to God and therefore to God's community. All that we are and all that we have is therefore God's, and belongs to God's family, the church – not in

theory, but in practice. The question is not: 'What percentage should I give?' but 'Why should I hold back anything, after being saved from the certainty of hell by a loving God who gave his very life to redeem me?'

The New Testament Christians shared two things together in their house churches, material and spiritual blessings: 'No one claimed that any of his possessions was his own, but they shared everything they had . . . There were no needy persons amongst them. For from time to time those who owned lands or houses sold them, brought the money from the sales, and put it at the apostles' feet, and it was distributed to anyone as he had need' (Acts 4:32–35).

They also shared spiritual blessings: 'When you come together, everyone has a hymn, or a word of instruction, a revelation, a tongue or an interpretation' (1 Cor. 14:26). Paul encouraged the Christians to 'speak to one another with psalms, hymns and spiritual songs' (Eph. 5:19), and said to Timothy, 'The things you have heard me say in the presence of many witnesses entrust to reliable men who will also be qualified to teach others' (2 Tim. 2:2).

Christians knew that they no longer belonged to themselves; Christ owned them, and everything they had. When Christians come together, they share what they are and what they have, whether it is spiritual or material. In practice each house church had a common fund, into which all of them deposited money, clothes, valuables. Everyone had something to share and therefore was able to serve others, which made everyone able to appreciate and value each other.

This may sound to some like social romanticism, an ideal picture of a bygone era, but that does not mean we can simply ignore the God-given concept of sharing. Paul later had to collect money from other churches for the church in Jerusalem, which only goes to show that the concept of sharing material blessings is meant to be extended beyond the boundaries of the local church. No God-given concept is foolproof, so long as the weakest link – we humans – is present in the chain: in our weaknesses, like Ananias and Sapphira, we create less than glorious exceptions to the rule. However, this radical biblical lifestyle of sharing saves a lot of everyday expenses, establishes a deep bond of community amongst the Christians, and is in itself a witness to Christ sharing His own life and death with us, so that we may live with Him.

4 Praying together

'They devoted themselves to prayer' (Acts 2:42). Prayer is the heartbeat of a relationship of a child of God with his father in heaven. Whenever Christians come together, therefore, they will pray for each other, pray for the authorities, pray for peace, come before God in petition and thanksgiving, pray for their enemies, bless those who curse them, practise exorcisms and pray for healing.

Prayer is a two-way communication, and as we talk to God, God might want to talk back to us. He often does this through prophets, tongues which are interpreted, dreams and visions, or angels. 'God does nothing without revealing his plan to his servants the prophets' (Amos 3:7). Prophecy has been an integral part of house churches: 'Two or three prophets should speak . . . you can all prophesy in turn' (1 Cor. 14:29). Unlike traditional churches, house churches did not have a set agenda for their meetings, a liturgy. The living Christ *was* the agenda. So, if a house church did not know what to do next, they could simply pray and prophesy, so that God might reveal what He wanted them to do next, or what He wanted them to pray about next. Supernatural messengers, messages and prophecy helped to

pinpoint sin (Acts 5:3; 1
Cor. 14:24), give special
tasks to the disciples (Acts
8:26), identify spiritual
potential (Acts 9:10–19),
arrange divine appoint-
ments (Acts 10:9–47),
develop apostolic break-
throughs (Acts 16:6), and
simply encourage individ-
uals (Acts 18:9–11).

As people confess their sins in front of each other and forgive each other, they stop being hypocrites, break the power of hidden sins in their lives, confess their own need for grace and forgiveness, lose their face and gain the love and respect of fellow sinners redeemed by God.

In the prayer Jesus taught us, he encourages us to
pray: 'Forgive us our sins' (Lk. 11:4). In a family that
shares their lives together no misconduct can be hidden
for very long. Families provide a healthy accountability
and check for each other. Similarly, house churches as
spiritual families are an ideal place to be accountable
for each other's conduct, which naturally involves the
confessing of our sins: 'Confess your sins to each other
and pray for each other so that you may be healed,' says
James 5:16. As people confess their sins in front of each
other and forgive each other (Col. 3:13), in whatever
cultural format is appropriate, they stop being hypocrites, break the power of hidden sins in their lives, confess their own need for grace and forgiveness, lose their
face and gain the love and respect of fellow sinners
redeemed by God: they leave the darkness and live in
the light (1 Jn. 2), humble themselves and experience
how God will lift them up (Jas. 4:7–10). They repent, not
in order to avoid the consequences of sin, but because of
shame for what they have done. This also reinstates a
healthy and natural form of church discipline, so well
known to the New Testament church.

Sheep and goats: the small but decisive difference

'When the Son of Man comes in His glory' Jesus will not
divide the sheep from the obvious wolves, as we might
expect, but the sheep from the goats. To the casual
onlooker, goats almost look like sheep on the outside,
but they behave very differently: they seem to have a
much more negative character, are less gregarious, less
fellowship-loving. This is highly significant. Jesus
makes a decision about where a person is going to
spend eternity, in heaven or in hell. The defining factor
in this passage is not whether we belong to the right
church or have once said the right creed or prayers, but
whether we lived a living faith. Jesus had already
warned sternly that 'Not everyone who says to me,
"Lord, Lord," will enter the kingdom of heaven, but
only he who does the will of my Father who is in
heaven' (Mt. 7:21), which will cause some consternation
amongst folk who were only into driving out demons,
prophesying and performing miracles. Jesus sends
them away in the strongest possible terms: 'I never
knew you. Away from me, you evildoers!' (Mt. 7:23).
Jesus does not want to have anything to do with such
people in eternity. 'Faith without works is dead,' says
James.

The conclusion of all this is simple. Jesus expects us
to live a living faith, to live the truth He preached, or
even we preach. And when Jesus was asked to explain
more clearly what He meant, He described someone
who has experienced house-church Christianity: 'I was
hungry and you gave me something to eat, I was thirsty,
and you gave me something to drink, I was a stranger
and you invited me in, I needed clothes and you clothed
me, I was sick and you looked after me, I was in prison
and you came to visit me' (Mt. 25:35,36). House-church

Christianity is about sharing lives, about being gregarious sheep in the power of the Spirit of God. We eat and drink together; give a bed to strangers who pass through; share clothes; look after our sick people; and if somebody is in prison – presumably not because they stole something, but precisely because they are Christian, persecuted for their faith! – we would visit them and probably risk being incarcerated with them. Why on earth would we do this? Because we are family. 'Whatever you did for one of the least of these brothers of mine, you did for me,' says Jesus. He did not speak of His natural family and physical blood relationships; He considered 'whoever does God's will' as His 'brother and sister' (Mk. 3:35), i.e. fellow Christians.

The solution is not to try to delegate all this to charities, to paid pastors, counsellors and prison ministries through a tax-deductible donation. 'The Way' is to do it as a regular lifestyle ourselves. The way we live makes a difference, even about heaven and hell. That does not mean we are saved by works rather than grace. But it means that our life shows our faith, at least in the eyes of Jesus. And I am not prepared to argue with Him about that. It seems clear that Jesus strongly advocates a lifestyle for his followers which can easily be lived out in informal, relational and organic house churches, spiritual families who take expert care of each other and of those whom God wants to touch through them.

House churches in the Bible

This book cannot provide an extensive exegetical study of house churches in the Bible. Other works, however, have done this, especially *The Church in Thy House* by Dr Met Castillo and *The Church in the House* by Bob Fitts. A short overview reveals that:

Not only individuals but whole houses are recipients of the gospel

⟨ Mt. 10:1 'As you enter the home, give it your greeting. If the home is deserving, let your peace rest on it; if it is not, let your peace return to you. If anyone will not welcome you or listen to your words, shake the dust off your feet when you leave that home or town.'

⟨ Lk. 10:5 'When you enter a house, first say, "Peace to this house".'

⟨ Lk. 10:7 'Stay in that house, eating and drinking whatever they give you, for the worker deserves his wages. Do not move around from house to house.'

⟨ Acts 10:22 'The men replied "We have come from Cornelius the centurion. He is a righteous and God-fearing man, who is respected by all the Jewish people. A holy angel told him to have you come to his house so that he could hear what you have to say".'

⟨ Acts 10:30 'Cornelius answered: "Four days ago I was in my house praying at this hour, at three in the afternoon. Suddenly a man in shining clothes stood before me".'

⟨ Acts 16:15 'When she and the members of her household were baptised, she invited us to her home. "If you consider me a believer in the Lord," she said, "come and stay at my house".'

⟨ Acts 16:32 'Then they spoke the word of the Lord to him and to all the others in his house.'

Pentecost happened in a house

⟨ Acts 2:2 'Suddenly a sound like the blowing of a violent wind came from heaven and filled the whole house where they were sitting.'

Christians regularly meet in homes

⟨ Acts 2:46 'Every day they continued to meet together in

the temple courts. They broke bread in their homes and ate together with glad and sincere hearts.'

⟨ Acts 5:42 'Day after day, in the temple courts and from house to house, they never stopped teaching and proclaiming the good news that Jesus is the Christ.'

⟨ Acts 8:3 'But Saul began to destroy the church. Going from house to house, he dragged off men and women and put them in prison.'

⟨ Acts 9:11 'The Lord told him, "Go to the house of Judas on Straight Street and ask for a man from Tarsus named Saul, for he is praying".'

⟨ Acts 12:12 'When this had dawned on him, he went to the house of Mary the mother of John, also called Mark, where many people had gathered and were praying.'

⟨ Acts 16:40 'After Paul and Silas came out of the prison, they went to Lydia's house where they met with the brothers and they encouraged them. Then they left.'

⟨ Acts 18:7 'Then Paul left the synagogue, and went next door to the house of Titius Justus, a worshipper of God.'

⟨ Acts 20:20 'You know that I have not hesitated to preach anything that would be helpful to you but have taught you publicly and from house to house.'

⟨ Acts 21:8 'Leaving the next day, we reached Caesarea and stayed at the house of Philip the evangelist, one of the Seven.'

⟨ Rom. 16:5 'Greet also the church that meets at their house. Greet my dear friend Epenetus, who was the first convert to Christ in the province of Asia.'

⟨ 1 Cor. 16:19 'The churches in the province of Asia send you greetings. Aquila and Priscilla greet you warmly in the Lord, and so does the church that meets at their house.'

⟨ Col. 4:15 'Give my greetings to the brothers at Laodicea, and to Nympha and the church in her house.'

⟨ 1 Tim. 5:13,14 'Besides, they get into the habit of being idle and going about from house to house. And not only do they become idlers, but also gossips and busybodies, saying things they ought not to.'

⟨ Philem. 2 'To Apphia our sister, to Archippus our fellow-soldier and to the church that nmeets your home.'

⟨ 2 Jn. 10 'If anyone comes to you and does not bring this teaching, do not take him into your house or welcome him.'

Practical aspects

Homegroups are not house churches
There are many reasons why the traditional home group, Bible-study group, prayer group or even youth group is the fiercest competitor of a house church. The concepts look similar, but are really miles apart, because they build on different values, and a different understanding of church. Where the home group is a small part of the big and 'real' church, a 'mini-version' of the church, the house church in itself is the church in its fullest and most holistic sense.

Who leads house churches?
House churches do not have leaders in the technical sense; they have elders. Elders are responsible members of society who are able to assume a fatherly or motherly role in the house church, and who need to meet biblical qualifications (1 Tim. 3). These local elders are empowered and counselled by apostolic people, who usually function beyond the borders of an individual house church and who steer the churches together and sometimes even make decisions in tandem with them (Acts 15:2,4,22,23).

Baptism

House churches are fully functioning churches, and therefore usually handle baptisms themselves, unless they want to team up with other house churches for a larger baptism celebration. Baptisms can happen in a bathtub, a barrel, a pond, a well, a swimming pool, a river, a lake or the sea. Baptism normally happens through immersion in water after new Christians have professed their faith, following the New Testament pattern. In some cultures house churches prefer to baptize people immediately after conversion; in other cultures they prefer the candidates to undergo some time of preparation. Paul was baptized three days after his conversion (Acts 9), the Ethiopian eunuch immediately on the spot (Acts 8); Peter encouraged the 3000 converts at Pentecost to be baptized that same day (Acts 2:41).

Weddings

In some cultures weddings are performed by religious officials, in other countries, by government officials. Jesus never performed a wedding. The only wedding Jesus was ever part of we read about in John 2. Jesus, despite his qualifications, was not conducting the wedding. He added the wine, and left the functions of society to those who are concerned about it. He does not seem to have been concerned about conducting or presiding at any kind of social functions, nor did He prepare His disciples to do so. He was concerned with a spiritual kingdom. He never conducted or even attended a burial: in fact he said, 'Let the dead bury their own deed' (Mt. 8:22).

In some cultures and countries established churches might specialize in solemnizing marriages for all Christians – not only members of their own churches – if the government requires them to do so. In other cases, the house churches are usually not concerned with these issues. Society can take care of them.

Children and house churches

Children are needed to humble us with their questions, break up our endless 'adult' discussions, bring us down to earth from our pious clouds, and act as natural evangelists and bridge-builders. They also help us to prove the fruits of the Spirit – patience, for example – and will serve as heaven-sent spies to spot instantly any trace in us of religious superstition and hypocrisy.

Since house churches are spiritual families, children are a natural and important part, just as they are a source of constant joy – and embarrassment – in a natural family. Children are needed to humble us with their questions, break up our endless 'adult' discussions, bring us down to earth from our pious clouds, and act as natural evangelists and bridge-builders. They also help us to prove the fruits of the Spirit – patience, for example – and will serve as heaven-sent spies to spot instantly any trace in us of religious superstition and hypocrisy. Children have a ministry to us adults which is at least as important as our ministry to them. They are, in short, as important to house churches as they are to families. Any couple that has a baby needs to answer the question: Are we now born into the life of our baby, or is the baby born into our life?

If we see a house church as a programme-driven event with discussion topics, tasks, objectives and an agenda to achieve – which of course Jesus never taught – we might feel that children only 'disturb the grown-ups', and therefore need to be separated, put into children's groups with their own programmes to keep them entertained and educated. Certainly, it is a positive and natural thing for children to do things together

with others of their own age. But it is precisely the times
of eating together, laughing and crying together, in the
context of a wider family – young and old together –
which show children from an early age how people live
in community, and what it means to be at home with
one another and for one another. A special time for children can very well be a common exception, but not the
rule. Otherwise children will, from an early age, be
quickly alienated from church. Church, again, is not a
meeting; it is a way of life. If we have children, they are
part of our life, and therefore of our house churches.

Obedient children are a qualification for leadership

In 1 Timothy 3 one of the prerequisites that Paul lists for
any elder or deacon is obedient children: 'If anyone does
not know how to manage his own family, how can he take
care of God's church?'

'That will never work in Switzerland, because our
children simply do not listen, and will constantly
scream and take over the programme. They can't even
sit still for one minute!', a married woman with a number of small children told me once sternly.

'Don't tell me this,' I replied. 'Explain to God why the
times have changed and His rules do not apply any
more today.'

This is why planting house churches does not start on
paper. It may well start in the children's room, with
Christian parents rediscovering a Spirit-filled way of
bringing up their children in their respective cultures,
not according to the pattern of this world, but according
to the values of the Kingdom.

Young mothers with small children

The following experience may not be applicable or even understandable in many cultures, but it will give you an idea of how mothers, together with their small children – one of the biggest potentials and resources of the church – have been locked up in a system of church that is less than ideal for them. Many young mothers are only noticed in church when, unable to keep a baby silent, they hurry out of the 'worship service', followed by the less than favourable glances of the congregation.

Not long ago, I was having lunch in an English town with a young couple in their flat. They had two children, aged 3 and 1. Between bites of Yorkshire pudding and sips of Darjeeling, I quite innocently asked the wife, 'So, you enjoy your Home group, then?'

She glanced at her husband, then somewhat furtively at me, and said, 'Well, you know . . .' and then petered out.

Her husband jumped in, in a hopeful tone 'Yes, we do, very much,' trying to smooth over the situation somewhat.

'I wonder,' I said. 'Let me guess. Every Sunday is a little shop of horrors. If the congregation only knew what kind of a drama precedes your entry to the service (punctually five minutes late), you wouldn't be an "elder couple" very long, right? The kids are fussy, the toast is burnt, Grandma is sick, the dog has made a mess, Dad can't find his tie and your scarf is ripped. Then you stand there in the service, agitated and nervous, but trying not to let it show – covering over with an "Everything's all right! Please don't ask about me!" spirituality – until the weekly reprieve comes, when the Pastor says, ". . . and now the children can go to Sunday school!"

'Now, at least on Sundays, the kids have Sunday school, but what about Home group? Wednesdays at 7.30 just don't work like that. Is that the way it is for you?' I asked. 'Are you starting to think that your children are keeping you from getting closer to God?'

Pregnant silence.

'And then, here I come, and I have the gall to ask if you enjoy Homegroup. Aren't Homegroups typically a mini-Sunday service, but without a "Reverend" and an organ? But there's an additional difficulty for young families: what will we do with the kids? A babysitter? Or maybe the kids have to be in bed by 7.20 so you can meet everyone at the door with friendly smiles and witty greetings as they arrive.

'How's this for an alternative? The house church – in the form of a neighbourhood or street church. It might start as early as 4.00, not 7.30. The wives from the neighbourhood get together, have coffee and fun together with the children, sing, pray, talk, cry and laugh together. Then at five o'clock the husbands start to trickle in from work, but instead of going to their own homes and dinner tables they're also going to the neighbourhood church tonight.

'At 6.10 that unsaved husband of one of your neighbours furtively comes in the door – for the first time and after your eleventh invitation, and that mostly because he was invited to supper, not to a Bible study. He's nervous and stiff and shifts uneasily back and forth on his chair. His countenance says, "I know that you all want to convert me. I haven't the foggiest idea how you're going to do it, but I'm expecting the worst." At that instant, your one-year-old comes crawling in and makes a beeline for his trouser leg. When he manages to grab the trousers he coos, "Abudah!" and smears some unidentified substance on them. Then he laughs as only a one-year-old can. In that second, a miracle of transubstantiation happens. In an instant the stiff neighbour and the house-church elder have become "daddies", glance at each other and start laughing. The little guy hasn't just eased the tension but brought human warmth into what your neighbour had expected to find a cold, formal, religious exercise. Suddenly, neither the atmosphere nor your neighbour are the least bit stiff. Everyone's much more natural and relaxed.

'At about 6.30, everyone sits down to a "potluck" dinner, or perhaps a large pot of spaghetti or, as they do in China, a large pot of noodle soup. There's some teaching at the table, but it happens as in the New Testament: conversations and discussions during, not after, the meal. People talk of their joys and sorrows, tell success stories and bloopers, trade insights on razors and cars, pray for and prophesy over each other, joke with the kids, who are not hindering but enriching the situation, and collect some money for an unemployed widow who's moved into the area.

'Pretty soon it's 7.30, and time for a collective bedtime story before everyone leaves, told by one person to all the kids (from 6 months to 80 years old). Perhaps this is when the unsaved neighbour is hearing – and understanding! – the gospel for the first time . . . How would all that suit you?' I asked.

'It's too good to be true,' she said. 'But what'll our pastor think . . . ?'

Gently I interrupted her: 'Let's face a tough one. Where's the easiest place for a man to be spiritual? Isn't it hiding behind a pulpit, where one can preach to a faceless crowd of distant people through a microphone? And where's the hardest place to be holy? Isn't it at home, in the presence of your kids and spouse, where everything you do and say is tested for real-life value? But that's also where the gospel has the biggest impact, because the message of an extraordinary life in an ordinary setting is its own litmus test and is much more authentic than an artificial message delivered in an unnatural setting. After all, when Jesus asked His disciples to go as His messengers two by two, He asked them to find a house of peace, eat what they give you, drink what they give you, heal the sick, tell them the Kingdom of God has come, and stick with them – do not go from house to house. Not complicated at all, is it?'

Recapturing the Homes

I believe that over the centuries, the church has hidden from the place of painful failure in real and everyday life at home, and has escaped into artificial preaching centres, large cathedrals, Bible schools, programmes and seminars. But God is today reclaiming our very homes for Christ. As our homes are again becoming the natural habitat for the church, the down-to-earth community of the redeemed, Christianity in return becomes a powerful testimony at the place where it counts most: next door.

Psychotherapist Larry Crabb, in his recent book *Connecting*, says it like this: 'Maybe the center of Christian community is connecting with a few, where ordinary Christians, whose lives regularly intersect, will accomplish most of the good that we now depend on professionals to provide. That will happen as people connect with each other in ways that only the gospel makes possible.'

Chapter 4

The Fivefold Ministry

God's resources and structure for multiplying house churches

Every growth form in life is based on the multiplication of organic cells. This is true for the church too, as organic, relational households of God. Once we have discovered that the church is not a series of organized and conducted meetings in religious buildings, but a supernatural communal life form, the species of the people of God, as they follow their master together, we may have to rethink how this life form multiplies in a healthy and organic way.

'If you want to build the church, use women'

David Yonggi Cho once said: 'If you want to build an organization, use men. If you want to build the church, use women.' We men like to have things under control, and therefore we are fascinated with computers, engines and robots. As long as we pour water and oil into them and provide some grease here and there, our beloved machines keep running, and we are happy. The problem is that the church is not a machine but a life form, not an organization, but an organism. One of the less obvious facts of church-planting today is that a significant

·percentage of churches seem to be planted by women. It seems clear that God's Spirit is challenging the women to get out there and save the country, as we men still sit and feel the need to discuss some more theology and strategy, and, like myself, write one more book.

'Theo-matic' growth

In his landmark book *Natural Church Growth*, Christian A. Schwarz says: 'We can learn about the church by carefully pondering and analysing the lilies – how they grow. The growth of plants and other living organisms reveals that they have a 'biotic' potential, the inherent capacity of an organism or species to survive and reproduce. This type of natural growth is not mechanical or artificial. It is God-given.'

Is this also true for the church? I believe so. The principle can be seen in Mark 4:26–9, in the Parable of the Growing Seed. 'A man scatters seed on the ground. Night and day, whether he sleeps or gets up, the seed sprouts and grows, though he does not know how. All by itself the soil produces corn.' The words 'All by itself' are the translation for the Greek word *automate*, which means automatically. This growth-automatism is actually a 'theo-matism', since God Himself is the actual cause of growth; it is He who 'gives the increase' (cf. 1 Cor. 3:6). This has very serious consequences for our thinking and practice. For a church to grow, we must *release* the biotic growth potential which God has put into it, rather than *inject* this potential into the church by whatever means we have in mind. The growth potential is already there and wants to get out, and then the growth will happen 'all by itself'. God has kept this part for Himself for good reasons.

No more manufactured churches

> *If we cannot make revival happen, we can at least stop hindering it!*

We will all agree that the church cannot be manufactured: there can be no man-made revival, no man-made church growth nor a manufactured church-planting movement. We cannot even 'make', manufacture, produce, or hammer out a good sermon: we can only 'make' a bad sermon, which is bad simply because we 'made' it. So what is man's role in this? If we cannot make revival happen, we can at least stop hindering it!

Proper ministry consists in releasing the growth automatism by which God grows His church, not manufacturing it. If we have in the past hindered this biotic growth potential, we might need to repent, get out of God's way, observe His ways carefully – by watching the lilies, for example, as Jesus recommends – and then humbly join in the process at a later stage.

Technocrats

In the past, many churches and missions have tended to think the other way round: with the aid of heavy programmes and almost superhuman and tireless effort, constantly teaching and preaching and organizing and fund-raising, they have tried to instill the necessary quality into the fellowships and groups they have planted. This is like trying to push a car sideways, painfully inching along, instead of turning the key and allowing the in-built engine to drive the car. 'The gospel is the power (*dynamis*) of God,' explosive like dynamite, says Paul (Rom. 1:16). If we try to produce the gospel ourselves, we might be like someone who heats up uranium 235 over an open fire, rather than allowing the necessary nuclear reaction to take place, which will release unbelievable atomic energies from within. We might want to enlarge the balancing wheels of the bicycle of the church, not realizing the awesome gift of balance which God has given even to small children.

If we try to handle the church like a company with the best management principles and foolproof methods, we might start to do the things of God in our own strength, not using God's in-built power and growth potential at all. In fact, we might be found fighting against it, because it upsets our preplanned agendas. As a result, we would become 'technocrats', who control and rule through the help of methods and technical devices. With the very best of intentions and probably pure motives, we may produce useless machines, because our minds – and therefore our methods – had been corrupted. God has provided everything we need for the growth and multiplication of the church: the secret and the power are in the seed! We need to make proper use of it.

How to keep disciples immature through teaching

'I have been teaching my church for five years now, and they still seem so weak,' said one young pastor to me.

'How many have you taught how to teach?' I asked him.

'What do you mean?' he said.

'You have already answered my question,' I replied. 'The teacher's job is to teach them how to teach, and not endlessly do it for them. This, in fact, is a way of artificially keeping people in perpetual immaturity, prolonging their baby status in the name of great and wonderful discipleship teaching!'

The organic growth potential seen numerically

Most people come across the house-church model for the first time do not see immediately its potential for growth through organic multiplication. But the right quality in the right structure produces a huge dynamic for growth. How can the quality of relationships become so good that there can be a fast multiplication of churches without losing the quality? The answer is obvious: it happens *in proportion to the intensity of lives shared in house churches*, a dynamic which is rarely experienced in traditional churches. Since there is sometimes in traditional Christianity not much sharing of lives, this fact – and its potential – is often overlooked.

I agree with those who say that building communities is not primarily a matter of numbers but of quality. Nevertheless, quality which does not sooner or later lead to quantity is, to me, suspect. I am intersted in spiritual quality in the right place in an appropriate structure in the right order of magnitude and properly distributed. It is instructive to have a look at the numerical potential of organic house churches.

Elephants or rabbits

A case in point is the different reproduction patterns of elephants and rabbits.

Elephants	Rabbits
only fertile four times a year	almost continuously fertile
only one baby per pregnancy	average of seven babies per pregnancy
22-month gestation period	1-month gestation period
sexual maturity: 18 years	sexual maturity: 4 months
maximum growth potential in 3 years: from 2 to 3	maximum growth potential in 3 years: from 2 to 476 million

Typical growth patterns of house churches

House churches are not multiplying like rabbits, but this example shows the theoretical potential of rapid multiplication. A typical house church may have between six and twenty people, and usually doubles itself once every six to nine months. For our example we take an average size of 12 people per house church, and a less-than-average doubling rate of 12 months. We also assume that in the first year of operation, the house church actually does not double itself at all: it may have a leadership problem, or some other starting problem. We remain slightly pessimistic and also assume a 25 per cent fallout rate, and periods of growth and consolidation, which means that one out of every four house churches which are started will eventually close down within any given five-year period for any number of reasons. This will give us the following scenario:

After year	Number of house churches	Number of people
1	only 1, not 2	12
2	2	24
3	4	48
4	8	96
5	12 (= 16 less 25%)	144
6	24	288
7	48	576
8	96	1152
9	192	2304
10	288 (= 384 less 25%)	3456
15	6912 (= 9216 less 25%)	82,944
20	165,888 (= 221,184 less 25%)	1,990,656

This scenario, which has truly happened several times in history as well as in recent times, will incorporate almost 2 million people in a house-church movement within a period of 20 years. The process may be

accelerated through contextual factors, a shorter multiplication time-span, revival, persecution, or may be slowed
down by other factors. The core observation, however, is
that the growth is through multiplication, and the multiplication is exponential, not linear.

From addition to multiplication

House churches are a multipliable structure. They can
multiply literally endlessly, as long as they are provided
with the essentials. Two of the essentials for house
churches are biblical quality and leadership.

Most of today's structures for developing leadership
are addition-based. We teach young leaders a set of
classes and go through some programmes which have a
similar 'output', a similar number of 'graduates' each
time. We may put people through the Bible school
system and faithfully add 50 or 500 each year to the
number of ordained pastors and missionaries. But just
as some are graduating each year, a certain number of
leaders that are retiring or dropping out. Moreover, just
adding leaders for the multiplying units of house
churches is not enough. Addition cannot keep up with
multiplication, because ongoing addition produces
linear growth: two plus two is four plus two is six.
Ongoing multiplication produces exponential growth:
two times two is four, times two is eight.

If we try to provide leaders for a house-church movement through a structure that is addition-oriented, not
multiplication-oriented, the leadership development
model itself very soon becomes the limiting factor in the
multiplication process of the churches, and the growth
stops. God does not want to give birth to babies only to see
them die of malnutrition and cold weather.

Another 200-barrier: when addition stops multiplication

If we have multiplying house churches, which create an exponential growth rate, we need a leadership development structure that grows as fast as the churches multiply. The leadership structure itself therefore also needs to multiply. Either we start multiplying all our seminaries and Bible schools, or we find another way.

If we draw a linear-growth (leadership development) and an exponential-growth (house-church multiplication) development, they intersect each other at the point where the number of house churches starts to exceed the number of leaders. This results in the movement coming to a grinding halt, because the fledgling house-church movement runs out of quality and leaders. The support structure has not grown fast enough, and so the whole movement is in danger of becoming shallow or even cult-like. This choking point, interestingly enough, often happens when there are around 150 or 200 churches in a given movement, for similar reasons that a traditional one-pastor church usually experiences the '200-barrier' described in Chapter 1. The one leader simply cannot care for more

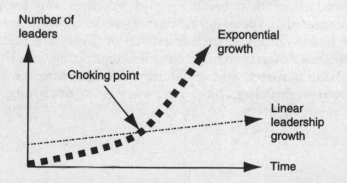

people, and the growth stops. Usually this might create
a new denomination in the process. There is, however, a
way to break this in-built structural growth problem:
we can simply avoid it from the very beginning and
provide structures which will help to multiply leaders.

Multiplying the fivefold ministries

The answer to the structural growth problem is the so-
called fivefold ministry of Ephesians 4:11–13: '[God]
gave some to be apostles, some to be prophets, some to
be evangelists, and some to be pastors and teachers, to
prepare God's people for works of service, so that the
body of Christ may be built up until we all reach unity
in the faith . . .'

The fivefold ministry functions as the self-organizing
powers of the church. They are part of the built-in 'biotic
growth potential', an internal structure, part of the spiritual DNA of the church, which forms itself within the
body of Christ just as a human body forms its own lymphatic system, white anti-body system, a blood circulation
system etc., with an amazing and in-built ability to grow
organically with the general growth of the human body,
and maintain or even cure itself.

I should underline that the fivefold ministry is
standard biblical teaching and practice, and by no
means only a speciality of particular denominations or
of house-church Christianity. All of these five ministries have their own task to fulfil in equipping the saints
for the ministry, and constantly circulate through the
(house) churches, like their very own breathing or
digestive system.

Empowering people for the ministry

The most important aspect for house churches is that these ministries can also multiply themselves: apostles spotting and training other apostles, prophets spotting and training other prophets, and multiplying themselves through the simple and biblical process of discipleship. This way, the leadership structure can grow exponentially together with a multiplying house-church movement. In the words of Barney Coombs: 'Jesus takes beggars and turns them into princes. He gets hold of six foul-mouthed fishermen, a despised tax-gatherer and five other nobodies, and transforms them into the élite of Heavenly Jerusalem'.

The bottom line of this process is the empowerment of exponentially more people to do the work of God. It is to find, nurture and release talented and supernaturally gifted people into their God-given calling in order to bring out God's best in them, and to do this systematically and strategically.

Giving away ministries to others

After the age of Constantine the church became a channel for the distribution of resources to members rather than challenging members to become resources, says Bill Beckham. The biblical calling of the apostle, prophet, pastor, teacher or evangelist is not to assume or usurp 'the ministry' and perform it oneself as others look on, but to train God's people for the ministry, to equip others. They are evangelistic, prophetic, teaching, pastoral and apostolic trainers, not demonstrators; teachers, not one-man-shows. An evangelist's true fruit is not a convert, but more evangelists. Strangely enough, exactly the opposite of this biblical model has become the norm: specialist teachers, evangelists, pastors, apostles and prophets move about at a breathtaking speed, constantly overworked and under stress, slaves to their diaries. Unlike Jesus, they are difficult for others even to approach, with more than just their blood pressure in danger. They give seminars and speak at conferences, at which they show to the amazed masses the latest state of the art in their specialist area, and do exactly the opposite of their true and God-given task: instead of equipping God's people for the ministry, they *perform* it for them in front of them. Instead of teaching them how to teach, they just teach. Instead of equipping them to be evangelists themselves, they simply evangelize. Instead of training people how to prophesy, they prophesy and go away without leaving disciples behind. This not only sets unhealthy standards, but leaves both the teacher and the students unfulfilled and empty, because they have not done what God wanted them to do, i.e. to be discipled into these ministries, to learn each other's secrets, to be initiated into the multiplication process themselves. This creates a new caste of clergy and laity, and ultimately fails to prepare God's people to do their ministry. The five ministries are given by God to be given away, to be used in equipping others to do the work of the ministry, which ultimately means multiplying the structure through which the ministry is operating: the house churches.

The five fingers of the Hand

Gerald Coates, leader of the Pioneer movement in England, compared the fivefold ministry to the five fingers of the hand. The apostle is the thumb. He gives stability, holds the counterbalance, and can literally touch all the other fingers. The prophet is the index finger. He points at you and says: 'You are the man!' The evangelist is the middle finger, the longest of all and sticking furthest out into the world. The ring-finger resembles the pastor/ shepherd, caring for internal relationships. The little finger is the teacher: he can worm his way deep into any ear, and there share the truth of the gospel.

The pastor

The pastor, in the charismatic and biblical – not the traditional – sense, is by nature a shepherd: he stands in the midst of the flock of sheep. Everything mills around him; but nowhere in the New Testament do we find a pastor truly leading a congregation. He is by nature a very loving person who can create a family atmosphere. To him, relationships are the most important, simply because he is interested in the flock's long-term spiritual well-being. The good shepherd knows the names of the dolls of the children of the adults he is caring for; he is interested in every last detail. There's only one problem: a person's greatest weakness almost always lies in the shadow of their greatest strength. The pastor tends to lose the big picture, because he is 'lost in relationships'. With this ministry usually goes a natural 'professional blindspot'. However, his motto is 'Relationships are everything!' The pastor focuses on redeemed relationship with God, and redeemed relationships with each other, and helps others to function in this relational way also.

The prophet

The prophet is way ahead of the flock of sheep, perhaps five miles beyond the next hill. He is on the lookout. There he hears God's voice and sees visions, enters the throne-room of God and glimpses something. It may actually be very good that he is often away from the flock, because few really understand him. He is interested not so much in people and what they think of him, but in God's voice for the situation. Added to that, he often has a complicated and disorganized personality exactly because he is so uniquely gifted. Can you imagine spending a relaxed half-hour drinking coffee with Jeremiah? He would probably tear you and me apart, and use the coffee for an illustration.

A prophet's perspective is radically different from that of the pastor. He hears from God and quite mercilessly questions everything, including the pastor, from God's perspective. That, however, is his healthy and God-given duty. For that reason, there is also a historical tension between the pastor and the prophet: one is a defender of the status quo, who wants to maintain the community; the other questions everything and is seen (rightly) by many others as a threat, because he disrupts things and wants 'movement now'. The shepherd, in many pictures, not only has a stick in his hand to tend the sheep and keep away the wolves; he may also be quick in using that stick to keep away prophets. And yet both views are valid, because both are serving God and the same flock – one with loving attention, the other with a prophetic view. Both are necessary!

The prophet's motto, describing his ministry, is 'vision'. Prophets often have the unique ability to see and hear what others do not see nor hear. These supernatural revelations need to go through a process of healthy interpretation in the church (1 Cor. 14:29) and application. The prophet is groomed by a direct calling from God, and then usually sent 'pouring water over the hands of a master prophet', as in the case of Elijah and Elisha (2 Kgs. 3:11).

The apostle

The apostle is not as far from the flock as the prophet. He is about three miles away, just on top of the next hill instead of being on the other side of it like the prophet. From this commanding point he can see the big picture and study his map, looking for the next green pasture. He generally has no time for house visits and small talk; 'the world is his church'. Like Paul, he is never really satisfied: after Rome, he wants to go to Spain! His core word is 'strategy', his heartbeat is 'missions': he wants to see God's plans come true for nations. Apostles are very much like generals in an army. They carry the main burden and responsibility for the advancement of the cause. The apostolic ministry is a founding ministry: it can create something out of nothing, create a foundation in the desert. In many ways it unites all other gifts in itself. The apostle may function as a supernaturally gifted problem-solver and talent spotter. And if the pastor – the word is mentioned only once in the New Testament – is something of the equivalent of a spiritual 'uncle', very caring and loving, but not ultimately responsible, then the apostles, 22 of them are mentioned by name in the New Testament, are the spiritual fathers who carry the last responsibility, the real agony and joy.

The teacher

The teacher, using the picture of his relationship to the flock of sheep, lives at a critical distance from the flock. He sits on a vantage point half a mile from the flock, so that he can send out his dogs in time to deal with a sheep which is misbehaving or one that is unconsciously separating itself from the flock as it grazes. His motto is: 'The truth, and nothing but the truth!' The teacher is interested in quality, in the details, which he finds even more fascinating than the big picture. He is often a 'footnote' person in the truest and best sense of the word, who likes details and needs to know everything exactly. He has a passion for teaching itself, and his gift is to empower others to teach others how to teach. He is, like Jesus, his master Rabbi, leaving behind not primarily teaching notes but literally his spirit.

The evangelist

The evangelist circles the flock, also half a mile away – just enough so that he doesn't smell like the sheep pen and frighten the wild sheep away, but close enough to be able to lead them to the flock when he finds a lost sheep. He has three aims and passions: that people find Jesus, find Jesus, and find Jesus. He introduces a healthy outward focus to the churches, and is even involved in discipling new believers into maturity by literally 'reading the gospel to them', 'evangelizing' them, filling them with the good news. Biblically the evangelist does not lead the extension of the churches, but works in partnership with apostolic and prophetic people, who bear the main responsibility for laying the foundations of the churches. The evangelist empowers others to be evangelists, not in order to create evangelistic enterprises in themselves, but so that the house churches can become or remain an evangelistic movement.

Avoiding ministry projection

One of the greatest errors of our day is that we have allowed and even encouraged 'spiritual gift projection'. Gift projection happens when a Christian who has received a particular spiritual gift assumes that his gift is the most natural thing in the world, and that all other Christians would automatically achieve the same results if they acted just as he does. He overlooks the fact that God has made each of us unique and given each of us special gifts. At one stage or another, it might be God's plan for a Christian to stop *having* a gift and start *becoming* one, where someone would stop just prophesying, and become a prophet. Whoever measures someone else against himself is comparing apples with oranges and is doing himself and others a great disservice. He also complicates the lives of other Christians with unrighteous comparisons and simply sins against the body of Christ, in which not everyone is a mouth or a ear.

'Ministry projection' makes the problem worse. In ministry projection, the teacher looks at the evangelist and says: 'You and your evangelistic campaigns! Theological training, that's what really counts. You have only one problem: you should be a bit more like me!' The pastor looks with horror at the prophet and says: 'You and your visions. Long-term relationships are what counts!' He grasps his shepherd's crook, meant for keeping wolves at bay, and starts driving the prophets away.

When a teacher builds a church

If you leave a teacher to develop a church all by himself, he will build it around his unique gifting of teaching. What else could we expect? He might convert a church into a lecture hall, or plant Bible schools or other teaching centres. These sometimes might grow into impressive preaching cathedrals, if he has the necessary rhetorical giftings, where people from far and near come to be amazed. But often enough when the talented man leaves, the centre disappears also. A teacher does not really lay foundations; but he explains them brilliantly.

The evangelistic model of church

Evangelists often seem to live in one endless rally, and if you leave them to build a church, they will create a most fascinating series of events and exciting programmes, with a lot of adrenaline per minute. But ultimately it will have only one message to tell. An evangelist will be able to gather many, but is usually not gifted in building them together. Very soon the people will get tired of this one-

sided spiritual diet and leave, looking for more. Maybe
the evangelist also spots the problem, and leaves before
the people do, or – a most elegant solution – becomes air-
borne and itinerant, with a basic equipment of 10 or 20
evangelistic sermons, looking for people who have not yet
heard them.

The pastoral model of church

One of the strongest messages of a charismatic shepherd–
pastor to the world is, 'Come to me, all you who are heavy
laden, and I will listen to you and counsel you.' And come
they do. If the shepherd is left all to himself, his ministry
will naturally create counselling centres, which ultimately
may grow into a spiritual hospital, where people come to
have their wounds cared for in the power of the Holy
Spirit. Pastors, like good uncles, have difficulty in saying
'No'. The result is often a choking effect created by the
very best gifting in them: they are swamped by more
needy people than they can handle, and the growth limits
itself and stops. They quickly become 'maxed out' and
reach their capacity.

The predominant role of apostles and prophets in church-planting

Important though spiritual hospitals may be, they
cannot replace what apostles and prophets are
uniquely gifted for: to build a supernatural base and
foundation for a multiplying church movement, to
accept nothing as impossible, to respond strategically
to visions and supernatural revelations, to be prophetic
talent spotters. They are not so much human-centred
and felt-need oriented 'tenders' like good pastors,
teachers and evangelists, but God-centred: they have

the God-given ability to see beyond things, beyond human needs and problems, and take hold of the tasks and visions of God. They do not just want to build 'a church', they want the whole city or nation! They live in the future, for the future, from the future, constantly pregnant with future developments, and they can therefore pull and lead the church into the future, and prevent it from becoming a traditional institution only celebrating the past, or a fossilized monument of history long gone.

The church is 'built on the foundation of the apostles and prophets, with Jesus Christ himself as the chief cornerstone' (Eph. 2:20), writes Paul. John writes to the church in Ephesus 'that you have tested those who

Like a foundation for a house, much of the work of apostles and prophets is not always seen but felt.

claim to be apostles' (Rev. 2:2) after almost all of 'The Twelve' had died. This suggests simply that the service of apostles continues beyond the 'age of apostles', as Watchman Nee says in his book *The Orthodoxy of the Church*. Like a foundation for a house, much of the work of apostles and prophets is not always seen but felt. That is why they are described as being 'first of all' (1 Cor. 12:28), because they are also 'called in' first of all to do the foundational work for 'founding churches', the site- spotting, earth-moving, excavating, foundation-laying, so that others, like carpenters and plumbers and electricians, can build on that foundation. Would you like to live in a house where the foundations were laid by a carpenter? I admire carpenters, but I would not want to live in such a house. That is simply outside their brief.

Instead of pastoral, evangelistic and teaching models of church, apostles and prophets build prophetic and apostolic churches. The apostle, mentioned first in all the biblical lists of ministries, is one 'sent to attempt to solve the unsolvable for the purpose of facilitating the increase of the church of Jesus Christ in quality as well as quantity,' says Barney Coombs in his excellent book *Apostles Today*.

Playing together, not against each other

We need to stop playing these ministries off against each other, and start recognizing these unique giftings in each other. They are all valid parts of the whole picture, each a unique 20 per cent of the whole 100 per cent of all ministry, with the apostolic and prophetic ministries having a special and slightly more prominent role than the others. The teacher will never be able to take over or replace the ministry of a prophet or apostle; the pastor will not be able to do the work an apostle is called to do; and the prophet might fail miserably if asked to be a shepherd, but flourish if he is allowed to function within his anointing, and prophesy and teach others how to prophesy. The five ministries are meant to function in harmony and synergy, and complement each other perfectly.

A house church is led by elders. Not every individual house church of 15 people will have its own apostles, prophets, evangelists, pastors and teachers sitting all together in one small room. Those ministries are equipping ministries, going beyond the scope of a local house church, and function translocally, affecting the whole area or, especially in the case of prophets and apostles, even beyond that.

Building a spiritual gene-pool for the local church

The devil's plan has long been for the pastors to stand in one corner, the prophets in the other corner looking out of the window, while the teachers sit in the library, the evangelists drink coffee outside and the apostles roam overseas. In order to see the fivefold ministries working together again, they need to be identified afresh. These ministries then need to recognize each other – which might involve some solid repenting to redeem past misunderstandings and correct misconceptions of each other. Then they need to become friends with each other, because 'everything significant in the Kingdom of God is built on redeemed relationships,' says Roger Forster. Then they need to form teams, usually based on a locality – the city, the region, the district, the state, the nation – and start to multiply themselves, prophets multiplying prophets and evangelists multiplying evangelists 30-, 60- or 100-fold, and finally forming the equivalent of a spiritual gene-pool, an equipping and resource centre for the whole body of Christ in that locality and beyond.

From this leadership pool, the right person with the right gift can be dispatched quickly to add to the spiritual diet if needed somewhere, to solve a crisis, or give a specially needed input in any given church or area. The apostolic and prophetic equippers and servants of the Body, similar to civic servants, form a spiritual senate and council for the city or region or nation. One of their jobs is to work hard to avoid the formation of another spiritual dominating élite by forgetting titles and fame and being humble and accountable to each other. Their task is to be responsible for the corporate identity, calling and redemptive purpose of the church in a city or region, for truly speaking with one voice to the nation, for city-wide celebrations and regular apostolic and prophetic envisioning of the church on a wider basis. Business as usual for them will be to make themselves available to any house church that needs them, constantly circulating 'from house to house', pouring themselves into God's people as they multiply the house churches.

Are you the man?

Where do you start to develop this spiritual gene-pool?
With those who have a passionate, supernatural vision for
it. Those who can and do cry for a city or region or nation
should be the ones to initiate the process; no one else will
truly have the anointing for it. It will have to be apostolic
and prophetic people, because this is part of their God-
given nature. John Knox, the reformer of Scotland, an
apostolic man, once prayed: 'God, give me Scotland or
I die!' This is the kind of prayer that should be naturally
on your lips before you do this. Pastor Colton
Wickramaratne of The People's Church in Colombo, Sri
Lanka, himself an apostolic and prophetic man, fre-
quently says it this way: 'God's method is a man. Are you
that man?'

The first step in many areas is to recognize, form and
multiply the individual ministries. We need to do what we
are made by God to do. You may work as a pastor today,
but really be a prophet. Or you may try to be a teacher, but
you are a pastor, and you long to get in touch with people,
away from all that paper.

Three areas of responsibility in the church

Rather than developing three layers of hierarchical 'leadership levels', house churches are organically maintained
and multiplied through the ministry of three types of
specially gifted people:

1 Elders

The house churches are led by elders, whose function is to
father or mother the church. They bring redeemed
wisdom to the church, overseeing the flock like a father
overseeing his children, showing them how to live, and

they add authenticity through a proven family track record and balanced and mature lifestyle.

2 Fivefold ministers
The elders are equipped and trained by people who have been called by God for one of the fivefold ministries, apostles, prophets, evangelists, pastors and teachers. Those ministers circulate within the house churches 'from house to house' and function as a spiritual blood-circulation system nurturing all house churches with the elements necessary to become or remain healthy and therefore to multiply. Those ministries are like sinews and joints, linking the various house churches together to be a whole system. Their ministry transcends the individual house church and serves the body of Christ like a spiritual genepool, which the house churches of an area or a region, and sometimes beyond, can draw upon.

3 Apostolic fathers
Those spiritual equippers of the fivefold ministry are related to a third group of what I call 'apostolic fathers', people with an apostolic and prophetic gifting plus a special calling and charisma from God for a city, a region or a nation. These apostolic fathers, usually recognizable by the almost unbearable agony and spiritual pain they bear for a place, a city, a nation or a people group (Gal. 2:7–9), become the local backbone, the regional or national 'pillars of faith', anchoring the whole movement of house churches locally and being responsible for celebrations and the city church that will emerge. Since they usually have a true kingdom mentality, a broken spirit because of the spiritual burden they carry, they are least viable to build a massive movement and kingdom around themselves, but truly function as serving all – and therefore leading

all – not top-down from the lofty heights of a hierarchical power-pyramid, but down on earth, alongside other equippers (Mk. 9:35).

The *deacons* can be seen as functioning together with the elders (Phil. 1:1), but also as the secretaries and assistants of those apostolic fathers, taking care of administrative needs and social aspects, and keeping the apostles' hands free to do their work (Acts 6).

Most leading companies know that their future depends on the quality of the next generation of their leaders. So they employ so-called human-resource companies and placement agencies, or send out their own talent spotters, who roam the universities and schools to find the kind of gifted people of the calibre the company feels they need to employ. The body of Christ could learn from that. We need a supernatural talent-spotting ministry, or even a plan, systematically identifying and recruiting those gifts in each other and in the churches, and then helping those junior apostles and prophets or pastors-to-be to become apprentices with their own role models, people who are miles ahead of them in spiritual maturity and experience in the very ministry area they feel called to serve. Those disciples and apprentices can carry the suitcases of their masters, or 'pour water over the hands' of a senior prophet, and rub off as much as they can, 'catching the spirit' of someone ministering in the spirit. 'Just imitate me,' as Paul puts it. As an apprentice without a master does not make much sense economically, a disciple without a master does not make much sense spiritually.

Healing the church trauma

Many apostles and prophets today are not in church at all, because there is little room for them in traditional pastor-centred churches. They have been pushed to the side; they are often feared because they seem so strong, radical and different. Many have been not only marginalized but rejected, and as a result have given up on church almost completely, maybe with a last flicker and a spark of hope still burning in them. Many of them are in business today, or have become medical doctors. More and more of them know deep down that they are made for more than just earning 10,000 dollars a month operating on ulcers, avoiding the church that hurt them, spiritually surviving by TV and radio, and attending an occasional conference or a Christian businessmen's 'chapter'. Those rejected, undiscovered or underemployed apostles and prophets suffer from what I call the 'church trauma', a very deep and tricky wound inflicted on them by the very institution of healing, the church, which did not live up to its own calling and which – an almost devilish scheme – has badly hurt those whose ministries it needed most. Many of those Christian businessmen therefore heavily support anything but the church, invest in 'parachurch' ministries and missions – called 'para-', meaning 'alongside', church because there is no place for their vision within the church – , as long as they can stay clear of the church which has hurt them. The tragedy of this is that the church is God's mission. Someone needs to find them, go to them, apologize to them profoundly, heal the 'church trauma', speak to that glowing spark and fan it into a flame, and then recruit them, helping them to see how God sees them, and release them into their apostolic and prophetic potential for the building up of the church.

Does this strike a chord?

If you stand next to a piano and sing a tune, some of the piano-strings reverberate with the melody and give an echo: they resonate with the frequency of your tunes. This is also true spiritually. Sometimes I explain the fivefold ministry to participants of a seminar, and afterwards ask them to identify themselves and physically stand in their respective five corners. Usually, a small percentage of participants keeps sitting, because they still do not know where they belong. I then ask some representatives from the pastors, evangelists, prophets, apostles and teachers to come from their corner and pray a short prayer for and over those who do not yet know their calling. Then we ask those still sitting whether they have felt or experienced anything special while one of those ministers prayed, whether it struck a spiritual chord in them. If yes, they are then encouraged to join the respective group to which they felt they responded spiritually, and go to their corners, where I ask those waiting there to lay hands on them and pray, 'to fan into flame the gift of God which is in you through the laying on of my hands' (2 Tim 1:6; cf. 1 Tim. 4:14).

What is the next step for your area?

It depends where you are, and what ministries have been founding or dominating your area or even your church in the past. If there was an overabundance of pastoral and evangelistic ministry in your nation or people group, you may need to consider complementing the effects of these good ministries with apostolic and prophetic and teaching ministries, so that the spiritual ground has all the nourishment and care it needs to develop strong fruit.

Watering flowers with ice-cubes?

I believe strongly in the pastoral ministry. I also believe strongly in the other four ministries, the apostles, prophets, teachers and evangelists. As water is found in three forms – ice, water and steam – the five ministries are also found today, but not always in the right forms and in the right places. They may be frozen to ice in the rigid system of institutionalized Christianity; they may exist as clear water; or they may have vanished like steam into the thin air of free-flying ministries and 'independent' churches, accountable to no one.

God is transforming the core quality of the five ministries, captured and frozen into neat packages by the era of Christendom, and gently warming them up, bringing out the best in them for the task of watering His creation, the church. In fluid form, the five ministries will also find it easier to relate to each other and function and flow together.

Many in the churches today have hurt or even ill feelings about the fivefold ministry, especially about the apostolic and prophetic ministries, because they may have encountered them in the wrong form or package, either as steam or as ice. But that should not lead us to throw out the baby with the bathwater.

The lesson of Liebig

German biologist and chemist Justus von Liebig discovered over 150 years ago that soil only needs four fertilizers or minerals for the healthy growth of a plant: nitrogen, lime, phosphoric acid and potash. As long as all four minerals are present in the soil in sufficient quantity and harmony, growth occurs 'automatically'; the soil is truly fertile, and has all it needs to produce a good crop. If one of the fertilizers is lacking, let us say lime, the growth will be limited and halted by this limiting factor. The soil starves for lime, and you can add as much nitrogen, phosphoric acid and potash as you want, but you will not change the situation, you even damage it, unless you add lime.

Treatment of overacidic soil

Let us, for the sake of illustrations, equate evangelism with phosphoric acid, prophecy with potash, teaching with nitrogen, and pastoring with lime. If you have a soil thoroughly treated with phosphoric acid (evangelism) and nitrogen (teaching), it soon reaches a saturation level where any more of phosphoric acid and nitrogen will actually have a bad effect: it will make the soil acidic and have the opposite results to the ones we desire. What the soil needs now is not more phosphoric acid and nitrogen, but potash and lime in sufficient quantity, so that those minerals can catch up, and harmony in the soil is restored.

This could potentially hurt the producers of phosphoric acid and nitrogen, because they might feel rejected; but in effect they are only complemented by lime and potash, so that their good contribution, together with the other necessary elements, will reduce acidity and make the soil fertile ground again.

Phosphoric acid around the world!

Someone might stand up in a Christian conference and say: 'Phosphoric acid (evangelism) did it for my church! When I applied phosphoric acid, my church exploded. It was just what I needed, and it is just what you need, too! Brothers and sisters, I have a message for you: you need phosphoric acid. You may not know it, but you need it! Before you even ask, I have the answer: phosphoric acid! It worked for me, it will work for you. Let us start a ministry, "Phosphoric acid around the world", and tell everyone the blessings of phosphoric acid which will change any church for good.'

What would you think of such a man? Would you allow him to speak again at the conference? I would not. I rejoice for what happened to his church, but I would beware of copying him, because the situation in his area may not at all correspond with that in my area. Contextualization – the importing of a foreign idea into native soil – might be a nice idea, but fresh incarnation is better. Given the historic developments in the area of our farmer, he might have been starved of phosphoric acid, but he might need lime! If I take the advice of the phosphoric acid enthusiast, I might spoil the ground and do something very bad with something very good. The message again is that we should not copy someone else's experiences and methods, but be apostolic and prophetic ourselves, creative and sensitive to our own situation.

Every good agriculturalist can test the soil, finding out its quality and what fertilizers it needs and in what quantity, in order to produce a good harvest. This would be, in this illustration, the job of the apostle. Like the wise farmer who knows which of the four minerals are needed, the apostolic ministry would see which of the four ministries are necessary next in order to create a healthy balance that will truly develop a good soil. In a similar way you may remember the spiritual DNA, made up of the four genetic letters: guanine, cytosine, thymine and adenine. They are put together in a double-helix structure, which defines what letters correspond and complement other genetic letters, and the very way these letters are arranged will define how the organism grows. If we equate, for illustration's sake, those four genetic letters with the four ministries: evangelism, prophecy, teaching and pastoring, this creative act of putting them together in the right order would fall to the responsibility of the apostle, God's 'master-builder.'

Chapter 5

House Church or Cell Church?

Thirteen reasons why house churches are the natural solution

David Yonggi Cho, pastor of Yoido Full Gospel Church in Seoul, South Korea, has made the cell-group system world-famous. In more recent times, it was due to the material published by Ralph Neighbour, Jr, Bill Beckham, Larry Kreider, Larry Stockstill and others that the concept of the 'cell church' has gained worldwide momentum. 'Cells form the basic unit of the Cell Church,' says Neighbour. All or most members of a cell-based church are part of a small group or cell, usually meeting once a week, and typically meeting additionally in a celebration, a large gathering usually lead by a 'senior pastor'. Structurally the cell church forms a pyramid, with the senior pastor on top, followed by assistant pastors, regional and zonal pastors, 'down' to the cell leaders with their respective cell-leader assistants.

Although I share with many of my contemporaries an in-built aversion to 'top-down' language and elaborate systems and Plan As and Plan Bs for all eventualities, I can wholeheartedly agree with Ralph Neighbour's diagnosis of much of the traditional church in the first chapters of his book *Where Do We Go From Here*? He points to the programme-drivenness of a meeting- and event-oriented church as one of the core culprits, replacing life fellowship with running the 'right' agendas and having exciting programmes. Neighbour then goes on in his substantial book to explain in detail many aspects of a cell-based church. He suggests, for example, structuring cell meetings around the four Ws: welcome, worship, words and works. The welcome is an icebreaker to get people involved; the worship is about meditations, readings or songs; the word is the application of last Sunday's sermon; and works means to reach out practically to the *oikos*, the immediate circle of friends and relationships a person has.

However, I also share with many insiders and observers of the cell-church movement today a certain suspicion: could the unthinkable have happened, that the cell church has developed many excellent programmes to prevent itself becoming a programme-based design, and in so doing has become what it fears most – a programme-based design?

God's hand in the cell-church movement

I want to leave no doubt about it: I clearly see the hand of God in the cell-church and related movements. I believe God is the prime initiator of a paradigm shift and resulting changes in terms of church of such radical and global proportions that many of us would be simply shocked or startled, if we were to see the whole picture. I myself readily agree that what I write here is only a small part of the whole truth, and needs the complementary work and input of many others. The impending changes will be so immense, that even many contemporary prophets will be ill prepared. I agree that it is difficult to swallow the whole issue and the implications of house churches in one big bite, let alone take them seriously and implement them by tomorrow night.

I see the cell church as one of God's halfway houses, giving some limited focus and vision, so that we in our own limitations can better glimpse the way ahead.

God is a gentle global teacher; He teaches us step by step, first ABC, than DEF, and finally XYZ. Through the cell church He teaches a return to smallness in a language that many traditional programme-based churches can and do understand quite well. The fact that the cell church itself clearly carries some genes of a programme-based design does not really disturb me, since I see that this can serve as a beautiful bridge of understanding for those yet to cross the river back from organized cathedral-type religion to an organic and relational understanding of the church as a way of life, at home where we are at home. In this sense, I see the cell church as one of God's halfway houses, giving some limited focus and vision, so that we in our own limitations can better glimpse the way ahead. It may be also God's gracious hand to slow down our traditional and global church bus to negotiate the more radical bend to house-church Christianity ahead. If we are not slowed down by warning signs that we understand and heed, we will be ill prepared and possibly overturn at the corner with disastrous results. God does not want to overturn us and create chaos, but to help us to negotiate the future. He therefore sometimes has to slow us down to prepare us for what He sees, but we don't. Often our very own overactivist mentality does this nicely, and in times of 'burn-out' and breakdowns many new prophetic insights have been born, because we had the time to pray and think, to again be quiet and still before the Lord.

I have seen and heard about numerous cell-church movements or national adaptions of a cell-church idea which are functioning much more like house churches. I am only too happy about it. My intention here is not to create an artificial division at all, but to point out a spectrum and a continuum of a reformation process, of which, I am convinced, the cell church is an important part. I am in great sympathy with the cell church, because I completely share the concern for developing a New Testament church, a working structure that truly disciples people and ultimately disciples nations. My intention here is not at all to create an artificial polarization, but to point out some key differences between the house-church and the cell-church concept. For that purpose I list some key differences between the two systems, knowing that there are many models and structures developing today, and necessarily there will be some variations and even overlaps between the two.

Core differences	Cell church	House church
1 philosophy	'Chiefdom'	acephalous, headless tribe
2 reflects	city culture	village culture
3 flourishes in	warrior nations	peaceful nations as well
4 cell is	part of larger unit	the unit itself
5 administration	Jethro system	fivefold ministry
6 programme	agenda-driven	house church is the agenda
7 structure	pyramid	flat
8 leadership	leaders ladder	elders and apostles
9 centre	headquartered	decentralized
10 celebration	must	optional
11 visibility	high	low
12 set-up	evangelistic	apostolic and prophetic
13 'big wing' is	denominational church	the city church

1 Chiefdoms and acephalous tribes

If we compare cell churches and house churches, they might simply echo the age-old distinction between chiefdoms, tribes with a headman and acephalous or headless tribes. Cell churches would then reflect the chiefdom pattern, house churches the make-up of the headless tribal societies.

2 *City and village culture*

Many of today's cell churches have developed in cities or metropolitan areas, whereas house churches have flourished both in cities and villages. I think it is important to note that most cell churches are city-bred. Although, as some have contended, the story of redemption starts in the Garden of Eden and ends in the new city of Jerusalem, many people today do simply live in both worlds at the same time, the city and the village. A person might dwell in a city, but still live in a village within the city, in a colony, housing estate, apartment block, gated community, slum or neighbourhood quarter.

The cell church offers a visible island in the urban sea of humanity, a castle rising above the masses, where people can seek and find refuge under a standard-bearer's flag or in the shadow of a great man of God. This is one application of the cell-church model which may not always be the case. It is true that many people in cities seem socially lost, without identity, waiting for someone to come along to offer them a place to belong. But that is only true on the surface. Underneath, many people even in cities actually do 'belong' already, to a club, a clan, a group of some sort, a gang, a modern 'tribe', or feel a strong part of their geographic location, their apartment block or neighbourhood watch group, for example. They still have their tribe, their village, even within the city.

Almost all nations, with the obvious exception of typical city-nations like Singapore or the Vatican, retain most of their heritage, typical life-patterns and cultural traditions and strongholds in the village. Of this many nations are increasingly aware and proud: 'India lives in a village,' exclaimed Mahatma Gandhi. But what if the church in India, for example, lives in the cities? Can a city church disciple villages? The statistics say no. The consequences are simple enough: a church developed in the city, on average, will not win the villages. If we do not win the villages, we will not disciple the whole nation. As much as we need to win the cities – which we could also see as a huge network of villages and neighbourhoods – we need the type of church which can penetrate and win the villages, too. If we can disciple the neighbourhoods, we can also disciple the nation. House churches seem to be able to do both.

3 War and peace

Some tribes are traditionally warriors, like the African Masai, the Japanese, or the Norwegian Vikings, while others have a more peaceful mindset and history like the Dravidians of South India, the Finns, the Filipinos or the Kalahari Bushmen. Some nations, more than others, have developed a warrior culture: some are simply more peace-loving and settler-minded. This is expressed in the way they see their nation and see themselves as individuals, in the films they produce, in the role of the army or the law, and whether they like to have a king or a president. In some countries the majority of people have come simply to expect others to tell them what to do; in other countries that same behaviour would be highly offensive. In some countries people are highly formal and ritualistic, in others extremely low key and cordial. Some countries feel as if you enter an army camp, with tight controls from top to bottom, where nobody moves without prior permission; other countries are more like a campsite, a loosely organized and quite a pleasurable mess. In many western countries, from the time of Thomas Aquinas in the thirteenth century, individualism and, later, democracy have been valued above all else, where each person is in charge of their own life; in other nations individuals feel much

People growing up in a 'warrior' culture will much more expect and accept that others tell them where to sit and belong, what to do and how to behave.

more part of the 'Ummah', the tight-knit community, and others are generally in charge of their lives.

Churches growing in particular cultures and nations always reflect, to a high degree, this 'war or peace' mentality. People growing up in a 'warrior' culture will much more expect and accept that others tell them where to sit and belong, what to do and how to behave. From childhood their lives will be filled with little rituals and ceremonies, ribbons and badges, titles and career ladders, and there will always be a standard-bearer to which they should rally. Small wonder if someone expects the same in church. The cell church, I believe, reflects that pattern, and rightly so. However, people growing up with a peaceful, democratic, socialist or even communist background have something in common with today's Generation X culture in the West: they will instinctively question any self-imposing authority, be it political, economical, or spiritual. They will resist a church with a military touch and a spiritual general on top, and value an organic and relational church with servant leadership. This is one more reason why I favour house churches. They effectively function in both war and peace climates.

People growing up with a peaceful, democratic, socialist or even communist background have something in common with today's Generation X culture in the West: they will instinctively question any self-imposing authority, be it political, economical, or spiritual.

4 Interdependent status

Where the cell is an important part of a larger individual church, it 'belongs' structurally, for example, to the Yoido Full Gospel Church in Seoul or the Faith Community Baptist Church in Singapore. The house church does not organizationally 'belong' to a larger unit in that sense. It is usually part of an interdependent – not independent! – network of similar house churches or, often in cases of severe restrictions on Christianity, functions completely on its own. They are not part of a larger, 'real' or denominational church: they are the real thing all by themselves.

5 Jethro or the fivefold ministry

In tune with a stunning absence of the fivefold ministry, many cell churches favour the so-called Jethro principle, a system of administration which delegates authority to several levels of leadership. Jethro, Moses' father-in-law, advised him (Exod.18) to delegate judging the people of Israel to 'rulers and officials over thousands, hundreds, fifties and tens', because otherwise he would be overworked.

We should notice, however, that the Jethro principle is basically a policing structure enforcing law and order, not designed to build and empower the New Testament fellowship of grace and love.

We should notice, however, that the Jethro principle is basically a policing structure enforcing law and order, not designed to build and empower the New Testament fellowship of grace and love. Moses was a mediator between the people of Israel and God, and this is exactly what Jesus did away with, as He himself became the mediator once and for all, opening access to the throne of grace for all people washed by the blood of the Lamb. Are we trying to do the new in the power of the old? In a cell church the unquestioned leader is typically of a Moses type, the 'senior pastor' with his 'cabinet of ministers', delegating his authority to a myriad of levels of responsibility and leadership with an enormous amount of counting, administration, bureaucracy, and, may I say it, control.

This appears to me like a Protestant attempt at Catholicism, a Protestant emulation of an episcopal and hierarchical system. Is it a Freudian slip when we read in *Church Growth and the Home Cell System* (Seoul, p. 122) that 'every week new souls are being added to the central computer'? What must it do to a person's ego to know that he or she is number 5432 in the tracking system of the church computer? Few people want to be run and tracked by others, and live a life where every move is controlled and observed by the watchful eye of Big Brother. I have been introduced proudly into a number of large computer-operating rooms of cell churches as if they were the Holy of Holies. Sometimes I walked away with the feeling that the greatest unspoken fear of this church is that someone might fail to do their duty or walk out of line, the senior pastor might fall ill or die, the electricity fail, or a computer virus creep in, and the whole church fall apart in an instant.

'The growth of the (Cell) Church should only be limited by our anointing and vision,' says Lawrence Khong; and Markus Koch, working with the Christliches Zentrum Buchegg, a cell church in Zürich, Switzerland, goes on to suggest that 'a church should be led by *one* pastor'. This traditional one-pastor thinking

I am suggesting not only that any of them can go astray, but also that we should not build too much on just one person's charisma.

does not differ much from the congregational model of church. In fact, the very life and quality of the church would depend very highly on the quality, vision and energy of the senior pastor. Knowing many Christian leaders – and myself! – I am suggesting not only that any of them can go astray, but also that we should not build too much on just one person's charisma.

The 'stock' of senior pastors available today is quite limited, too. In every nation the number of persons with the calibre of a Lawrence Khong, Yonggi Cho, Ralph Neighbour, Kriensak Chareonwonsak, William Kumuyi, Gerald Coates, Max Schläpfer, D. Mohan, Bill Hybels and Cesar Castellanos is simply limited. They may not be just 'senior pastors' at all, but truly people with an apostolic gifting and calling much larger than their current set-up, and should not, and probably will not, confine themselves just to their own church in the future or even now.

A house church, in contrast to all this, is much less threatened by an electrical power cut, because there is not much data to lose. The elders of house churches are in relationship with people doing the fivefold ministry, through which God empowers, anoints and encourages others to do the work of the ministry. This fivefold ministry is low key and quite invisible. The idea is not delegating authority top-down to build an ever-increasing pyramid touching the sky, but empowering each other to spread out and generate a movement which can, if necessary, slide under the carpet and continue out of sight.

6 Do we have a programme or are we the programme?

In a typical cell church there is an agenda to accomplish and a fairly set pattern to follow for each cell. This agenda could be handed to the cell leader on a sheet from the senior pastor or a responsible person, or discussed with

the cell leaders on Wednesday in order to rehearse for the
cell meetings on Thursday, or the agenda might be contained in the agreed pattern for such meetings. Yonggi
Cho advises other ministers 'never to delegate the important responsibility of writing the teaching lessons and
having seminars with the homecell leaders to others'.

In contrast, the house church ideally is the agenda itself.
Since a house church is typically part of an apostolic network within which the fivefold ministry is operating, it is
prevented from becoming a pious club, an isolated social
gathering or a fellowship with 'koinonitis' – a form of 'fel-
lowship-infection' of an inward-looking and self-centered
Christian group – not by a programme but by the way it
functions and relates to other house churches.

Although Christians in house churches read and discuss the Bible, it is not a Bible study; although they pray, it
is not a prayer meeting. Since Jesus is a person, the idea of
having each meeting with that person structured around
the same old pattern seems to be as creative and inventive
as a bridegroom bringing his future bride each day the
same set of flowers, singing the same songs, and declaring
his ardent love with the same poems. I suspect after a short
time she would be less than excited to receive him and listen to his programme.

Much of the programme-drivenness of the traditional
church stems from the fact that most meetings are usually
arranged in such a way that there can be no (unpleasant)
surprises, like 'lay people' exercising gifts to the embarrassment of a religious professional. For the very fear of
something going terribly wrong, many of them have
developed democratic forms of administration. Democracy may look like the safest form of church government,
but it has proved to be the very one which quickly leads
into spiritual oblivion and facelessness, because it has the
ability to block out prophetic direction in the name of the

numerical majority. Usually it introduces bureaucracy as the most inhumane and legalistic form of administration by accountants who will make sure that the letter of the law is followed. It is yes or no. Instead of people symbolically sitting in the Garden of Eden under the tree of life, we end up all sitting – and arguing – under the tree of the knowledge of good and evil, and who is right becomes more important than who we are in Christ. Church programmes then start to become foolproof, follow an agreed pattern (unpack the guitar and songbooks, sing, pray, listen to a Bible study or sermon, pray again, close the meeting), where simply nothing can go wrong. In such a context, I suspect, not much can go right either.

Nothing is wrong with singing, praying and having Bible study in itself. But if it becomes the dominating programme whenever Christians meet, it will soon become a tradition. This is also why a preoccupation with Bible studies or even prayer can easily kill a healthy community, because it values and emphasizes one agenda over the others. This ultimately attracts and involves people quickly into a programme, which is easy for the first few months, but then not only generates the need to go on inventing follow-up programmes to the last follow-up programme, but starts to actually wear and burn out the people. 'When we realized this with a shock, we closed down all our prayer meetings,' says Pastor D. Mohan of the 12,000-member Assemblies of God Church in Madras, India.

In a house church the idea is to come together in order to be together in the presence of Jesus, who, yes, might very well have an agenda for the asking, and will gladly reveal it through his Holy Spirit and anyone present with a prophetic ministry: 'When you come together ... two or three prophets should speak' (1 Cor. 14:26–9). The core reason Christians come together is to share and transfer life, and since life is not predictable, their meetings are not really predictable either. That this very issue of unpredictability makes house churches more attractive, at least for teenagers, may be a pleasant side-effect.

An agenda can potentially even harm or prevent community and fellowship, because it may introduce an overriding focus to the community and squeeze it mechanically into a predefined direction. The very agenda-drivenness of the cell church introduces a condition, and conditional fellowship is limited fellowship. Many such programmes or agendas develop because Christians are told that their meetings are for evangelistic purposes and reasons. This evangelistic structure carries an in-built evangelistic pressure to perform, which accounts for much of the startling burnout figures of cell churches.

In house churches, the people are the resources, Jesus is the programme, fellowship is the reason, multiplication is the outcome, and discipling the neighbourhood the goal.

Programmes can, however, sometimes serve as a temporary method of ingraining a mentality or a pattern of behaviour into people. Once they have achieved that, the programme can be discarded and life can go on. I heard about one of the best of such programmes for cell meetings from my friend Steve Dixon of the cell-based Kings Church in Slough, England. They call it L.I.F.E.: L stands for dealing with life issues, I for intercession, F for fun, fellowship and food, and E for evangelism.

Rather than seeing church or cell groups as a series of programme-driven weekly meetings at 7.30 p.m. in Cherry Tree Lane, house churches see their essence as sharing lives, and they could meet every day as in New Testament days, or any other number of times that suited them. Here, the people are the resources, Jesus is the programme, fellowship is the reason, multiplication is the outcome, and discipling the neighbourhood the goal.

7 Pyramid or flat structure?

Almost everything that man touches – buildings, companies, politics – grows into a bigger and higher structure, with any amount of levels, stairs and pyramid schemes. Beyond the tabernacle, which was a tent, the temple was the only building God ever designed, and it was flat, not multi-storied. The cell church usually develops quickly into a pyramid structure with the Senior Pastor on top, followed downwards by Assistant Pastors, Directors of Pastoral Care Departments, District Pastors, Sub-District Pastors, Section Leaders and finally, at the bottom, the Home Cell Leaders with their Assistant Home Cell leader and Spiritual Parents. A pyramid or power-based structure brings with it the danger of political corruption: the closer you are to the man at the top, the more power or influence you might have. In such a set-up, spiritual authority is in danger of being replaced by the mere distance from the source of power, which is the unquestioned leader himself.

> *The various tasks are not executed by people within a hierarchy, but by people uniquely gifted for a special ministry relating to each other as redeemed friends and submitting themselves to each other.*

The house church has, in comparison, a flat structure. The various tasks are not executed by people within a hierarchy, but by people uniquely gifted for a special ministry relating to each other as redeemed friends and submitting themselves to each other. In the New Testament there is no inferiority or superiority amongst members of the church, but equality: no one is more important than the others (1 Cor. 12:21–5), but everyone has simply to fulfil a different function within the body. Ministry is therefore not delegated top-down but earned through a spirit of humble servanthood. As I set out in the previous chapter there, are three main areas of responsibility:

a. the house churches are led by *elders*;
b. the elders are constantly equipped and trained by people who have been called by God for one of the fivefold ministries;
c. those spiritual equippers relate to what I call *apostolic regional fathers*, people with an apostolic and prophetic gifting plus a special calling from God for a city, a region or a nation. Those apostolic fathers, usually recognizable by the almost unbearable agony and spiritual pain they bear for a place, a city, a nation or a people group, become the local backbone, the regional or national 'pillars of faith', anchoring the whole movement of house churches and being responsible for any celebrations and the city church that will emerge.

The house church is typically part of an interdependent network, a truly self-regulating system of interrelated elements or clusters of elements. 'The biotic principle of interdependence states that the way the individual parts are integrated into a whole system is more important than the parts themselves. This is nature's blueprint: structured interdependence,' says Christian Schwarz.

The structure is flat, because there is no one 'higher' or more important than the other person. This also has consequences for the potential corruption with money and power in the church, from which the traditional church is not exactly free and immune, because it is not all that impressing to be the humble elder of 13 others or simply to serve a number of house churches as a teacher, pastor or evangelist.

8 Led or fathered

We humans love leaders, and chuckle knowingly when we drink out of a coffee mug with the slogan: 'Lead, follow, or get out of the way'. In the days of Saul, God wanted to be King of the Israelites, but the nation wanted rather to follow the ways of the nations and have a decent king. Today we are in the

The whole world wants leaders, not servants, and so does the traditional church. Maybe we want what God is not willing to give.

same danger. The whole world wants leaders, not servants, and so does the traditional church. Maybe we want what God is not willing to give, and instead of seeing the futility of our attempts, we carry on with what we think is persistence. Just like a human body, the body of Christ has not many leaders but many different members, all with different functions. As those members function together in collective obedience to their head, so the whole body is literally led by the head. To call one member a leader over the others – and in spite of the presence of the head – would be grossly misleading. Jesus is the head of the church, and that is all the leadership it truly needs. The church is led when its members obey its head. The church experiences leadership as they collectively obey their head and function together in unity.

If we want to see a biblical – and not political or management – kind of leadership, we must stop blindly assuming and usurping leadership of the church, as if it is the most natural thing to do. Man assumes there must be leadership in anything he touches. It is part of his creational brief. However, the church is an exception, because it is not man's invention or property. It is truly God's. This is something which runs so contrary to our human thinking: supernatural faith in a God, who has things under control when they long seem to have slipped out of our hands, is required to be true and faithful stewards of His church. That is also why God mainly rules His church through apostolic and prophetic people who usually have the charismatic gift of faith more than others. Rick Warren, senior pastor of Saddleback Community Church, puts it this way: 'For a church to grow, both the pastor and the people must give up control.'

Leadership in the political sense of assuming the last responsibility, filling a ministry slot and function within a job description within a programme, or taking on some delegated authority from someone else, is simply not good enough for the church. That will choke its development as Saul choked Israel, or bygone bishops who behaved like little kings choked the development of the church and led them into meaningless and religious chiefdoms. The body of Christ requires humble and faithful stewards, functioning in obedience to Christ and in mutual love, respect and submission to each other, not highly professional and individual great 'leaders' in their own right, who build their little kingdoms around their personality or personal gifting. The church requires Christ-like stewards managing God's *oikonomia*, or household, well, who know that they themselves are led by Christ, who is neither dominating and order-giving nor works with assistants, but has absolute faith in His father and has *therefore* been entrusted with the world.

Cell churches are very leader-intensive; they require leadership at many levels. House churches, in contrast, are basically not led, but fathered. A cell group usually has a leader and an assistant leader; a house church has an elder. There is a huge difference. I am the father and husband of a small family, but few would call me the leader of my family.

It is part of a father's brief to lead, but it is not necessarily part of a leader's brief to father. House churches are by nature spiritual extended families, extension centres of the heavenly father's heart, who expresses His passionate heart for His children through special people whose hearts are beating to the rhythm of God's own passion. No church in the New Testament is said to be 'led' by a pastor or any other leader; but there are always God-ordained persons – stewards – who carry a special responsibility for the church, namely the elders, the apostles and prophets. Again, this does not mean that they are leaders. Few would turn to a steward to ask for his business card. The stewards of the church are servants, and the more they serve, the more they will ultimately lead (Lk. 22:26) in a way which is upside-down to the way the world expects leadership. An obedient and humble servant can lead because he is led. Leadership, if at all, is therefore a function of obedience. Many house-church movements in the world have no leaders in the political sense; they are served by anointed stewards, who function very much like spiritual fathers and mothers, as in the case of Yuan Allen in Beijing, the 'Father' of the Chinese house-church movement.

For a cell church with a pyramid structure and 'leaders' trained at every level, it is quite possible that a new professionalism and clericalism enters through the back door. In addition, many cell churches have a 'leaders' ladder', where a person can work himself 'up' from assistant cell-leader level to assistant to the senior pastor. Quite apart from the danger of possible competition in such a 'career structure', it means that a person usually performs his task only for a short time, and then moves on or up. What if God has called a person simply to be an elder, and never fashioned him or her to become assistant senior pastor at all?

9 The headquarters question

The cell church usually has an impressive headquarters, typically as an expression of the unique ministry of its senior pastor and his close associates. House churches are typically a decentralized system with many different centres – i.e. homes! – which can change at any time, if needed. I was reminded of this while speaking recently in Yuan Allen's house church in Beijing, which is networked invisibly 'under the carpet' with many other house churches. All this happens from a single bedroom with a few chairs and a minute porch, all located in a small alley too narrow for a car to pass through, just behind a bustling market.

House churches seem to demonstrate more of a flexible, pilgrim mentality: they are on the move, just as God's Spirit is on the move. The cell churches are more settled than that: they have developed roots and a more or less huge administrative structure, and usually broadcast the message that they are 'here to stay'. One of the negative aspects of a headquarters is that it generates the need for a lot of organizing and administration.

The biggest problem with organizing the church is that it introduces bureaucracy. Bureaucracy is possibly the most dangerous, cruel and inhuman form of administration, because it will only take yes or no for an answer. 'Did you fill out the form properly, yes or no?' A bureaucratic system of administration throws the door wide open for the kind of people who ultimately would account, organize, administrate, manage, sell, run and finally control – and therefore kill – the church. Howard Astin in his book

Body and Cell comments that some cell churches feel very 'regimented'. This can be avoided quite easily in house churches, because everything here is relational, and things are therefore simply more humane. There is not much more to organize than

> Since there is a head – and naturally a headquarters in heaven – we can relax on earth and have as many small outlets of this heavenly chain of churches as possible, because God does not lose track of them.

in living in an extended family. We do not have to assume control of the church as if it were a company which needs Total Quality Management, a modern business philosophy which leaves no space for unforeseen developments and has 'all bases covered' for maximum quality and therefore maximum customer satisfaction, which means maximum profit. With the church, we can have a more humble approach, knowing that God is in control. Since there is a head – and naturally a headquarters in heaven – we can relax on earth and have as many small outlets of this heavenly chain of churches as possible, because God does not lose track of them: He has the final oversight. In frantically trying to help God run His business by establishing visible and impressive cathedrals and headquarters on earth we might, unwittingly, have actually hindered Him, because these structures may have shouted glory to men on earth so loud that the glory of the Lamb was drowned in the process.

10 The role of celebrations

The cell church typically requires both sociological sizes, the cell and the celebration, to function well; both are necessary wings of the 'two-winged church', as Bill Beckham illustrates it. The house church can exist independently of celebrations, especially in a hostile environment, and still spread out. They can celebrate through the way they are linked together in an interdependent structure, whereas in the cell church the celebration, complete with worship band and preaching by the senior pastor, can often become a way back into the very congregational structure they have tried to leave behind. The celebrations of cell churches often have a denominational character – it is our brand of cell groups that meet in our celebration – whereas the house churches favour and support more the regional or city-wide celebrations, where the whole local church comes together as the sum total of all Christians in an area. One builds a new denominationalism; the other builds the Kingdom. Which is more biblical?

11 High and low visibility

Low visibility of human structures also means high visibility of God's hand.

As the house church can function with or without a celebration and the necessary administrative headquarters to run it, it is obviously much less visible. In many nations or cities house churches can function for a long time without being noticed at all by the public. The interdependent network structure of a house-church movement links the churches 'under the carpet', through an invisible and flat structure, so that even the celebration happens as the fivefold ministry rotates through the house churches and carries with it good news, greetings, gifts and vision. This also means that house churches are less prone to corruption through insecure and therefore power-hungry people attracted by powerful and impressive structures like flies to the honey. This type of Christianity makes a much more humble statement about itself, which is specially important for areas of the world with a lot of religious bigotry, where religious movements try to outdo each other by competing to see who can have the highest steeple or tower attached to holy buildings. Low visibility of human structures also means high visibility of God's hand in all this. Finally, a low-visibility structure is much more persecution-proof and prepared for all apocalyptic eventualities than massive cell churches with a vulnerable top man and a vulnerable hub.

12 *Evangelistic or apostolic–prophetic foundations*

Many have correctly understood that the cell church is an evangelistic model of church. Because many feel that 'evangelism is the need of the hour', we might feel prone to go with the flow and build evangelistically. However, as I have pointed out above, the long-term driving force of a church is not its evangelistic vision, but a solid apostolic and prophetic foundation (Eph. 2:20). In this way, the apostolic outward focus and a prophetic vision for the past, the present and the future, is literally built in. I believe that often the house churches are 'apostolic and prophetic', because that is exactly the way the New Testament apostles and prophets built the church. Evangelists have never played the main role in propagating the church: this has always been the ministry of prophetic and apostolically gifted people. The apostolic and prophetic church as a new way of life is good news in itself, and does not really need evangelism as an activity to drive it, with all the unhealthy pressure to perform that comes with it.

A good example of this is Argentina, a country that has been experiencing revival since roughly 1982, when it lost a war with Great Britain, and much of its national pride was sunk with its flagship, the *General Belgrano*. Gifted evangelists like Carlos Annacondia, Hector Gimenez and

Omar Cabrera sprang up and had massive evangelistic rallies of almost unheard-of proportions, counting the 'decisions for Christ' by the tens of thousands. However, I was told that Carlos Annacondia and others have honestly asked themselves, 'Where are all those people we led to Christ now?' Omar Cabrera, in a Dawn-related conference in Miami in November 1998, pointed out that many pastors in Argentina, including himself, have found it difficult to incorporate the many who made 'decisions for Christ' into existing or newly planted churches.

Argentina, as a study in September 1996 revealed, has one of the lowest church-planting rates of all of Latin America. All that 'Extraction Evangelism', as I call it, trying to extract individuals from their families through an individual and purely verbal 'decision for Christ', is not only breaking existing social structures and is therefore hated by parents of converted children around the world, it has also not led to much church growth either. There must be a missing link. 'Evangelism which pulls individuals out of their family context and provides no new context is half-baked and may well do more harm than good,' says Alan Tippet.

Argentinian Alberto de Luca, together with a growing number of pastors, sees church-planting and multiplication as the prophetic way forward. They are developing now a national church-multiplication strategy. In other words, they are moving from being evangelism-driven to functioning in an apostolic and prophetic way to see their country discipled. Good evangelism supports and functions in unity with the fivefold ministry, never isolated as a single force or cure-all for the lost or unheard witness of the church.

I have mentioned above that the cell church seems to be an urban product, a model of church grown in the city or a metropolitan climate. The city develops a particular culture, quite different from the villages. In a village, each person is directly responsible for his actions. In an atmosphere of tight social control he cannot escape because everybody knows everybody. In a city, however, an individual quickly drowns in an anonymous mass and may start to feel that he does not have to stand up for the consequences of his actions, because he can always disappear into the faceless crowd. The city breeds a philosophy of its own, a 'hit and run' approach, where any salesman understands that he needs to quickly touch as many people as he can with his product, because next moment they are gone. This philosophy has moulded much of today's evangelistic thinking, and much of today's evangelistic thinking has, in turn, flown into the cell-church approach. But as long as the church thinks the evangelists are the prophets, the true prophets will not be heard.

13 How big is big?

Bill Beckham introduces a helpful picture of the church: the bird with two wings. The one wing is the cell structure, the small gatherings of believers; the other wing is the big worship service, the celebration. A one-winged church, one with only a celebration worship service, where the cell-system was lost in the sands of church history, is a restricted creature, only flies in circles, and cannot really soar like an eagle any more. It therefore needs a second wing. I completely agree.

However, the core difference between house church and cell church in this regard is that cell churches typically develop a 'branded', denominational type of celebration, such as a 'Faith Community Baptist Church Celebration'. The natural second wing for the house churches is the city church, ideally the whole body of Christ of a city or an area, who meet and celebrate in the largest possible numbers, regularly or irregularly, without a denominational label, just as the Christians of the city coming together and acting as one body. Instead of having a focus and identity on church level 1 (the house) and 3 (the city or region), a cell church usually focusses on level 1 (the house or cell) and 2 (a congregation), a certain cluster of 'branded' cells within an area.

Transitioning for ever?

Cell churches have done only half a paradigm shift, they have not fully concluded the circle and not yet finished the 'second reformation'. But they are a brilliant start in the right direction.

One of the most striking aspects of cell churches is that most of them seem to be constantly 'in transition'. Transition could easily become the outstanding constant of the cell-church movement. Lawrence Khong of Faith Community Church, Singapore, a passionate and visionary man of God, mentioned in a brochure in 1998 that they were now in their 'tenth year of transitioning'. In my view, cell churches have done only half a paradigm shift, they have not fully concluded the circle and not yet finished the 'second reformation'. But they are a brilliant start in the right direction, given the fact that a large proportion of the churches in the world are built according to the congregational model of church.

I believe that God wants us to go full circle, returning back wholeheartedly to the New Testament God and consequently His model of house churches, incarnated in apostolic and prophetic ways into our soil, time, people group and culture, because God wants once more to turn the world upside-down.

Lamb or Lion?

In biblical revelation, we meet Jesus in many forms; one of them is the Lamb of God, and one is the Lion of Judah. My impression is that house churches are much more 'Lamb', much more fragile and vulnerable in nature, than the cell church, which sometimes reminds me of a Lion, a kingly structure. We all know there will be the time when Jesus will come back as the world ruler and establish His dominion visibly. But we are not there yet. In the here-and-now we are experiencing the Messianic Kingdom, but in many ways we still do not experience it fully. We are strong in weakness, the meek shall inherit the earth, lasting things for the Kingdom of God are accomplished 'not by might and power, but by my Spirit'.

In house churches, as I hope I have made clear, so many things can go wrong, and probably will go wrong. If anything positive happens and is achieved through house churches, the ultimately glory will not go to an ingenious system, a fantastic human pastor, an anointed concept, but to the Lamb of God Himself, who has done the humanly impossible and seen His lambs safely through into the final Kingdom. Like Himself, they have been beaten, ridiculed, mocked, harmed, and maybe crucified on earth. But they will rule for ever in His Kingdom to come.

Chapter 6

Developing a Persecution-Proof Structure

'Blessed are you when you are persecuted': how to develop a persecution-proof spirit and thrive under pressure

As much as people loved Him, the life of Jesus was almost always threatened. He was a stumbling-block to the religious leaders, to the political leaders, and He upset and challenged to the very core the nice business-driven world of the civilized and ordinary citizens. As a result, He was questioned, threatened, tempted, tricked, persecuted and finally betrayed, captured and killed. The miracle is that He survived it all, He was 'proof' to all this suffering. In fact, He survived even His own death.

His disciples lived in a world of fierce and brutal religious persecution. They were in and out of jails, had little academic education, no massive church buildings or mission headquarters. At one point they had favour in the eyes of the public, and at another moment, were feverishly persecuted and had no foundations and donors to appeal to for financial support. Still, Jesus told them to go and make disciples of all nations.

Jesus must have known something which we are sometimes in danger of overlooking. His own ability to survive, His supernatural power to live, to achieve His purposes against all possible odds, His own resilience, was to be built into the church, His body on earth. Maybe Jesus foresaw that His church had fascinating and God-given supernatural abilities: it can thrive on chaos, blossom in the darkness, be rich in poverty, grow in the desert, flourish under pressure and sing in jail.

Where do we look for inspiration?

Many insights, lessons and advice for church growth or church-planting on the market today come from the non-persecuted churches rather than the persecuted church. Not that there is nothing to learn from peacefully settled churches: far from it. But statistical evidence and missionary research, such as that carried out by David Barrett and his associates, shows that the church grew and still grows most vigorously under a certain level of persecution and affliction. As Mao Tse Tung closed out all western missionaries from China in 1949, the church began to be persecuted – and grew like never before. According to some researchers, up to 10 per cent of China is now evangelical, the largest single evangelical block in the world. Similar observations come from Ethiopia, Russia, Vietnam, Sudan and Cuba. But the eyes of the church are often where the eyes of the world are too: on Dow Jones indexes, and the centres of political and economic power. Many want to learn from the powerful how to *dominate* the world; only few people want to learn from the meek how to *inherit* the earth.

As a result, many church growth and church-planting lessons from Djibouti, for example, go unnoticed, because most Christians do not even know where Djibouti is. They know about Wheaton, Pasadena and Colorado Springs, Brownsville, Toronto, Oslo, Rome, Stuttgart, London and Bern, and consequently learn lessons from the teachers to whom they look up.

In 1998, German evangelist Ulrich Parzany received a medal for his outstanding achievements in the area of youth work in Germany. In his response he said: 'They crucified my boss, Jesus Christ. I am being honoured. What did I do wrong?' Jesus sent us as lambs amongst the wolves, not as wolves amongst the lambs. This means that there are lessons to learn from the lambs who have been amongst the wolves. It also means, that it is difficult, if not impossible, to preach the message of redemption from a position of power. More and more Christians are realizing today that there is power in weakness, strength in humility, and that a powerful mission agency is a contradiction in terms.

Thank God for pressure

We are tempted to think that Paul's words, 'In fact, everyone who wants to live a godly life in Christ Jesus will be persecuted' (2 Tim. 3:12), must have been written for another place and another time, maybe another world. However, Jesus said in Matthew 5:10–12: 'Blessed are those who are persecuted because of righteousness, for theirs is the kingdom of heaven. Blessed are you when people insult you, persecute you and falsely say all kinds of evil against you, because of me. Rejoice and be glad, because great is your reward in heaven, for in the same way they persecuted the prophets who were before you.'

Today we are in danger of turning those words on their heads, and defining blessings and curses according to the patterns of the world, not according to the values of an upside-down Kingdom of God. We feel we are blessed when we are successful and remunerated, honoured and quoted, given seats of honour, and when we are admired and glide pain-free through a peaceful and safe life without problems. We behave as if religious freedom is a status of blessing, and persecution is inherently bad: we may even pray to the very God who sent the persecution to 'kindly protect us from it'.

Three kinds of persecution

There are three kinds of persecution:

⟨ *external*, by national or local government, or other religious groups;
⟨ *internal*, where Christians fight and persecute each other, withholding blessing from each other, and filling up countries with 'angry brothers' (Mt. 5:22–4);
⟨ thirdly and probably worst of all, *no persecution at all*, because the church is not worth being persecuted; its values and its lifestyle have blended with a godless society, the salt has become saltless and is simply trodden under the feet of society unnoticed.

In this regard it is helpful to re-examine the role of persecution and suffering in regard to the church. Some insights stand out:

1 *Jesus was persecuted because he did not keep religious laws:*
John 5:16 'So, because Jesus was doing these things on the Sabbath, the Jews persecuted him.'

2 *Christians are supposed to have enemies in order to love them:*
Matthew 5:44 'But I tell you: Love your enemies and pray for those who persecute you.'

Romans 12:14 'Bless those who persecute you; bless and do not curse.'

3 *Jesus predicted persecution:*
Matthew 10:23 'When you are persecuted in one place, flee to another. I tell you the truth, you will not finish going through the cities of Israel before the Son of Man comes.'

Matthew 13:21 'But sice he has no root, he lasts only a short time. When trouble or persecution comes because of the word, he quickly falls away.'

Luke 21:12 'But before all this, they will lay hands on you and persecute you. They will deliver you to synagogues and prisons, and you will be brought before kings and governors, and all on account of my name.'

John 15:20 'Remember the words I spoke to you: "No servant is greater than his master." If they persecuted me, they will persecute you also. If they obeyed my teaching, they will obey yours also.'

4 *Persecution is not an extraordinary but a normal part of the Christian experience of 'everyone who wishes to live a godly life':*
Romans 8:35 'Who shall separate us from the love of Christ? Shall trouble or hardship or persecution or famine or naked-ness or danger or sword?'

1 Corinthians 4:12 'We work hard with our own hands. When we are cursed, we bless; when we are persecuted, we endure it.'

2 Thessalonians 1:4 'Therefore, among God's churches we boast about your perseverance and faith in all the persecutions and trials you are enduring.'

2 Timothy 3:11,12 '. . . persecutions, sufferings – what kind of things happened to me in Antioch, Iconium and Lystra,

the persecutions I endured. Yet the Lord rescued me from all of them. In fact, everyone who wishes to live a godly life in Christ Jesus will be persecuted.'

5 *Persecution is a blessing, not a curse:*
    Mark 10:29,30 '. . . no-one who has left home or brothers or sisters or mother or father or children or fields for me and the gospel will fail to receive a hundred times as much in this present age (homes, brothers, sisters, mothers, children and fields – and with them persecutions) and in the age to come, eternal life.'

    2 Corinthians 12:10 'That is why, for Christ's sake, I delight in weaknesses, in insults, in hardships, in persecutions, in difficulties. For when I am weak, then I am strong.'

6 *Jesus identifies with the persecuted church:*
    Acts 9:4,5 'He fell to the ground and heard a voice say to him, "Saul, Saul, why do you persecute me?" "Who are you, Lord?" Saul asked. "I am Jesus, whom you are persecuting."'

    Acts 22:7,8 'I fell to the ground and heard a voice say to me, "Saul! Saul! Why do you persecute me?" "Who are you, Lord?" I asked. "I am Jesus of Nazareth, whom you are persecuting," he replied.'

    Acts 26:14,15 'We all fell to the ground, and I heard a voice saying to me in Aramaic, "Saul, Saul, why do you persecute me? It is hard for you to kick against the goads." Then I asked, "Who are you, Lord?" "I am Jesus, whom you are persecuting," the Lord replied.'

7 *Persecution has a long history:*
    Exodus 1:12 'But the more they were oppressed, the more they multiplied and spread; so the Egyptians came to dread the Israelites.'

Acts 7:52 'Was there ever a prophet your fathers did not persecute? They even killed those who predicted the coming of the Righteous One. And now you have betrayed and murdered him.'

8 *The gospel spreads because of persecution:*
Acts 11:19 'Now those who had been scattered by the persecution in connection with Stephen travelled as far as Phoenicia, Cyprus and Antioch, telling the message only to Jews.'

9 *Avoiding persecution can be avoiding the cross:*
Galatians 5:11 'Brothers, if I am still preaching circumcision, why am I still being persecuted? In that case the offence of the cross has been abolished.'

Galatians 6:12 'Those who want to make a good impression outwardly are trying to compel you to be circumcised. The only reason they do this is to avoid being persecuted for the cross of Christ.'

The blood of the martyrs is the seed of the church

It has been pointed out countless times that persecution helps the church to be pure and holy, to pay the price of the gospel and be less concerned with luxuries, and that the blood of the martyrs has always been – and still is – the seed of the church. We can draw at least three important conclusions for the house churches:

1 Persecution is normal, peace is the exception
If the Kingdom of God is conflicting at the deepest possible level with the kingdom of this world, disturbances and conflicts, or even a state of war, are the necessary outcome. At this present stage of history, God's Kingdom and 'the

world under the rule of the evil one' are simply not compatible; they are unreconcilable, like water and fire. Jesus came to destroy the works of the evil one, and this will not happen in diplomatic peace talks. The church as Jesus' body on earth will be drawn into this conflict. Persecution, therefore, is business as usual for the churches; peace and harmony are the exception.

2 Persecution reforms the inner quality and structure of Christianity, and therefore restores apostolic church patterns

Jesus says, 'Love your enemies.' Many pastors know that even after many hours of motivational sermons as well as Bible studies, few Christians truly manage to love their friendly neighbours, let alone the unfriendly ones. Persecution changes all this by regularly upsetting the status quo and changing comfortably settled Christians into pilgrims. It uproots complacency and restores the pioneer spirit. It liberates Christians from their fixation with big buildings and involves them in a movement. The disciples, commanded by Jesus to be 'my witnesses in Jerusalem, and in all Judea and Samaria, and to the ends of the earth' (Acts 1:8), only began to reach beyond Jerusalem after God allowed persecution (Acts 8:1–4). Persecution restores the church back to the likeness of its persecuted founder, Jesus Christ. Jesus said: 'Blessed are you when you are persecuted.' Persecution, therefore, restores an amount of 'blessedness', which in itself is a quality, with which God is gifting the church.

This also has structural consequences, because during persecution the church needs to 'live out of suitcases', needs to have a 'moveable structure', live and grow in a flexible tent rather than a solid immovable structure meant to stay here for ever. It needs to have forms that are dynamic, readily adaptable to any change. The house church perfectly fits this description.

Sometimes persecution may be God's last word to a sleepy church which has afforded itself the luxury of sleeping through all the apostolic and prophetic wake-up calls in the past. Persecution is a wake-up call few will be able to miss. This way God may bring back a mentality of urgency and mission, and restore the apostolic nature to the church. As they are scattered, they may again go and 'preach the word wherever they went' (Acts 8:4), which is what they should have done in the first place.

3 *Persecution purifies the agenda of the church*
A settled streamlined church that is absorbed within its own culture will soon develop values, priorities, habits and agendas, that are not in line with God's priorities of upsetting the status quo by introducing the Kingdom of God. The early church had few of the projects – social, political, ecological, evangelistic or holistic – in which the church engages itself today, and it still grew and flourished. In times of persecution, the agenda of the church is reduced to absolute Kingdom essentials: spreading itself thin, carrying on as the yeast that leavens the dough, and keeping on discipling the nations. A degree of persecution also helps to prevent corruption in the church, because no one wants to be much of a king or a star in a secret, half-legal society of fairly unimpressive little groups.

Standing in good company

We must find a healthy way between, on the one hand, unhealthily glorifying persecution like the early Church Father Irenaeus, who reportedly even 'lusted for the beasts in Rome', and, on the other hand, appealing against every discrimination to the Human Rights Commission of the United Nations, the secretaries of the World Evangelical Fellowship or the local newspaper. We need to see persecution and its purposes from God's perspective, which may be different from our own feelings and desires. We need simply to be prepared to stand joyfully in the company of the main accused, Jesus Christ Himself. If any person who wields some amount of religious, political or economic power today truly begins to understand the total claims of Jesus Christ, and rejects them, he will naturally join in the age-old cry, 'We do not want him to rule over us! Crucify him!' (cf. Lk. 19:14; 23:20) – and with Him all those who carry His name.

The message of 40 million martyrs

At the time of the death of Stephen (Acts 7), 2000 Christians were martyred in Jerusalem, according to F. L. Plotter in his book *Martyrs in All Ages.*

⟨ Philip, after a revival happened in Phrygia, was imprisoned, bound and hanged.
⟨ Matthew was reportedly martyred in Ethiopia.
⟨ James, the brother of Jesus, as an old man of 96 was thrown from the pinnacle of the temple and stoned, and after that his brains were dashed out with a club, according to Josephus.
⟨ Matthias was stoned, beheaded and crucified.
⟨ Andrew preached in Asia, and ended up crucified by order of Algenas, proconsul of Achaia.
⟨ Mark, says Eusebius, was sent to Egypt, planted a church in Alexandria, and was dragged to death.
⟨ Peter, says a tradition, died in Rome, crucified head downwards.
⟨ Paul probably died a martyr's death in Rome.
⟨ Jude, some early writers say, was crucified in Jerusalem.

〈 Bartholomew was flogged and crucified.
〈 Thomas allegedly died a martyr in India, killed by a
   spear.
〈 Luke was probably hanged from an olive tree in Greece.
〈 Simon the Zealot preached in Africa, and was later cru-
   cified in Britain.
〈 John, as an exception, died a natural death in Patmos at
   the age of 98.
〈 Timothy, bishop in Ephesus, was martyred.
〈 Barnabas was killed by Jews in Syria.

From here a long list of martyrs – Ignatius, Simeon, Clement,
Zenon, Faustius, Jobita, Justin Martyr, Polycarp and many
others – is written throughout history.

   David Barrett of the Global Evangelization Movement
has documented around 40 million Christian martyrs
since Christ died, averaging 160,000 per year, 'not counting those just harassed and kicked out of their houses or
denied their social status because of their Christian faith'.
Barrett anticipates that this figure will rise to an average of
300,000 martyrs each year by the year 2025.

You cannot burn the church

The true church of Jesus Christ cannot be burnt. It is not
made of wood, hay, straw even stone, but of the redeemed
people of God. If the most visible aspects of traditional
Christendom, such as church buildings, can be attacked,
houses usually won't be. In almost every culture the home
is a safe and quite protected zone: 'it is simply poor
upbringing to attack a private home,' says Dr Met Castillo.
I am not saying that the church is immune to persecution
in homes; but it is not only the most natural but also the
safest possible place for it.

Flexible structure

In many countries the house churches have long been, and still are, the spiritual backbone of Christian movements, even under fierce persecution or surveillance as in Russia, China and some countries in the Middle East. Since house churches fit invisibly into the existing architecture of a

> *Since house churches focus on sharing lives, not on performing religious worship services, they can easily exist without alerting the neighbours or the secret police.*

nation, they are able to respond flexibly to any pressure or new situation. Since house churches focus on sharing lives, not on performing religious worship services, they can easily exist without alerting the neighbours or the secret police through loud music, clapping, dancing, loud prayers and sermons.

Some house churches even rotate, meeting somewhere different each time, the next meeting place only known to the members. This could be a hotel room, a bus rented for an outing, under a tree, or in the houses of various members. In some countries people even start coming in ones and twos from early in the morning, in order not to arouse suspicions. If anyone should ask too many nosy questions, it is amazing just how many birthdays, weddings, anniversaries and reunions of all kinds some families can have nowadays.

Avoid creating your very own 'persecution'

A young man in a church stood up and told how he boldly went into the market-place in a village where the locals adhered to a non-Christian religion. There he started to preach loudly. 'They were soon harassing me, finally beating me, and then chased me out of the village. But I am proud I took a stand for Jesus,' he exclaimed. I asked him: 'Who told you to offend them? What would Jesus have done in that village? Maybe He would not have openly agitated them at all. He did not want to deliver a bomb, but to win their hearts. Perhaps Jesus would have started by having dinner with a man of peace in the village, and might not have been chased out at all.'

In a city in India an evangelistic crusade drew massive hostility from non-Christian activists. Some Christians, feeling threatened by their minority status, got excited and started fighting with the police. The result was law suits, arguments, discrimination, and some Christians ended up in jail.

I was once invited to preach in a small village church in Tamil Nadu, South India. The church of about 35 people met in a rented building on the main road. If there was one thing that could be said about the worship and singing, it was very loud! This church had hired microphones and a big loudspeaker: the sound could probably be heard for 500 metres. Fifty metres away there was a political meeting going on. Every five minutes someone from there would come and politely ask the church to please be more quiet. The leaders of the church eagerly pointed out to me: 'See, we cannot have undisturbed worship. We need the financial help of the West to build our own church building.' 'There might be a much simpler and cheaper solution to your problem,' I said. 'Pull the plug! In such a small family gathering you really do not need a loudspeaker at all!'

We need to avoid a wrong sense of competition and religious pride, the eagerness to go to any lengths to fight for our 'human rights' or 'minority status'. We may also question whether the word 'crusades', referring to evangelistic rallies, is still an appropriate word for today's world. If there is true persecution arising, it should happen because of the stumbling-block of the Cross, not because of our own lack of wisdom.

No peace ahead

Jesus never predicted a more peaceful and harmonious future for the church, living around a romantic village church building surrounded by lush greenery and scenic hills. He prophesied increased heat, persecution and even tribulation. 'When you are persecuted in one place, flee to another' (Mt. 10:23); 'You will be handed over to be persecuted and put to death' (Mt. 24:9). The future scenario for the world which Jesus paints in Matthew 24 and other places is not at all of a peacefully united world, harmoniously coexisting and trading with each other and sending and receiving nice Christmas cards and embroidered tablecloths for the whole of our lives. Jesus speaks of a terribly war-torn and increasingly bitter planet, deeply distressed, nation rising against nation, ridden by famines and earthquakes and, worst of all, a loss of love and increase of hatred.

Be prepared

The political, religious, and even economic climate of the world is heating up ideologically and spiritually. Noah did not wait until it began to rain to start building the ark. For a similar reason we need to be prepared today for what is coming tomorrow:

1 We need to develop a persecution-proof quality or mentality, and prepare ourselves to again become worthy to be persecuted, by conforming to the patterns of the Kingdom of God, and to stand up for the name of God,

even if this means we lose face and respectability in society. This preparation starts with a revival of New Testament quality of Christianity in all of us, today, a fire burning again in us that no one can quench.

2 We need to let an appropriate structure of the church emerge out of this mindset, and again embrace the New Testament form of house churches, because they will be able not only to sustain the life of the church, but also to allow it to flourish and grow, even under pressure and persecution.

Then we need to consider the consequences of this decision, pray on our own and together with our families, friends, churches, organizations and co-workers, listening to God for His direction, and starting to take the appropriate measures. Now.

The Mennonites in Ethiopia

The most explosive growth period of the Mennonites in Ethiopia started when two of their presumed pillars of growth were taken away: their church buildings and their pastors.

It is a well-known story how the Mennonite Church of America used to do traditional mission work in Ethiopia. In 1982 the Meserete Kristos Church had around 5000 members. Then the communist government took over. The government confiscated all church buildings and properties, and threw most of their leaders in jail. The Mennonite church became, almost by government decree, a lay-driven, house-based movement. But instead of slowing down the church, the drastic measures of the Communists had the opposite effect. After ten years the Mennonite movement had grown to 50,000 people. The most explosive growth period of the Mennonites in Ethiopia started when two of their presumed pillars of growth were taken away: their church buildings and their pastors.

'Now we have a good, two-step plan for the growth of the church anywhere,' exclaimed a pastor humorously at the end of a seminar. 'Close down all the church buildings, and ask all pastors to kindly take a long vacation!'

When did persecution start?

Although God's elect, His people, prophets and godly kings, have almost always been threatened and persecuted, the days of persecution for the New Testament church did not start by accident. 'And Saul was there giving approval to his [Stephen's] death. On that day a great persecution broke out against the church at Jerusalem, and all except the apostles were scattered throughout Judea and Samaria' (Acts 8:1).

In Acts 7 Stephen had preached his sermon before the religious authorities, and almost all he said was acceptable to them, until he reached one single topic, touched one wound, dared to tackle one hot item which was the King of all Taboos. When they heard *this*, 'they were furious and gnashed their teeth at him . . . they covered their ears and, yelling at the top of their voices, they all rushed at him . . . and began to stone him'.

What had they heard to lose their minds in such a manner? What terrible and explosive subject did Stephen touch? He had said: 'The Most High does not live in temples made by men.' Stephen had questioned the core of their belief, the temple, the religious building.

Although the tabernacle and the temple, with the worship related to it, were at the core of Old Testament religious practice, the New Testament brings in a totally new dimension of worship, where the Spirit of God seems to clearly dissociate Himself from bricks. From now on, the people themselves are the temple (1 Cor. 3:16; 6:19). What does this do to the old temple? 'One greater than the temple is here' (Mt. 12:6). It replaces it with the temple of the body (Jn. 2:19–21). It closes the chapter about stone temples and temple-centred worship, and opens a new chapter. Worship no longer happens in Jerusalem or Samaria, at special 'house of the Lord', tabernacles, holy places or buildings, nor around holy symbols such as stone altars, but 'in spirit and truth' (Jn. 4:23,24), because God is spirit and truth. The temples are gone for ever, never to return. Even in heaven, there will be no temple: 'I did not see a temple in the city, because the Lord God Almighty and the Lamb are its temple' (Rev. 21:22).

When Jesus spoke to the Samaritan woman, she immediately brought up the topic of religious worship, obviously at the core of her heart. 'We worship at this mountain, you Jews say we should worship in Jerusalem. Who is right?' 'Nobody,' answers Jesus. 'The time is coming and has now come when the true worshippers of God will worship God in truth and Spirit,' not in a place that is more holy than any other. The whole concept of a 'house of God', a temple as a religious or holy place, an abode of God with His people, has completely vanished from the New Testament.

In the New Testament, God never asked anyone to build a religious house for Him. 'Heaven is my throne, and the earth is my footstool. What kind of house will you build for me? says the Lord. Or where will my resting place be?' (Acts 7:49). He much rather builds ourselves into a spiritual house, the church, makes us part of His household, and builds a house for us in heaven, in the city to come.

Religion – the core of the problem

'Religion is for unbelievers; it's the business of the god-less,' says Swiss theologian Karl Barth. Religion is what man makes out of God; Christianity is what God makes out of man. Christianity, therefore, is no religion. It is a living relationship with a living God. The moment Christianity becomes religion, it dies. The word 'religion' comes from the Latin *religare*, and literally means to tie yourself back, to rest a secure anchor at a safe place, so we are not swept away by the current of life into unknown and dangerous waters. Religion tries to reach up to God, and throw an anchor into a safe place beyond the line between humans and God, the secular and the saint, then it safeguards that anchor and line at any cost. Not only does religion not see that Christ has done all that for us: it does not want to see it.

The religious man cuts a tree in the forest, carves an idol out of it, places it before himself, falls down before it and exclaims, 'Save me!' (Jer. 10). He makes his own arrangements with the spiritual world, and if he is particularly inventive and influential, he may even found a new religion to deal with God here in this part of the world. Religion wants to be on the safe side in spiritual things. The more insecure someone is deep inside, the more fantastic is the amount of time and energy he or she will spend on defending their religious convictions and sacred cows, in order not to reveal their deep doubts and lose face. Religious people needs daily assurance of the things they are not sure of, need to touch what they know they cannot touch, need to smell the unsmellable. Religious people want to feel God, hear God, drink God, eat God, internalize God, and would love ultimately to possess God and put Him – or at least something related to God, something holy – onto a throne and into a safe, then close the heavy metal door and put the key under the mattress. Then they will hire a sacred priest or holy man to safeguard the shrine for good money. Later they will build a religious house around the idol, the safe and the priest, and visit it once a week, give donations and ask blessings. This way religious people have created a temple for themselves, because they are the genius behind it, and they know ultimately that they sit on the throne themselves. That is what troubles them most. But, that they have been deceived by the devil who lusts to detract worship away from God any way he can, has not yet crossed their mind.

Religious people love the feeling of excited goosebumps as they participate with feverish fervour in religious ceremonies with candles, holy music, smells and bells, and awe-inspiring rituals; and they will defend their religious traditions and practices to almost any extreme and argue about it without any logic, because they ultimately argue about themselves.

The root problem is that they know deep down that they are lost without God, but they are too proud to say so, because of peer pressure from friends, family and society. No one has told them yet that there is a way to deal with their pride and sin, the cross of Jesus Christ.

Deeply insecure people are the ideal market for insurance. Deeply insecure people in the area of religion will buy almost anything from the religion's sales representatives – do this, that and the other – in order to have at least the feeling of safety.

In Islam, for example, there is no concept of assurance of salvation, except, some say, to die in a Holy War. Even after observing all religious laws, there is no guarantee that Allah will ever let you go to paradise; he may just feel differently on the day you happen to die. That makes people deeply insecure, and deeply insecure people are the ideal market for insurance. Deeply insecure people in the area of religion will buy almost anything from the religion's sales representatives – do this, that and the other – in order to have at least the feeling of safety. This pattern cannot calm the empty agony of peacelessness and search going on inside people.

Religion is ultimately false worship, pseudo-sacred beliefs and useless practices inspired, empowered and defended by 'the spirit of this world'. Many Bible teachers have pointed out a connection between religion and the whore of Babylon, 'drunk with the blood of the saints... For all the nations have drunk the maddening wine of her adulteries ... and the merchants of the earth grew rich from her excessive luxuries' (Rev. 17:6; 18:3).

> *Religion is like a built-in feature of every person on earth.*

Since every person has been born a sinner (Ps. 51; Rom. 3:23), everyone has a wounded consciousness, knowing they are guilty before God. The easy answer to calm this trouble is religion, which is like a built-in feature of every person on earth. The world steams with religion, even if it comes in the form of agnosticism and liberalism, to which teachings its adherents cling with passionate religious fervour. We do not have to do anything to become religious; it is creational, natural, and it creeps in without our being aware, like an ugly spirit raising its head while everyone sleeps. Religion builds up like static energy when we walk with plastic shoes on a carpet. It needs the power of the Holy Spirit, constant prophetic and apostolic ministry, and the ongoing equipping of the saints, to maintain a non-religious, alert and sober spirit, to be free from religion and liberated by Christ to worship Him

> *If I were the devil I would certainly let loose on the followers of Jesus the most deadly plague there is on this planet: religion.*

in truth and spirit. If I were the devil and wanted to stop Christians from being effective witnesses to Jesus, I would certainly let loose on the followers of Jesus the most deadly plague there is on this planet: religion. I would look for the weakest members of the church – who sometimes look to be the strongest! – whisper into their minds the age-old, tried and tested words 'Did God really say?' (Gen. 3:1), undermine their faith in God's word and God Himself, instil in them the hunger for more security, power, glory and fame – and then feed them the ready-made poison of religion. What a triumph for the devil if he can arrange the ultimate demonic scheme: to persecute the church in the name of the church, to persecute the people of God in the name of God and get the functionaries of organized religion to hold the head of the organic body of Christ under the water as long as possible.

In establishing house-church movements, therefore, we need to soberly beware of religious cults emerging around special names, allegedly effective rituals, traditions, moral laws, spiritual practices and methods, pseudo-holy worship patterns, and religious experiences that are supposed to be the norm. We need to literally 'earth' any religious energy which builds up regularly, like static electricity, by coming to the cross of Christ and asking Him to set us free individually and corporately from the religious spirit, and to fill us with His Spirit again and again, until the earth is filled with the fragrance of God, 'believers are a letter read by all men' and 'the manifold wisdom of God is made known through the church' (cf. Eph. 3:10), through simple and supernatural house churches in which the people of God share their lives with God and each other. Those houses literally will change the earth.

We also need to understand that, in the days when Stephen spoke against the temple, not only were Saul and his men stirred up to bloodthirsty fanaticism, but literally all hell broke loose. The core of the religious and demonic system to keep people in blindness and ignorance – and therefore lost for eternity – was under direct attack.

Unprecedented growth, unprecedented persecution

As God's Spirit resurrects and literally reincarnates the body of Jesus in its organic and original form, and as Jesus, the head of the church, restores apostolic and prophetic patterns to the church, there will be an unprecedented and explosive growth of house churches in many nations. Innumerable people will be saved and incorporated into the churches, the poor and the rich, the rural and the urban populations alike. But we should not forget for a moment that, alongside this final harvest movement, what Jesus predicted will come true: persecution will mount like never before, because the devil will realize that now the church really means business. The church is now structured and equipped with the harvesting tool which he dreads the most and which he has spent almost 2000 years trying to obliterate from the planet: the simple, non-religious household of God in the form of house churches.

This global movement, emerging from the shadows of history and religious tradition, is empowered to, and actively does, storm against the 'gates of hell', preventive mechanisms, spiritual roadblocks and religious mindsets and probably even cherub-type demons like the figures God had placed before the Garden of Eden to prevent Adam and Eve from re-entering paradise.

Those gates or portals (Mt. 16:18) can be interpreted as a devilish equivalent to the 'beautiful gate' of the temple where the lame man was healed after Peter and John prayed for him (Acts 3). The outer court of the temple was not the inner sanctuary itself; it was a first stage of the temple. In the same way, the 'gates of hell' might be portals and heavily guarded gateways and entries trying to keep people inside the gigantic waiting room of hell, a place where, if nothing happens, billions of people will die and glide into a godless eternity in hell. As American intercessor Cindy Jacobs said, 'The church will have to possess the gates of the enemy.' As Jesus has clearly predicted, those gates will not prevail and hold their captives forever.

We need to be ready for the moment that happens. In terms of our vision, our readiness, our flexible structures, we also need to be ready for any number of people that God Himself will choose to add to His church. Just like in the time of Elisha (2 Kgs. 3,4) we need to 'make this valley full of ditches', and 'ask all our neighbours for empty jars', so God, seeing our faith, can pour out His water to fill those ditches, and His oil to fill those jars to the brim.

Chapter 7

No Progress without Change

The art of transitioning, or how to avoid doing the new in the power of the old

A camel train was trotting through the desert. Suddenly someone was missing. They finally found him, sitting under a tree in the last oasis they had passed. When they asked him why he had stayed behind, he said: 'My body moved so fast during the journey. I need to wait for my spirit to catch up with me again.'

In a similar way, many Christians find their spirit sometimes going far ahead of their present-day realities. As in a vision or a dream, they suddenly feel lifted away from their familiar life and soar above the current plains and deserts, driven to unknown lands by the wind of the Spirit. When they wake up from their vision or dream, they feel challenged to go where they have not gone before. They experience the classic tension between a vision of the future and the realities of their present situation.

This seems to happen to many Christians in regard to the nature of the church. Many, therefore, feel the need to allow their body to catch up with their spirit again, and for the structures to match the new quality of church they are discovering. To turn around the illustration of our lost camel driver: their spirit has gone away into the future and is now resting under a tree in an oasis far ahead, while their body still toils under the sun of the desert and wants to catch up.

The leader of a denomination once asked me after a seminar: 'I am 100 per cent convinced about house churches. But the denomination I lead is based on the traditional church model. What do I do now?' He had seen a new vision of church, but, as a responsible leader, saw his present-day realities and realized that he had some catching up to do now with his structures.

In almost every meeting, seminar or conference on the subject of a relational, organic, house-based church movement the same question inevitably arises: 'I understand what you're saying, and I'm totally with you. But I have this church at home. It runs on the traditional pattern. How do I change the system without destroying the church?!' I call this the 'How to cross the river without getting my feet wet' question. Can we really have progress without change? I do not think so. But the painful part is: all change is personal. It upsets routines and traditions. But if we want to see new things happening in and through the church, we need to be prepared to make personal changes first, changes in the family second, and changes in our ministry third.

After a seminar in an Asian country, the leader of a denomination came up to me with the same question: 'I am personally involved in pastoring a church. What would you suggest I do now?' It was 10 p.m. I had spent the whole day talking with a group of pastors and we were walking on a lush green towards our sleeping quarters. I said rather casually to him: 'Do you know what? I would stop pastoring in the traditional sense. I would realize, in your case, that I have a more apostolic role, lay down my office, get my hands free, and start fathering and equipping a new generation of house-church planters.' 'That is the answer I have been looking for these last seven years!' he exclaimed.

Not everything new is good, and not all change is helpful. Although it is already a well-known story, I still love this following letter, because it reflects, not a theological conviction, but a philosophy that simply cannot see necessary and good change, because it wants to defend the status quo:

31 January 1829

To President Jackson

The canal system of this country is being threatened by the spread of a new form of transportation known as 'railroads'. The federal government must preserve the canals for the following reasons:

1. If canal boats are supplanted by 'railroads', serious unemployment will result. Captains, cooks, drivers, hostlers, repairmen and lock tenders will be left without means of livelihood, not to mention the numerous farmers now employed in growing hay for the horses.

2. Boat builders would suffer, and towline, whip and harness makers would be left destitute.

3. Canal boats are absolutely essential to defend the United States. In the event of the expected trouble with England, the Erie Canal would be the only means by which we could ever move the supplies so vital to waging modern war.

As you may well know, Mr President, 'railroad' carriages are pulled at the enormous speed of fifteen miles per hour by 'engines' which, in addition to endangering life and limb of passengers, roar and snort their way through the countryside, setting fire to crops, scaring the livestock and frightening women and children. The Almighty certainly never intended that people should travel at such breakneck speed.

Martin Van Buren,
Governor of New York.

(from: 'Dynamic preaching',
Net Results Magazine,
March 1991)

Four phases of a paradigm shift

If we want to see practical changes, our paradigm must change first. A paradigm is the way we see and interpret the world according to an in-built pattern or worldview, seeing things through a specific type of glasses. A paradigm shift is a process which typically has four stages:

1 *'Search for it!'* A paradigm shift usually starts with a crisis in our old worldview, which may be related to a personal crisis. Crisis gives birth to creativity. Without asking pertinent and pointed questions, without a burning search for new answers there will be no room to accept even a new insight, let alone even a new paradigm. False contentedness is the biggest enemy of change. Typically, a paradigm shift starts with a crisis, where our safe and sound world, our traditional way of explaining things, simply falls to pieces. This crisis can be caused by an accident or a revelation, a negative or positive experience with something that simply does not fit into our world. The Chinese word for crisis is *wu-wei*, and means change as well as the opportunity for starting something new.

2 *'Preach it.'* In the second phase, we find what we have searched for. I call it the 'eureka phase', because this part of a paradigm shift is usually accompanied by the

overwhelming feeling of thrill and excitement of someone who has 'found it'. We may find ourselves standing up with our hands in the air and foaming at the mouth about our new discovery, wanting to tell everyone in an almost evangelistic or apologetic fashion about it. In fact we usually find only a piece of the truth, a fragment of a larger piece, but our desperate search has temporarily made us blind to the bigger picture. We have been thirsty for too long, and now that we have found a well, all we want is to drink, drink, drink. This is the most dangerous phase of a paradigm shift, as our excitement may drive us to immature and naive statements or actions, which are difficult to redeem later.

3 *'Live it.'* In this third phase we symbolically sit down, wipe the emotional foam off our lips, and start to become an integral part of our new-found paradigm. We stop preaching and defending it, and we live it.

4 *'Teach it.'* This last phase turns us into an agent of change, helping others to discover the paradigm we have found ourselves, and assisting them in making the necessary changes themselves.

Three options of change

One of the most devastating frustrations anyone can experience is trying to do the new in the power of the old. It is like preaching democracy from the loudhailers of a warship of a colonizing nation. Jesus in His teaching about new wine in old wineskins and the new patch on old cloth is crystal clear. He said that two so radically different systems as old wine and new wine cannot be mixed without doing damage to both the wine and the wineskins. The same principle is true for the new patch on old cloth (Mt. 9:16,17). That gives us three options for change.

1 *Do not change at all.* Keep going. Stay within your structure, maintain it, expand it, work from within it, because you realize that change will be too costly, too upsetting, too painful, or simply too frightening and insecure. God will bless you. Not everyone has an apostolic or prophetic ministry, unafraid of touching and changing 'touchy' subjects and people. Do the best you can to use your structure for good, and keep close and personal relationships – open doors and bridges of communication – to those who have taken another choice. You may need each other in the days ahead. Maybe God will open doors for co-operation in the future with people who will help you, your church, organization or denomination, to be ready to change. Prepare yourself for that day now.

2 *Attempt a compromise.* Try to 'dance at two weddings at the same time'. Pour new wine into old wineskins, or old wine into new wineskins, and try to live in both worlds. This is, from all I have seen, a sure recipe for disaster. You may very well enter a phase of transitioning – and never leave it.

3 *Prepare yourself for change.* Your spirit may have gone far ahead. Now the structures have to catch up with it.

Beyond the Titanic model

The best and most radical kind of change might be to start all over again. One pastor got up in a seminar and said: 'That means we have to close down all our churches!' He was quite serious. But with a church of more than 10,000 attenders, that is not easy to do. To change from one set-up to another means transitioning, crossing over from one camp to another. There are many ways to do it; all of them are dangerous and costly; they take time, and they still sometimes do not work. Companies spend millions on anticipating and implementing change in order to remain in business or gain markets. Management and change consultants like Tom Peters earn $50,000 a day for a seminar for business executives.

However, there are some changes that do not change a thing. They help us to soothe our minds and our emotions, give us the temporary illusion that we are doing something, but they are as harmless as a storm in a teacup. Someone might decide to paint the sanctuary a different colour, move the piano from left to right; or merge with another, similar, organization. I call this type of change the 'Titanic model'. When the Titanic struck an iceberg, no amount of changing the furniture, repainting the ship, or even restructuring the apartments, would do any good. They would have had only cosmetic value and become rapidly obsolete, as the ship itself was sinking into oblivion.

Yesterday's revolutionary is often today's church father

It may be observed that most changes in history did not come through safe democratic processes but from quite unbalanced persons, radical in most senses. Very few innovations or true, radical changes were initiated by committees and boards; most came from visionary people who saw what no one else saw, said what no one else dared to say, and did what was 'forbidden' and taboo in their time. Many of yesterday's revolutionaries, like Luther, Booth, Wesley, or Hudson Taylor, have become today's trusted pillars of the church. Many of them have created churches or movements, which today have become so vast and administratively complex, that the statistical probability of these organizations or churches entrusting decision-making power into the hands of just one visionary person is minute.

Yet change starts with people, and you may just be the man or the woman for the job. I encourage you to start doing this in the area of your personal or organizational jurisdiction, no matter how small or large it is. Start with what is at hand. George Bernard Shaw once said: 'The reasonable man adapts himself to the world; the unreasonable one persists in trying to adapt the world to himself. Therefore, all progress depends on the unreasonable man.' In this sense, how unreasonable do we dare to be?

Five models of transitioning

Except for the radical approach to change, i.e. starting all over again, there are five different ways of transitioning.

1 'Windows 95'
The well-known computer programme Windows 95 allows you to make changes in its configuration, which determines the way the computer understands itself and ultimately runs your programmes. Changing the configuration is like changing an entry in your own passport. If you want the new changes in the configuration to work properly, the software will flash you a message: 'You have to restart the computer in order for the changes to become effective.' Once you restart your computer, the new configuration will work, and your computer will run differently. In changing and transitioning from one model of church to another, this means that you might want to close down your existing work, and restart it according to a new 'configuration', a different set of values. This approach would allow you to close down a phase properly and in style, lay a new foundation, a new quality, and then build a different structure into a different direction.

2 *The 'Beachhead Principle' of the prophetic 20 per cent*

This approach involves carefully and prayerfully choosing those 20 per cent of people in your church, organization or denomination, who you feel will be well able, suited and gifted to lead your church or organization into a new future. They will build a 'prophetic beachhead', a base which you later expand as more people follow.

Form one or several house churches with them. Live and model the pattern for them and with them, without touching your existing structure or changing anything in it. For a while, which can be up to 6, 12 or 18 months, you will run a parallel structure, the old and the new model together. Once you have established a new pattern of behaviour and see that those 20 per cent you have chosen are well into the new paradigm and finding their way forward, empower them to multiply the pattern by leading others into the new paradigm themselves. They will then take people 'boatload by boatload' to the new beachhead, introduce them into the new church pattern, until no one else is willing to make the crossing. Then you declare a new phase open, give your marching orders for the new direction, and stop glancing over your shoulder to the other shore, where there will always be some of those standing who were simply not ready to do the crossing. You will have to leave them behind, because you know that you need to move on.

In any process of change there are four different groups: firstly, a small group of 'pioneers', who live on the masthead and see what others do not even want to see; secondly, a slightly larger group of 'early adapters', who accept a new vision early if it is new and endorsed by some credible witness. The third group is a large group of 'late adapters': they will accept new things only if they are new, come endorsed and are made the new law. Fourthly, there is a last and again relatively large group of 'laggards',

Even Christian traditionalists may slip into a spiritual ancestor cult. It is a cult, because the adherents revere those who handed down to them cherished practices, faith systems and beliefs more than Jesus himself, the one who makes everything new.

hard-core traditionalists, who always seem to remember 'the meatpots and onions of Egypt' and will not change, no matter what. To wait for them to accept change is futile. They won't. They are under 'future shock', as Alvin Toffler says, the paralysis of fear that grips those who feel overtaken by developments.

In almost every church or organization you will find those for whom the traditional values of the past are more important than being pro-active, prophetic and ready to change. In many Asian and African nations there is a strong ancestor cult; similarly, even Christian traditionalists may slip into a spiritual ancestor cult. It is a cult, because the adherents revere those who handed down to them cherished practices, faith systems and beliefs more than Jesus himself, the one who makes everything new. You may want to mentally prepare yourself and your church to ultimately lose them. They will not be lost to the Kingdom of God, but will either find another group or church, or start their own.

3 Morphing – the seamless transition

'Morphing' is the almost imperceptible change from one picture into another, with such fine graduations that the process is almost seamless. In the context of church change, this process is determined to make the shift from one pattern to the other without losing anyone, and so to make it as smooth and as pastorally sensitive as possible. It introduces a new pattern in incremental steps. It still is a tricky business, because it is like changing a horse into a rabbit at full gallop. The most vulnerable points are the times where the old pattern is no longer fully valid, and the new not yet fully evident. Additionally, it means endless discussions and attempts to convince traditionalists, and is advisable only for those with supernatural good humour, pastoral patience and prophetic wisdom. You can follow a set of stages: introducing and teaching a new set of values; gradually introducing new patterns of behaviour; changing leadership according to the new pattern; resettling on a new foundation and starting building. A small church or organization of up to 100 people or 'voting entities' may take from 1 to 3 years for this process. A medium-sized church or organization (100–500) may take between 3 and 5 years. A large church or organization (over 500) may take between 5 and 8 years or even longer.

4 Behind their back

This model is for the more desperate and adventurous. It happens in secret, like many inventions which have occurred under strict security for fear of being stolen or cloned prematurely. In this approach, you start from scratch without involving your church or organization at all in the new venture. You do it across town, in another place, behind the back of your group, so to speak. It allows a new experiment without getting the spiritual genes and structures mixed, and observation first hand of a new pattern. You might want to delegate some work in your traditional set-up to other people to free up more of your own time. As the model grows, you may, at some stage or other, introduce the two entities to each other.

5 Hong Kong style: multi-structured churches or organizations

As the gospel is dynamic and excellent, reflecting a God who is not mediocre and 'average' in any respect, we need to avoid institutionalized mediocrity as a 'balanced mix' between bad and good. A last resort could be therefore to attempt to work according to two separate value patterns at the same time, carefully kept apart from each other in order not to mix the unmixable. Many congregational churches have introduced multiple and different worship experiences, quite different from each other, but all organized by the same church. Some, like Holy Trinity, Brompton, an Anglican church in London, offer a traditional worship service, and a more family-type service a bit later, for different target audiences. Others, like Tilehurst Free Church in Reading, UK, offer cell groups for those who want them, and a congregational church service for those who prefer the traditional pattern. I call this the Hong Kong approach, because this is similar to the 'one country, two systems' pattern where China and Hong Kong function under one government, but with two administrative systems. One is based on socialist, the other on capitalist values. It may be a temporary compromise, but at some stages a compromise is better than a split.

Insights from the world of management

In business in a fast-moving world with ever-changing markets and products and an exploding technology, change is the only constant. Management advisers and business consultants know that if a company is unable to adjust to change and beat the competition, they are out of business and have to close down.

I resist naive attempts to compare churches with companies, because they are like apples and oranges. Business success and maximum profit strategies are a bit different from following the Lamb of God and carrying our cross; the church and business are built on very different foundations, and pursue different agendas: Mammon and God. But there are areas of overlap, especially in the area of organizing the visible part of the church. We can therefore risk at least a quick glance over the fence, to see how 'the children of the world', as Jesus says, handle it. The language in business with regard to transitioning and change is categoric: 'Whatever made you successful in the past, won't in the future. It is the end of the world as we know it,' says Tom Peters in his book *The Circle of Innovation*. That is why we need to 'think revolution, not evolution. Incrementalism is innovation's worst enemy,' he contends.

Frantic overactivity, in churches as well as in business, can often be a cover-up for deep-seated insecurity. Jim Utterback, in his book *Mastering the Dynamics of Innovation*, says about those unwilling to change because of new technological developments: 'They resist all efforts to understand innovation, and further entrench their positions in the older products. This results in a surge of productivity and performance that may take the old technology to unheard-of heights. But in most cases, this is a sign of impending death.' More important than attending the next seminar with 'new insights' might be, says Peters, to buy an eraser to wipe away wrong thoughts and teachings, which block new developments. We even need to develop a 'strategic forgetfulness', he argues. 'The problem is never how to get new, innovative thoughts into your mind, but how to get old ones out', says Dee Hock, creator of VISA. Many companies, according to Peters, need their CDO – a Chief Destructive Officer – whose job is regularly to tear down useless structures and procedures, avoiding personality cults, regularly slaughtering the holy cows that have crept

> *More important than attending the next seminar with 'new insights' might be, to buy an eraser to wipe away wrong thoughts and teachings, which block new developments.*

in to graze, and avoiding naive plans because the boss of the company has fallen in love with a product that no one else really wants.

Bless the mess

In search of excellence and new products and break-throughs, 'the size of your vision corresponds with the size of your waste-paper basket'. Business visionaries are immensely productive, but most of the time they produce useless rubbish, until that golden moment when they come up with one gem of insight or invention which will change the course of history. That is why we need to 'bless the mess', to encourage innovators, product developers and visionary and seemingly chaotic seekers of the impossible, the 'nerds', bespectacled and almost unsociable brain geniuses working away forever in those little shacks and laboratories like Microsoft's Bill Gates, who ended up leading one of the world's most influential companies. When Tom Peters is invited to a management consultation of a company in deep trouble, he says, 'in just a second, I have the answer. Of the 150 executives, 144 are between the ages of 48 and 59. I call them OWM – Old White Males. They talk alike, smell alike, dress alike, eat the same food and think the same thoughts.' No wonder, he concludes, that there is no creativity in an atmosphere of conformity – and no space for vision, because everyone tightly observes and controls the other.

Chapter 8

All Change is Practical

The last step you want to take determines your next step

'That means that we have to change almost everything we do!', exclaimed a well-known mission leader in India after hearing about house churches. However, not everything will change when we start to develop house-church movements. The eternal gospel, its content, living spirituality and many quality insights which the church of the past has discovered and taught us, will remain, and need to remain.

If we seriously consider house churches, however, it will have some very serious theological and practical consequences for the church, for church growth, for church-planting and also for missions. 'The truth will never harm a just cause', said Mahatma Gandhi. This material, however, is not intended to criticize any particular church. We have to move beyond that. In genuine love and appreciation for each other we are all called to be part of the solution, and not to remain part of the problem.

Many Christian leaders agree that sober thinking and even mission statistics will tell anyone that, even if we multiply what we do today by a factor of 10, it is not going to make a big difference in terms of discipling the nations.

Sometimes I am startled to observe issues and areas of ministry where seemingly no amount of empirical research and truth can change our thinking for good. 'How foolish to act before knowing the facts!' says a proverb. In many countries, the population may still grow faster than the church; evangelism can be a flash-in-the-pan; churches may be aging; the structures need to be changed; the majority population does not respond to the type of church we favour; and even large evangelistic projects and programmes may barely scratch the surface, if we compare their results with the huge population figures of today.

Are sacred cows standing in the way of the Lamb?

The key problems of churches and missions today, many contend, are neither money, nor the isms of the day, but 'in the hard ground of our own head', hidden in those unquestioned concepts, axioms, and long-grown convictions and man-made traditions.

It may be neither the first nor the last time that the people of God have been deaf to God's true intentions while dancing around a golden cow. Most leaders agree today that the obstacles to the extension of the Kingdom of God are much more inside our own thinking than out there. The key problems of churches and missions today, many contend, are neither money, nor the isms of the day, but 'in the hard ground of our own head', hidden in those unquestioned concepts, axioms, and long-grown convictions and man-made traditions which have become so dear and sacred to us that even daring to touch them is for many 'an act of heresy'.

This is the 'holy cow syndrome', where seemingly sacred animals (spiritual concepts) block the road for the

Lamb of God, daring to sleep in the streets and make the public drive around them, or causing a traffic jam as one of these dear animals feels it needs to stand in the middle of a main road and look unimpressed. Rather than passively 'accepting the cow', we sometimes need to sound the horn; and, who knows, the cow might move, so that the road clears and life goes on.

Pay the price

In house-church Christianity, one of the prices to pay is to stop the emphasis on individual freedom as against the collective obedience to Christ. If we want what Christ wants, we will no longer be willing to do just whatever everyone else wants to do, and how and when they want to, irrespective of the community they live with. No longer can we call our homes just 'our own' homes, or treat our cars just as 'ours' only. In the West, the lifestyle of many Christians is still centred around a career, TV, hobbies, privacy and pets, sugar-coated with a thin layer of Christian behaviour such as attending a church service, praying before meals and listening to Christian music. This is not much different from the lifestyle of the average person living in the West where, in one single lifelong orgy of individualism, almost everything is geared and structured for the pursuit of personal security, success and fun, and even individual spiritual growth.

In the non-western world, we need to overcome an addiction to wrong priorities, where family honour, clan and tribal allegiance often still come firmly before an allegiance to God; and where strong shame-oriented cultures make it difficult to say the plain truth and confess sins to one other, and where conversations and sometimes the whole of life remain on a polite, religious surface. In

*Christianity has
never really been
cheap: it always was
meant to cost our
very lives.*

other words, without our own transformation, which starts with repentance, the crucifixion of self and, yes, of some of our cultural values and habits, the giving up of a self-centred lifestyle so we stop conforming neatly and pain-free to the patterns of this world, there will be little redemptive power left to touch and transform our societies with the gospel. Christianity has never really been cheap: it always was meant to cost our very lives.

For almost 2000 years people have tried again and again to come up with a lucky compromise, a 'win–win' situation between the claims of God's Kingdom and the spirit of this world. One result was that some of the sad consequences of aligning ourselves with the world in order to be fashionable and modern have become an institutionalized part of the way we think and 'do church': some of it has become part of our heritage and cherished tradition, which may now be painful and difficult to rethink. However, Paul's message on the subject is short and simple: Since I became a disciple of Christ, I as my old self no longer exist, but Christ lives in me.

Cutting out the double standards

As any pastor of a traditional church knows, it is not only fairly easy but also quite common for Christians in a Sunday-morning-service-cum-Wednesday-night-Bible-study Christianity to live by double standards, to have a secret, second life hidden away for years from their own congregation or pastor, to harbour petty sins for decades without anyone knowing. This is also due to the fact that out of 168 hours in a week, Christians in traditional, meeting-oriented Christianity spend typically three or four hours together with other Christians per week. This is simply not enough time to effectively transfer life and Kingdom values, to develop deep relationships, to make disciples and to lay down our lives for each other.

House-church Christianity will greatly reduce this compromising lifestyle which tries to make the best out of both worlds, because it involves us deeply in everyday community and healthy ongoing accountability. This will cost us dearly. But if our lifestyle is in any relationship to the salvation of real people from a real hell, it is worth it.

*　　*　　*

Some practical consequences

In this small volume I would like to make a shortlist of the most important practical consequences of a house-church set-up, and some key issues we may need to address as we start developing a house-church movement.

We would stop doing church, and start being church

We would stop going to church, and start becoming the church, seven days a week. Church would cease to be an organized Sunday morning activity, and start being the corporate, organic, local lifestyle of Christians.

Church would again touch all of life, and be 'holistic'

When church again becomes part of everyday life, all of life starts to become touched and transformed by God. The gospel of the Kingdom would be expressed again in 'words, works and wonders', reflecting the triune and holistic God the Son, God the Father and God the Holy Spirit.

The end of the money problem

> *House churches would not cost money; they would produce money, which could financially support the fivefold ministries which in turn support them spiritually.*

Many traditional church-planting activities and mission movements have a significant limiting factor – money. They need money for outreach activities, buying a plot of land, renting or building a special building and paying the pastor's salary, as well as putting up a decent parsonage. Then they need money for chairs, a PA system and an overhead projector.

Not so with house churches. House churches would not cost money; they would produce money, which could financially support the fivefold ministries which in turn support them spiritually. House churches simply do not need a full-time professional pastor: any person with the qualification of an elder will do.

The end of the leader problem

After money, the second most well-worn outcry of the Christian church is: 'We do not have enough leaders!' For a typical congregational church movement, we need a large number of small geniuses, people who can handle any part of the various programmes, from preaching to teaching, marrying and burying, playing the organ, raising funds, organizing and conducting small and big meetings and conducting Bible studies at any time of the day.

By changing to a house-church set-up, the world would be full of potential leaders for house churches in an instant, because we would no longer require professional or semi-professional leaders to fit the congregational structure, but we would have a structure tailor-made for all the people. This would also solve the global problem of spiritual unemployment. Currently we have about 70 per cent of all Christians spiritually unemployed, without a way to get involved in their church systems, while the leaders of this very system still cry out for more leaders. In a house-church situation, everyone would participate and have a spiritual task.

The end of the building problem

Instead of having a problem with more and new buildings to buy, build, rent or lease, we would be able to use what is already there in abundance: homes of every kind and shape. We could simply use the existing houses and their facilities to multiply themselves.

A new quality of conversions

Most traditional churches organize outreach and evangelistic programmes in order to make more people attend the churches. Statistically, 1 in 100 of the people who 'make a decision for Christ' in evangelistic meetings (rallies, conventions, 'crusades') will actually start attending a church. That means Christians lose 99 out of 100 new 'converts'. This is not only costly in terms of money and people, but also speaks of a very low quality level of the conversions produced through such activities. Instead of making individual spiritual seekers parrot prayers – 'Repeat after me to invite Jesus into your heart' – house churches would allow much more 'relational conversions', often of whole families and households, who would help each other to 'stay converted' afterwards.

200 Houses that Change the World

For a quality conversion, contends David Pawson in his book *The Normal Christian Birth*, we need personal repentance, personal faith, personal infilling of the Holy Spirit and baptism. Very different from the rushed atmosphere of evangelistic rallies and follow-up meetings, the house church would be able to provide the natural framework for that, and so improve the quality of the conversion, reduce problems in the churches generated through half-baked conversions and improve the overall quality of the church in a locality.

Door to door?

'Do not go from door to door!' said Jesus (Lk. 10). Yet, many evangelistic activities have 'door to door' as their methodological and strategic foundation-stone. This has very serious consequences. In Luke 10, Jesus sends his disciples 'two by two', without money, and asks them to find a 'man of peace' in a village. They should enter his house, forming an immediate nucleus church with that 'third member'. Then they are to eat and drink 'whatever they give you'.

Eating and drinking is a very significant means of identification with a new group. If we appreciate what they eat, they might appreciate what we have to say. Many Christians today take their lunch packets with them for so-called village outreach, not trusting the villagers to provide them with clean and healthy food. But how can villagers trust those visitors with their eternal life in return? In many societies hospitality is a God-given task; if strangers come to a village and knock at a door, it is the task of that family to host the strangers. If, however, those strangers are seen leaving the first house and knocking on other doors, the villagers have only two possible conclusions: either there is something terribly wrong with the first house, that they could not host them, or those strangers are in fact not guests at all, but salespeople, criminals or members of a cult. In either case, the salespeople might win a few people for some time, but ultimately lose the village.

'Evangelistic door-knocking' is usually *extraction-oriented*: it involves knocking at a great number of doors to end up with a small handful of people, who then have to be 'followed-up'. Apostolic–prophetic church-planting usually works the other way round: it is *penetration-oriented*, and moves from the few to the many. It is more important to find (this is one of the places where the prophet comes in) and stay in the right house than to knock on the doors of many houses. First establish a quality house church and make this house of peace the foothold and beachhead for discipling the whole village or city.

Missions would be redefined

At the heart of much of our traditional and contemporary missions is the congregational understanding of church. From this static centre we 'reach out' to others in proximity of 'the church', trying to get them to 'come to church' too, and we call it evangelism. If we do this abroad or across significant social and ethno-linguistic barriers, we call it mission. If the house church, however, became the centre of our missionary understanding, the static church could stop just identifying and sending mobile specialists, the 'missionaries', and could rather start to send itself by simply acting apostolically as a whole. The church, in the best sense of the word, would again become the mission, the sender as well as the sent one.

We would 'send forth' the very multipliable units of the church, who can change with its spiritual DNA everything it touches, and can deposit its spiritual

202 ## Houses that Change the World

Instead of bringing more people to the church, we would be bringing the church to the people.

message into every culture and language. It would work very much like a virus infection, where the virus would introduce its own genetic code into every host cell that it touched, transforming it into its own image. Missions would regain the dynamics of yeast, which does not send informed emissaries of yeast: it sends itself. Instead of bringing more people to the church, we would be bringing the church to the people.

More action, less acting

The congregational type of church is geared towards stage performance. The emphasis is on 'conducting' the meeting, 'delivering' the message, 'performing' the functions, 'celebrating' the rites. The bottom line is that, with so many spectators involved, it is not a discipleship structure at all. It lends itself at least potentially to acting, going through the motions without emotions, performing the outward forms without content, while the spectators remain empty and void behind a pious smokescreen of court nods, hallelujahs

The congregational type of church lends itself at least potentially to acting, going through the motions without emotions, performing the outward forms without content, while the spectators remain empty and void behind a pious smokescreen of court nods, hallelujahs and amens.

and amens. The question 'Are you acting powerful, or are you a powerful actor?' could be settled by returning the church to normal life, away from artificially conducted meetings. The result? Authenticity and authority are restored locally, right there in the neighbourhoods. This would lead to less acting, and more significant action.

Combining local and regional dynamics, spiritual LAN and WAN

When computers are linked together by cables or telephone wires, we differentiate between a Local Area Network (LAN), and a Wider Area Network (WAN). The LAN could be part of a WAN. This will be exactly the way house churches will develop. A local network of interdependent house churches (LAN) would interlink with a wider network of house churches (WAN) in the district, the city, the state; they could exchange ministries and work together in a strategic partnership towards a goal of saturation church-planting.

A new era in reaching Muslims, Hindus and Buddhists

It is no secret that, given the current structure and set-up of the church, only marginalized and lower caste adherents of others faiths are joining the church in any significant numbers, with painfully few exceptions. More and more Christians realize that the very set-up of church is the biggest part of the problem. For many Muslims, Hindus and Buddhists entering a church building itself is a spiritual, cultural, social and philosophical problem. As relational family-style house churches develop themselves, very much according to the extended-family mentality in those three religions mentioned, they will open up a whole new perspective on helping people raised in Muslim, Hindu and Buddhist societies to follow Jesus Christ in an appropriate fashion. Already today we see that, of all possible church structures, house churches have by far the greatest potential to grow amongst Muslim, Hindu and Buddhist people groups. Many Christians have tried, for example, to bring Muslims to the churches. House churches would allow us to bring the church to the Muslims.

Thriving in socialist and communist cultures

Communism is, in many ways, an involuntary strategic ally preparing the mindset of the people for a massive house-church movement.

The traditional church has not done particularly well in attracting the attention and excitement of intellectual students, atheists, Socialists and Communists. But what are their slogans usually about? About redistribution of wealth, sharing resources and justice for all. These are all New Testament values, which the congregational church has preached, but not always lived.

Communism as an ideology is still a powerful attraction today because it focuses on injustice, the rights of the poor, and the redistribution of wealth, if necessary by force. The Communism of Lenin has spoken of 'power to the people', but the result was that the power was usurped by the élitist few who 'humbled themselves' towards the top of the power-pyramid.

As Christians we need to avoid a romantic version of 'early Communism' and all its dreamy songs and emotions, because Christianity also speaks of power to the people, but it provides a God-given delivery and accountability system for that power called 'the church', where God's power is facilitated through the humble services of crucified elders and members of the fivefold ministries.

The problem with Communism is that it does not deal with the root problem of corruption, the sinfulness of people, so those people who 'redistribute wealth' are as fallen and sinful as those from whom they take it; more corruption and dictatorship is usually the result. House churches with their emphasis on sharing material and spiritual resources and the absence of dictator-type leaders are particularly effective in current or historically socialist or communist societies like Russia, Cuba, China, Vietnam and Ethiopia. Communism is, in many ways, an involuntary strategic ally preparing the mindset of the people for a massive house-church movement. If any socialist or communist government keeps on failing to implement the 'communist paradise', the house church, without much propaganda, can deliver the goods. It can do locally what the government cannot do nationally. The house church has the answer to the questions socialists ask, and it provides the right structure for life in a working model, because it has found the solution to sin, the root problem.

The excitement level would rise

Far fewer people in traditional congregational churches are mobilized for actual ministry than in small house churches. Even in a traditional church of fewer than 100 attenders, says the research of Christian Schwarz, only 31 per cent are involved in a ministry corresponding to their spiritual gifts. In a larger church, the figure is only 17 per cent. It is a known fact that involved people are excited people, and uninvolved people quickly become bored. The house church with its participatory lifestyle is able immediately to involve almost everyone. As a result, more people get excited. Excited people excel, and excellent people attract.

*   *   *

Some practical issues to address

If we want to see new developments, we may need to do new things. In developing house churches we will need to address some practical areas. Here I list a few.

Restore the families back to the centre of the church

> *The planting of house churches, therefore, may very well start in the relationship of husband and wife and in the restoration of the family.*

Western Christendom and secularism has focused strongly on the individual, at the expense of the family. Stable and secure traditional families, even with a single parent managing the home and the children, are a much more stable social unit than today's double-earning initially childless, couples who may laugh at the Christians and scorn their traditions, but go on to shipwreck their own marriages and bodies for the sake of a short life in luxury. Once they do have children, they often produce insecure, troubled and violent kids. These almost parentless children grow up peaceless and restless, left to themselves, while their parents pursue a successful career or social significance. The family has been sacrificed on the altar of economic and social success, and only the church can break that cycle, because it has found a better and more humane way to live, not for Mammon but for God. The right relationship between man and woman as the core of the family is at the core of the house church. My friend Kari Törmä from Whole Marriage Ministries in Finland believes that 'we need to focus on the most demanding relationship in the world, the one between husband and wife, to create a healthy foundation for the church and society. Whoever can take care of his marriage and take care of his family, can also take care of the church.' One of the best things a father, for example, can do for his children, is to love their mother. Within a family house-church setting, true fathers and mothers can emerge, and healthy families can be restored. Children can contribute in their own ways to the house churches just by being what they are, bringing out the vulnerable and soft aspects of adults, taking the rough edges off them, making them laugh and cry, humbling and amazing them. The planting of house churches, therefore, may very well start in the relationship of husband and wife and in the restoration of the family.

Develop empowering structures

Jesus gave them power and the keys, and the early disciples turned the ancient world upside down (Acts 17:6). As Christians, we do not draw power from each other, but from God. Our job on earth, however, is to help bring out the best in each other. The core of the Great Commission is discipling, and discipling is basically empowering others as God has empowered us.

I came across a young and dynamic pastor, who served under a 'mighty servant of the Lord': he faithfully led the worship, did what he was asked to do, and humbly served the senior servant. However, he was never given real responsibility. After six years he was finished, ready to leave, an empty shell, rendered powerless. He changed his workplace, and ended up in another church network, where the senior pastor immediately saw the potential of this young man, how he could fit into his own vision and strategy. The young man fell from the frying pan into the fire. He was not discipled and empowered; he was used. If we do not disciple and empower others, as Jesus has done, we end up exploiting others, using them for our ends, even if we clothe this in very spiritual terms.

If the traditional congregational churches do not have discipling at their core, they will not be able to develop a structure that disciples and empowers people, let alone one that disciples nations. Quality defines the structure which in turn determines quantity. As a result, people will remain systematically undiscipled and powerless. If the traditional structure does not empower and disciple, what does it do?

How to empower others	How to exploit others
let them function	give them functions
believe in them	make them believe in you
delegate authority	require submission
further God's plan for them	make them part of your plans
invest in them	use them
love them and say so	love the task more than the people
give them what you have	take what they have
discuss with them	preach at them
spend time freely with them	require appointments
give them the keys now	hold back until you retire
serve them	let them serve you
praise them	accept their praise graciously
transfer masterhood to them	demonstrate masterhood to them

We need to recapture discipling as the heartbeat of the Great Commission, and live this out in our ministries and churches. House churches and the fivefold ministry are a God-ordained way to disciple and empower each other – and ultimately the nations. We need to do this not by accident, but on principle, and determine to develop structures and even strategies that support discipling and empoweringof others on local, regional, national and even international levels.

Develop disabled and senior elders

One way to empower others is to turn strategically to those who are considered weak in our success-driven and youth-oriented societies. Ten per cent of the world suffers from injuries and disability. Instead of trying to make the existing churches more accessible and open for the disabled – to get the disabled to church! – we should turn the other way round and get the church into the homes of the disabled. We need to encourage and equip disabled people, who are often enough housebound, to develop their home into a house church. Not only will this add ten per cent of the world's population to the list of possible house-church planters and elders, but you will hardly find more enthusiastic promoters of the idea.

Similarly, we need to empower not only BYM – Bright Young Men between 18 and 30 – who already enjoy the attention of society, but our seniors. Because a traditional church is often very programme-driven, there is little need for seniors. However, as we train and equip senior people to become elders of house churches, many of them will flourish, just like the churches in their homes will flourish. We could as well truly do with a good portion of redeemed wisdom and grey hairs in the affairs of the local church. They will become grandfathers with a vision!

Stop contextualizing, start incarnating

Jesus was Asian, not European. Most Christians and not-yet-Christians agree that we do not really need a contextualized, but still basically western, church in Asia or Africa or Latin America.

> *Each nation needs to develop its own models of church, incarnating Christ again into its own time, culture and soil.*

Each nation needs to develop its own models of church, incarnating Christ again into its own time, culture and soil. Contextualizing has been a helpful missionary method in the past, where the gospel and western expressions of church were adapted and made to fit into the local context of culture and language. Now that the church is literally present and growing in almost all cultures of the world, we need to allow the church to form its own expressions, its rural and its urban forms, speaking powerfully to its own cultural patterns.

Change our traditional worship patterns

Missions exist because worship does not. As the pouring out of the Spirit replaces the temple-centred worship rituals and patterns in the Old Testament, Christians are now called to worship God 'in spirit and truth'. We are in danger of overlooking, however, that true New Testament worship has much more to do with Spirit-filled obedience (Rom 12:1,2) than with music and singing 'worship' songs. Our worship must centre around the unquestioning readiness to lay aside life, limb, possessions, family, house, friendships, evangelical respectability, everything, to see the knowledge of the glory of the Lord covering the earth as the waters cover the sea. It may be quite appropriate even to recover some New Testament forms of worship, laying ourselves down flat on the floor to express speechless adoration and praise God (Mt. 28:9; Rev. 4:10), signalling to God that we are even ready to lay down our very lives for Him in obedience to His calling – while, at the same time, not forgetting to sing our songs. However, phrases like 'Let us now have a time of worship' or 'Let us now go into worship', meaning that we all have to stand up to sing some songs, may be less helpful than they sound, because they are a simple misnomer. 'It is important to note that the New Testament never mentions worship as the very reason for Christians to come together – they come for mutual encouragement and edifying each other (1 Cor. 14:26; Heb. 10:24,25) – but focuses more on the how, and not on the when and where of worship,' says Peter Ignatius of Christian Fellowship in Madras. The New Testament never refers to a meeting of the church as a worship service. Worship, in short, is not so much what we do but how we do it; not so much what we say or sing, but how we are a living sacrifice.

Introduce a new commitment level

Secret societies have flourished and are still flourishing, because of people's curiosity about the unknown, the secret. They want to belong to something special. Christianity in its house-church form has been a secret society. It still is, and probably will be or become again a secret or semi-secret society. This calls for more attention to the initiation process for novices into the church, and means that we have to require a higher level of commitment from anyone who wants to become part of a local church. After all, it is a commitment to become part of a spiritual family and share one's life with others, which is a very high commitment, much more than just a commitment to a membership of a voluntary club which is satisfied by attending once in a while. It is interesting that, rather than people flocking to places where they are unconditionally welcome, the number of people who are interested in joining a group is related to the commitment level required.

One pastor in Germany announced that 'The sermons in my church are intellectually so demanding that not everybody will truly be able to grasp what is being preached.' This caused a lot of people to come out of mere curiosity to see whether the preacher was right. The narrower the door, the more people seem to be interested in squeezing through it. In addition, as the initial commitment level for someone becoming part of a house church is raised, the quality level also goes up.

Recover tribal patterns of church

After being driven out of the Garden of Eden, the home which God made for Adam and Eve, mankind has basically been homeless. The place where humans and their creator God were supposed to meet was closed to them. This left a deep 'home-shaped vacuum' in the heart and mind of all humans, and explains the craving we all have to have a home, a castle, family and clan, a refuge where we are safe and secure, where we have an identity – and where we can, possibly, forget for a moment that God has driven us all out from His presence. 'Man is a tribal animal,' writes Peter Marsh in his book *Tribes*:

> The early population of the earth were basically hunters and gatherers, who formed hunting bands as an effective solution to survival. A group of 6–8 hunting males made up a typical band size of 20–25, including women and children. This size proved to be enough for hunting purposes, but not for social purposes like marriage. For that a larger unit of society was required. The ideal population of such village-units seems to have settled at about 500 men, women and children, and so emerged the tribe, typically embracing 20 hunting bands, each consisting of about 6 families.

Social identity is knowing who we are in relation to other people. Many scientists see the origins of basic human behaviour patterns in the area of territoriality, marriage, kinship, taboos, social interaction etc. rooted in the tribal format, which, they say, is still deeply buried in all of mankind. That is why they cannot and should not be suppressed; they are too basic. These tribal patterns emerge automatically, whether we look at traditional or the modern tribes of society, at fox-hunters or football hooligans, commandos or criminals, trade unionists or terrorists, Boy Scouts or Hell's Angels. All obey basically the same rules. There are modern tribal tendencies everywhere: in our committees, juries, teams and squads; councils, governments, board members, clubs, our secret societies, protest groups, clans or institutes, our childhood gangs, school reunions and our pop-group fan clubs.

Chiefdoms and 'headless' tribes
Anthropologists define a 'tribe' as a collection of groups of people who share patterns of speech, basic cultural characteristics and, traditionally, a common territory. They appear in two distinctly different forms: acephalous (headless) tribes lack a single head and a centralized authority, and the adult members are all part of the decision-making process and have roughly equal status; chiefdoms, by contrast, have a clear, centralized authority in the form of a chief, and develop a pyramid structure of authority.

Initiation rites
Initiation, the specially marked transitions from one stage of life to another, or the process of becoming part of a tribe, usually has four stages. First, there is the uninvolved outsider, who is not part of the tribe. He is suspicious of the tribe, and the tribe has been taught to be suspicious of outsiders. Then comes the novice stage, where a person enters into a probation and training period, usually accompanied by symbolic death rituals like circumcision, isolation or other forms of symbolic killing of the initiate, where he becomes dead to the normal life of the tribe. Through suffering and daring deeds the novice declares his commitment and shows courage. The third phase is the welcoming of the former novice as a full member of the tribe. The fourth and last stage is when a full member of

the tribe becomes an initiator himself, actively initiating others into the tribe and therefore caring for the ongoing life-cycle of it. This basic pattern is still observed in traditional and modern tribal structures.

Ordeals of initiation
When new boys are entering school, or freshmen enter university or the army, they are usually treated to some kind of humiliation or entry ordeal to show what material they are made of. Only then are they admitted to the academic tribe or become 'one of the boys' in the modern armed forces. Youth gangs often require prospective new members to show what they are made of before they are admitted to the tribe. Often they need to commit a crime, like stealing an apple or a car, to pass the test. In this way the new recruit is bound to the group through his shared complicity in illegal activities, with an unspoken threat hanging over his head: if you ever leave the tribe, the world will know about your crime. Many present-day tribes, like modern secret societies, have fairly rough initiation rites, such as having a rope tied around their neck to symbolize what will happen if they ever betray the secrets of their society, or having tattoos administered. Freemasonry, founded in 1717, still has nearly 500,000 men meeting monthly in England alone – not in spite of, but because of their 'archaic' initiation rituals.

House churches help release tribal dynamics for good
The congregational church in a standard size of 80 to 150 attenders is one of the only structures which breaks the tribal mentality, and violates deep-seated feelings and traditional habits in the process. This pattern does not conform to in-built tribal patterns, and restricts the natural flow of building relationships and social identity. The church is either much too large for the organic dynamics

of the small band, or too small for providing 'a village' for its members. The church has traditionally tried to over- come this by heavy organization and strong, authority- figure leadership as well as highly structured worship patterns. But whenever the size of a Christian community comes close to either 20 or 500, the two numeric poles of the tribal pattern of a hunting band or a village, special social and tribal dynamics are released, which would otherwise be kept dormant.

House churches and larger celebrations can immedi- ately recapture the social tribal dynamics of the 'small hunting band' of around 20 people, and have their other needs met in larger gatherings like the city church. Chris- tianity also has its initiation rites like baptism and sharing of material wealth with the community. There is even a very powerful Christian equivalent to the minor crimes which modern youth gangs require from new members to bond them to the tribe. It is the confession of sin. If some- one confesses his sin to the house church, he may lose face before the outside world and, as it were, die to a life of double standards, but is accepted in grace, forgiveness and love by his new spiritual tribe.

In terms of linking house churches together, cell churches tend to reflect the chiefdom-structure, while house churches and their flat structure, linked together in mutually interdependent ways, reflect more the headless tribal pattern. This could be one of the reasons why the cell church might be more appropriate for chiefdom cultures, and the house church more for democratic cultures.

Change our teaching structures

In an African country once, the electricity went off just as I was about to begin to teach some 200 pastors and evangelists. I chose six disciples (those who knew

English best), asked everyone else to pray for each other. Then I explained to my six 'disciples' a simple lesson, which took me 15 minutes. Then I asked them to choose six disciples of their own, and tell them exactly what I had told them. Then those 36 disciples of my six disciples were to choose another six disciples each (now covering all 200 people), and teach them the very same lesson again. After that I asked one of the last generation of disciples, who had learned the lesson handed down through two generations, to stand in front of us all and repeat the whole teaching – at the top of his booming voice. As his teaching was right, he got a thumbs-up sign; if he had introduced or been taught false teachings or 'extra flowers', he would have got a thumbs-down. As a result, not only was it good fun and saved electricity, but it made 43 of them do the actual teaching, and we could observe which of them were gifted and which others needed, let us say, more prayer.

How much do you really remember from your time of classroom teaching in school, where a teacher explained a subject in front of a class, and you all dutifully took notes so as not to fail in the inevitable exam? This is arguably the most ineffective type of teaching available to mankind, yet we have got so used to it that we reproduce it wherever we go, even in the life of the church. If we want to change the quality of teaching and learning, we need to change our structures accordingly, and move from static to kinetic learning. In the New Testament, the very model and way of teaching is geared to changing lifestyles through changing values. Since the house church is a structure that emerges out of a heartbeat of discipleship, we again could start to teach each other how to live and how to teach, not just spoon-feeding one subject after another. In Hebrew tradition there are so-called rabbinical thinking schools. The aim is to learn first how to think, how to handle and use one's God-given intellectual abilities, and then how to apply them to other topics. Usually, students going through this process of learning to think first, and then looking into other subjects, are able to handle even A Levels with ease.

Kinetic or dynamic teaching abandons classroom settings, lengthy sermons or Bible studies, and becomes again part of everyday life in the most natural place on earth, the home. Here we can teach each other by example, by questions and answers, drawing everybody into the teaching and learning process, building not individual head-knowledge, but consensus, corporate understanding and therefore spiritual momentum.

Chapter 9

QSQ

Values and content come first, methods and plans second, and growth and numbers last: how to think Quality–Structure–Quantity

QSQ: Quality–Structure–Quantity

There is a wonderful North-African dish called couscous, made of semolina, meat and vegetables, usually eaten sitting with your legs crossed on the floor in a tent around a large bowl, forming small balls of couscous with your hand and popping them into your mouth. When I am with my friends in Sudan and it is eating time, we all will usually stand in line for our meal. Each pair of people is given only one plate, and they both eat the portion of rice and sauce from the same dish, using that most flexible of all forks, the hand. Once in a while someone will tap your shoulder and, with the broadest possible smile, will transfer the leftovers of his own plate onto your plate, a sign of friendship and appreciation. As we allow even our sweat and saliva to mix, our quality of fellowship and bonding is built. In many countries legal contracts are still sealed by having a meal together as a sign of mutual agreement.

The message of QSQ, which stands for Quality, Structure and Quantity, is simple: reformation, revival, church growth and also church-planting seem to follow those three steps in that very order, each one related to the former one. Each one is incomplete – and even dangerous – without the other, and they follow logically and naturally.

More, better and smaller churches

The bottom line of what many of us see God doing at the moment around the world is this: He is bringing back Q, that is foundational New Testament, apostolic–prophetic Quality to His body. This new quality forms its own S, new Structures: they emerge from within, not through efforts from outside. These new structures will, in turn, prove worthy and capable of fast growth and multiplication – the second Q, the Quantity aspect. This may very well mean many more, qualitatively 'better' and – for some surprisingly – very much smaller churches than we are used to.

Quality

Quality – no longer the silent victim

The church is always in danger of reversing the order, and starting with quantity and methods, rather than with quality. There are two main reasons for this. The church is constantly tempted to listen too much to impressive people who seem on the outside to be like spiritual stars and sure-fire winners. Their simple message is: we have found a magic button to press for instant success and victory in Christianity. They strongly influence a slightly depressed church through an unhealthy focus on mere quantity, and sometimes encourage it to run evangelistic mega-projects that want to 'touch as many people as possible as quickly as possible'. This mindset, almost completely foreign to the New Testament, is overly driven by numbers and goals alone, and it basically tells the church to act now, and think later; to shoot now, aim later; to evangelize now, follow up later; to succeed now, do the patchwork later; to see the success story happen today, leave the reformation and quality control for others; to rush on to save another country or city, and let the local or national churches take the blame for a less than ideal follow-up.

The other reason is very simply the 'donor-dollar': the money given to missions and evangelism carries the agenda of the one who gives the donation. The Golden Rule is still valid: the one who has the gold makes the rules. Reflecting the mentality of many – but not all – financial donors today, this money is often even expected to yield a high return, preferably measurable in hard numbers and results.

The 1930s – when volume became the new God

'Once Quality was a natural fact of everyday trade,' writes Steve Smith in his management book *The Quality Revolution*. 'Then, during the 1930s, mass thinking began to take over. First came mass production, then mass service: "Pile them high, sell them quick". Volume was the new God.' The early decades of the twentieth century were also the time when many modern-day evangelistic operations and ministries were born, their general philosophy neatly fitting into the spirit of their time. An obsession with quantity and mass-ministry created a blindspot in the area of quality, which is often still evident today. Smith goes on to say: 'Many companies are blissfully unaware of the quality gap – the difference between the customers' expectations and the achievement of the company, partly because they are only really looking at themselves (their measures, mostly internal, may show that they are still improving satisfactorily), and partly because they don't want to know.'

'Quickly, quickly,' – act now, think later! – 'is a word straight from hell,' says Francis Schaeffer. But we often greet it as a revelation from heaven. If a focus on quantity replaces our focus on quality, then we will be tempted to use structures, i.e. means, methods, plans, techniques and projects,

If a focus on quantity replaces our focus on quality, then we will be tempted to use structures, i.e. means, methods, plans, techniques and projects, to attain only our numerical goals.

to attain only our numerical goals. Usually, quality is the silent victim of this action-driven and success-oriented process. However, we as the whole body of Christ will not be able to avoid paying the price and building a quality church somehow, either now or later.

The streets of Madras

Let me illustrate my point. At the time of writing this book I am living in Madras, South India. Our city is hit every year by extensive monsoon rain. This torrential downpour washes away many streets, and they are left in dire need of repair. Due to the lack of a proper sewerage system, it leaves half the city (and usually my office, too) flooded. After the rain stops, small groups of construction workers swarm all over the city, filling in the potholes with any conceivable material – dirt, sand, stones, pebbles, plastic bags and even pieces of wood – and they patch it over with a generous layer of tar. Through the onslaught of traffic, sun and further rain, this marvellous patchwork quickly deteriorates, the holes open here and there, and soon the road is ready for the next monsoon, mercifully initiating the repeating of the cycle. The steps taken here are quantity first (patch as many holes as quickly as possible), structure second (using fast-working groups of workers treating the streets superficially) – and the victim is quality.

It helps that India is receiving generous development aid from western countries for just that very purpose, to build and rebuild its roads. As long as the money keeps pouring in, that process will probably not change: after all, somehow or other it works. The price for quality, with the help of subsidies from the West, is this: there is no real progress, only a maintaining of the status quo.

Good foundations

Although most comparisons fall short of their purpose, I suggest that the quality of the church is, in some ways, comparable to the quality of a house. Its quality depends on six factors:

⟨ the character, wisdom and vision of the architect
⟨ the physical locality of the building site
⟨ the quality of its foundations
⟨ the building materials used
⟨ the quality of the master builder
⟨ the quality and enthusiasm of the workers.

Jesus has made it quite clear that God Himself is the inventor, visionary and father of the church; Jesus Himself, not just any sandy plot, is the rock and foundation for it (Mt. 7:24–6; 1 Cor. 3:11); and Jesus sees the 'right people' like Peter (Mt. 16:18) or 'a man of peace' (Lk. 10:6), not just any man, as a possible starting point – or building site – for the church. The apostolic and prophetic ministries are instituted, through the one who empowers those ministries, to lay the foundations for the church (Eph. 2:20); the company of the redeemed are the 'living stones' built up together (1 Pet. 2:5); and Jesus again is Himself the master-builder (Mt. 16:18), who uses apostolic people as His master-craftsmen or expert builders (1 Cor. 3:10).

Who builds what?

Still, there is a big difference between building a church and the mechanical process of building a house. We cannot just take 'six guaranteed principles' and, independent of its maker, build the house of God. God has wisely tied the whole process to Himself. In an act of grace and sovereignty, God reserves the right to give the increase as He likes, and supply the secret of growth whenever and wherever He pleases. Jesus, God on earth, has summed this up in His famous words: 'I will build my church.'

I see four possible interpretations of these words, of which I suggest we should only favour the last one. The interesting thing is that most of these interpretations are subtle and unspoken.

1 *"We will build our church."* We in our own strength and traditional methods will build our own kingdoms. The result is just that, a man-driven religious cult. Flesh builds flesh.
2 *"We will build His church."* This interpretation is more dangerous than the first, because it appeals to the go-getters, the doers and activists in each culture, and implies that we humans can build God's house; flesh can construct spirit, great human strategies and projects will usher in God's Kingdom. The result is usually the same as under 1, but has a more spiritually deceptive,

and sometimes even a triumphalist overtone. Some
even have called this approach 'modern witchcraft and
magic', because it tries to use means other than the Holy
Spirit for spiritual ends. The results are often enough
manipulation and spiritual megalomania.

3 *"Jesus will build our church."* This interpretation says,
in effect, that Jesus uses his resources for our ends;
spirit builds flesh. We are God's chosen few, the right
denomination or group, a holy – perhaps even the
only! – remnant, and so Jesus has now chosen to build
our church. Here humans are using God for human
ends; the church comes first, and everything else is
secondary to the goal of building a single denomination or organization, not His whole universal church.
Jesus, to put it in pictorial terms, pours His oil on our
fire, and the result may very well be nothing more
than a temporary human and religious kingdom.
There is another downside to this thinking: if nothing
grows and nothing happens, this must be God's will,
since surely nothing is wrong with us.

4 *"Jesus will build His church."* This implies that Jesus
Himself is the master-builder, and He offers a definite
invitation for any one of us to become His co-workers
(Col. 4:11) and help Him in building up His church
His way. This is somewhat humiliating, because it
does not underline our human efforts very much, but
rather stresses a spiritual partnership, with Jesus and
His Spirit being the senior partner. The result will
have God's stamp of approval, because He Himself
gave the very mandate to build, and His own spiritual genes are engineered into it. Spirit builds spirit.
Only by the grace of God will we be able to appreciate
the fact that this is the only way that emphasizes the
right name in the credit line of all church growth and
church planting endeavours: the Lamb of God.

Beyond renewal and reformation

Over the millennia, the great divide in Christianity has never really been between denominations, Catholics and Protestants, or charismatics and non-charismatics, but always between Spirit and Flesh, the breath of life and the odour of death, between

> We may be using and following a spiritual genetic code, a methodological pattern which may be brilliant in comparison to other church movements and streams, but one which is still not quite up to God's norm.

man-made religion and movements of God's Spirit. In many countries, right up to today, a number of renewal movements have been struggling sometimes even for centuries, to renew traditional structures, by calling the church back to either the word of God, the Spirit of God, or the original confession of faith of their particular church or denomination. When we read about prominent reformation leaders, or even ask outstanding leaders of present-day renewal movements, none of these three methods of renewal seems to truly work in the long run to the satisfaction of all involved.

The answer may be more radical still. Reformation and renewal of existing structures may simply not go deep enough. We may be using and following a spiritual genetic code, a methodological pattern which may be brilliant in comparison to other church movements and streams, but one which is still not quite up to God's norm. In short, if we compromise quality, no amount of quantity will ever do.

'Give me back my church!'

God is good, and He therefore sets good standards for the church of God. Normality, therefore, is only what stands up to God's norm, no matter what place a given concept of church has had in history or in our tradition, and no matter how many people have agreed to it in the past. God's Kingdom is no democracy. Many Christians today feel strongly that God is simply calling the church back to New Testament standards with sound apostolic and prophetic foundations.

When the meek inherit the earth

This means, in practice, that God calls all of us away from a spirit of complacency to a spirit of revival; from superficiality to depth; from lukewarmness to true heat; from mediocrity to spiritual excellence; from the pursuit of pleasure to a life of passion; from living in a fake peace with the world to a state of war under God's martial law; from conforming to the patterns of this world to being transformed into the image of Christ; from a silly and costly behavioural pattern of trial and error to a prophetic mode; from a settler mentality to a pilgrim mentality; from a me-focus to a we-focus; from individual thinking to corporate thinking; from hiding one's sin to living in the light; from proud boasting and preaching of ourselves to true strength in weakness, realizing that it is the meek that will inherit the earth, a statement of Jesus which turns any earthly wisdom on its head.

Being before doing

Some of God's essential qualities are love, hope, faith, truth, light, and compassion. The essence of God, His true qualities, is not related so much to what He does, but to what He is. Because God first 'is' the great 'I am', the one who simply 'was in the beginning', and only then 'does' what He does and did what He did as an outflow of His personality, so also we are called first to be, and then to do.

Because God is a lover, he loves. What God does, shows us who He is, and because He is a good God – a quality God! – His actions are good and of a supernatural quality. That is why the gospel is 'Good News', because it is the solid news about a supernaturally good God redeeming mankind from terrible sin by sacrificing His own son, liberating them from a bondage that was too great for them to liberate themselves, and releasing those held captive by a system of lies that comes straight from hell, providing them with a new system to live out their new life in Christ, a structure called the church, before which all hell is rendered powerless. The gates of hell will not prevail against the church which I build, says Jesus.

Structure

Structure is, according to the Oxford English Dictionary, 'the way things are put together', how things are organized. Since the Bible describes the local church as the body of Christ, the essence and qualities of God will have to be reflected in the local church, not in only one perfect and holy individual. For God, good does not at all equal numerical success. Much of God's qualities are relational, interdependent. They cannot be lived out individually, in a vacuum. It requires at least two to love. That also means that many of God's qualities, His spiritual genes, will be lived out in a corporate manner: they will be seen in our lifestyle, the way we follow Jesus. All that requires some structure, a more or less systematic way of doing the things which we do. I do not favour a perfect, perfectionist or any other legalistic kind of structure. The Bible encourages us to deal with each other with grace, forgiveness, love and truth – not truth alone! – in a spirit of warmth and mutual appreciation. At the same time we are not to ignore the supernatural pattern and purpose of the church of God, which is, for example, not a feel-good club for mere socializing, but has a divine destiny.

Structure and culture

Jesus became flesh and lived amongst us. He chose Bethlehem, 2000 years ago, a very particular spot in time and space. He lived, ate, spoke and related to people of His time in a special way, which is difficult for anyone to emulate because we live in a different time and culture. His incarnation meant that the eternal God became one of us, and we could see God in Jesus for the first time: 'If you see me, you see the Father,' says Jesus. If Jesus were to be incarnated today, say, in southern France, He would probably behave and act very similarly, and at the same time very differently, to the way he lived in Palestine. The quality of His life, His principles and destiny, would be the same, but the way He would speak and act, might be quite different. This means that the internal quality of the church, the body of Christ, might also be the same in each culture and time, but will differ greatly in its style, the structural outworking of its life.

Preach the church or preach Jesus

Vincent Donovan, a missionary to the Masai tribe, explains in his book *Christianity Rediscovered* that in the past Christian mission to this African people group has been mostly agricultural and social, focusing on schools etc. It hardly had any effect on the Masai. Donovan asked

himself the question: Can I leave behind everything the
other Missionaries do, and just take the message of Jesus
to the Masai? As a result, he saw 'whole villages come to
Jesus'. He sums his experience up in two lessons. The first
was that if you preach the church, the response will look
like the church that sent you out; preach Jesus, and the
response looks very different. The second lesson was that
he himself rediscovered the gospel afresh in the process,
as 'the church became flesh' again in unchurched cultures
and started to tell its own story.

Confusing culture with spiritual realities

Some young Christians from the USA were reporting in
an Asian church about some outreach they were doing in
Calcutta. They had genuine tears of brokenness in their
eyes as they talked about the people worshipping dead
idols in temples, and yet these young people did not
recognise the endless hours of TV in their country as
worshipping living idols of sport, music or film.

They had broken hearts over the abject material
poverty in Calcutta, and did not see the spiritual and
emotional poverty of countless millions suffering from
loneliness and meaninglessness in their home country.
They could not believe that people sacrifice flowers and
even animals to their gods, overlooking that it is quite normal to sacrifice even children and whole families on the
holy altar of success back home. They marvelled at the
smoke and incense-offerings 'those pagans do to their
gods', and did not see for one moment the smog caused by
every individualist jamming the roads with their own car,
industry polluting the atmosphere, and cigarette smokers
polluting the rooms. They said, 'These children here are so
dirty!', and yet they did not realize that most children in
their own country do not obey their parents and have

unbelievably dirty language, harbouring fantasies most children in Asia or the Middle East would simply abhor.

In short, they saw and judged the outside, not the inside. They were shocked by the culture, not by the spirit behind it, and they failed to see that it is no better at home than in Asia. Fallenness and sinfulness only looks different on the outside; its quality is essentially the same everywhere.

National sins and blessings

Like a human being, each nation and each tribe at any given time in history has its own way of doing things, its own values, language, patterns of behaviour, its communication systems, its do's and don'ts, its special strengths and weaknesses, blessings and sins. As there are liars and lawyers, murderers and mechanics, drunkards and drivers amongst men, you will find that each nation has a personality of its own, with strengths and weaknesses, special sins and special blessings, gifts and curses. Most nations and tribes, like individual humans, usually have a tendency to be blind to their weaknesses and sins, and tend to overestimate their strengths, and underestimate their weaknesses. Which nation comes to your mind when you think of national hallmarks like perfectionism, fearfulness, shyness, insecurity, megalomania, laziness, fear, pride, superficiality, militancy, obsession with martial arts, lust, gluttony, stinginess, corruption, loneliness, neutrality?

Patterns of the world – patterns of God

One of the most fascinating words for me in the New Testament is the Greek word *stoicheia* (Col. 2:8,20; Gal. 4:3), which, similar to the word *aion* in Romans 12:1,2, means 'pattern, life-force, principles'. 'Do not conform to the principles of this world,' says Paul. Originally the word *stoicheia* meant the principal elements of the world, like earth, water, fire, air. However, Paul attributes a much more spiritual significance to the 'patterns of the world'; he seems to see them like spiritual natural laws of a fallen world, demonically empowered principles that have formed its traditions, institutions and cultures, which 'automatically' take over and control each person born within its jurisdiction. 'You cannot understand Europe without the dimension of the demonic,' said German psychoanalyst C. G. Jung.

The two magnets

I would liken the effects of *stoicheia* to a gigantic magnetic field. As many of us have seen in a experiment at school, when you sprinkle iron filings on a magnetic field, they 'automatically' arrange themselves according to the magnetic patterns. If human 'iron filings' are sprinkled, i.e. born, onto such a pattern, they immediately start arranging themselves and, with the help of some spiritual peer pressure, stay arranged that way. This is not some magic principle, but part of the fact that this world has 'fallen into sin'. Sin can corrupt and pollute land, teaches the Bible (Deut. 24:4; Jer. 16:18; Num. 35:33; 2 Chr. 7:14; Ezr. 9:11; Gen. 6:11).

From Adam and Eve onwards we know that sin has a tendency to spread. We can therefore see sins of individuals – demonically enhanced, empowered and encouraged – growing into sins of groups of people, growing into community habits, growing into local traditions, developing into national institutions – and ultimately forming cultures, shaping the spirits, minds and the thinking patterns of millions of people almost 'automatically'. This influencees the human thinking within each culture, especially in the very elementary aspects of life, such as work, eating, money, honour, shame, children, how to behave and even how to think. When a person is born and brought up within a particular culture, he or she also has to drink and inherit this spiritual paradigm and pattern with their mother's milk, becoming part of an overpowering spiritual system of '*stoicheia* and *aion*' into which they are introduced through the sin of their parents – and ultimately through their own sin. From their perspective, however, such people would consider themselves as absolutely 'normal'.

Even the very pattern of people's lives, therefore, has an in-built message: it simply and clearly says to which system you belong.

The kingdom of God, in this picture, brings a completely different dimension to this set-up. A new, very powerful magnet, so to speak, is lowered from heaven to earth, creating its own magnetic field and influence, and changing the way people think, act and behave. Ultimately, some or many human iron filings change their magnetic allegiance and arrange themselves into this new magnetic field of the Kingdom of God. This causes no small confusion, since the two magnetic systems – the 'patterns of this world' and the Kingdom of God – are not the same, and pull people in opposite directions, arranging them in very different patterns. Even the very pattern of people's lives, therefore, has an in-built message: it simply and clearly says to which system you belong. Thus, the very lifestyle of Christians becomes a battle-cry, and may be the real down-to-earth arena of what we may call 'spiritual warfare'.

Three ways of church-planting

The gospel of the Kingdom challenges and changes the very essence, the core beliefs and values of a sinful, fallen and ungodly world, country, people group and culture. It crucifies the sinful patterns, and is able to redeem and use powerfully those aspects of a culture reflecting and institutionalizing the blessings of God.

In each culture there are therefore essentially three ways of planting and building the church:

1 One can try to fit in with the 'patterns of the world' in a given culture and nation, and arrange the church as neatly as possible into the accepted cultural pattern. This habit, sometimes hiding behind what is called 'felt-need oriented evangelism' or 'state-church Christianity', will probably look from the outside like a quick success; but it usually fails to penetrate deeply and cut through the spiritual roots and invisible plumbing through which sinful patterns and culturally accepted habits are sustained. The result is usually an adapted church, often with a phenomenal initial growth rate, but an untold and long-lasting depression afterwards, whereby the church is sooner or later absorbed, losing its power and finally its identity. It has merged with the patterns of this world.

2 The other extreme is to ignore the patterns of this world, of the local culture, the local 'way of doing things', and to create and remain on a 'holy island', so separate from the world that almost all meaningful communication and interaction breaks down. This mentality usually creates an 'island syndrome', and the church remains very different and therefore suspicious, truly foreign, small and again powerless to change people and to disciple and transform a country.

3 The third way, which I advocate, is not a middle-of the-
   road compromise, but finding a truly godly mix
   between redeeming and crucifying a given culture.
   Here we cannot rely so much on human wisdom and
   anthropological insights alone, but on divine revelation, prophecy and sound apostolic thinking.

This is also one of the many reasons why church-planting as a global partnership is so important. God may
use us to help each other recognize culturally and
nationally developed spiritual roadblocks, blind spots
and strongholds, which we have imbibed with our
mother's milk. We need spiritual crossfertilizing, helping each other to break through the inherited patterns
of *stoicheia*, without forsaking the good and godly parts
of our cultures and countries, and bringing out the best
in each other in synergy with one another.

Yuppies and savages dancing to the same gods

The idea of happy savages living in peace with nature,
and needing to be protected by anthropologists and
ethnologists from the outside world, reinforced by
government agencies, is overlooking the grim truth: the
life of the typical savage is just that: savage and wild.
They are forced to live in overpowering spiritual
circumstances, subject usually to cruel laws, vulnerable
to unreal demands of tradition, customs and demons,
who suck their life-power out of them and throw them
into an endless cycle of pleasing and appeasing distant
and angry gods. This is not very different from a
modern yuppie in the West, dancing to the tune of
career prospects, appeasing the cruel and costly God of
fashion, and trying to forget all problems in one
constant escape. He and the proverbial savage both live

the same lie: they have arranged themselves according to the same spiritually magnetic pattern, and are in need of the same redemption, but in very different forms.

A national church and the redemptive purpose of nations

Each nation or people group has its own identity and character, almost like a corporate personality. From there – and the fact that God is a God of the nations – we can conclude that each nation and people group has its own corporate identity, and therefore needs to grow its own type of

> *Jesus has to be incarnated in each nation and soil, and the result, His church, will be identical in its quality but very different in structure from the church in the neighbouring tribe and country.*

church, with its own structures and ways of organizing things. Jesus has to be incarnated in each nation and soil, and the result, His church, will be identical in its quality but very different in structure from the church in the neighbouring tribe and country. In addition, the collective body of Christ in a nation is called by God to find and fulfil its very own national redemptive purpose, to function within its very own collective supernatural gift, to fill its strategic place in God's global economy which no one else can take. Mission in each nation has therefore three main goals:

1 to develop a national ecclesiology, i.e. a national and not foreign expression of the church;
2 to disciple the nation through a multiplication of this type of church;
3 to define its own contribution towards world missions,

according to the redemptive purpose God has ordained for each nation.

More Southern Baptist churches for Northern Iraq?

If, for example, the church is incarnated in a highly militaristic and urban culture, where powerful kings have ruled society for a long time and the ordinary folk, deeply insecure, still feel the overriding need to be in the shadow of a strong general and leader, and want to rally around a standard-bearer because they would otherwise feel lost in the crowd, what would a church in this culture look like? The church would have an aroma of an army, organized according to military rank and file, where everyone has a title or a badge to show their position, and where the all-important role of a senior leader is beyond question.

But how would the church look in a rural and matri-archal society, where women are the decision makers? And what would it look like in a country with a basic democracy, valuing individual freedom beyond anything else, where strong leaders are regarded as highly suspicious and flags are a symbol of a militant past they want to forget as quickly as possible? Such churches would look look very different from each other.

Knowing the visionary, gracious and humble hearts of many of my Southern Baptist brothers, I am sure they will forgive me if I use them to illustrate this principle. In this sense that I have described, we do not need more Southern Baptist churches in Northern Iraq, but only churches which are born in Northern Iraq.

Same quality – different structures

The sum total of this is that churches incarnated in different cultures can be essentially of the same spiritual quality, but in their structure can look quite different. The western world has been brought up according to a Judeo–Christian value pattern, married for centuries to a Greek and Roman system of logic. This does not function 'east of the Jordan' very well. We must never compromise in the God-given quality aspects of the Kingdom of God, but be flexible and truly prophetic in the way we arrange things in the church, in the area of our structures. We may want to look for what anthropologists call a 'dynamic equivalent', a creative way to explain the unexplainable, like grapes to the Eskimos, snow to the Sudanese and sunshine to the English, that is true to the original message, but adapts the form to make sense to the listener. Quality is God-given, the structures will differ and are flexible expressions of the Body of Christ incarnated over and over again into a local and organic expression of the church.

This is also one of the reasons that church 'models' are very difficult to transplant, translate and contextualize into a different setting. We can learn from underlying principles of each church, but transferring the whole model itself will most probably lead to failures and delay the process of Christ taking root in any native soil.

Create, not copy

Many pastors I meet tell me, 'I tried it, and it did not work!' I guess that today there could be about 200,000 pastors worldwide who suffer from what I call the 'Yonggi-Cho depression'. Yonggi Cho is a most unusual Korean pastor, extremely gifted and capable of leading people and building a church movement. But most have not understood that his message is not 'Copy me, and you will get the same results', but 'Learn from the principles which God has shown me, and perhaps God will bless you, too'! A pastor may teach one thing but what the people hear may be quite different. This is why many have not understood that there are two reasons for Pastor Cho's success: the obedient Yonggi Cho himself, and the church growth principles he has discovered along the way. As a result, many followed his example and, unknowingly or willingly, have tried to copy him. A very few, extremely gifted men have succeeded to a degree – but most have failed. The latter group feel today more guilty and depressed than before, because they honestly feel 'I tried it, and it did not work', a clear symptom of the pathological pattern of 'copyism', a dangerous and deadly disease which has stricken many churches around the globe today.

Some time ago Pastor Colton Wickramaratne of Colombo, pastor of one of the largest and most dynamic churches in Sri Lanka, related to me how someone had told him excitedly about 'the wonderful model of evangelism called Evangelism Explosion. Pastor James Kennedy's Church,' so Colton was told, 'in Fort Lauderdale, Florida, literally exploded with this programme.' Pastor Colton had replied drily: 'How can I explode with someone else's explosion? Do I not sell myself too cheap by denying the creative and powerful potential God has given me – and each of us? As long as I am busy copying someone else, how can I be truly myself? By copying other people's story and model I might fail, therefore, to find and create the one single way forward which God has designed only for me – and no one else!'

In Europe, from 1986 to 1992 many churches copied John Wimber and his model of the Vineyard church. As a result, numerous churches today have a new, unwritten liturgy: one hour worship Vineyard-style, 45 minutes sermon, 20 minutes ministry time. Since 1994 John Wimber's model to be followed has been replaced in some churches by John Arnott's model of the former Airport Vineyard church in

Toronto, Canada. A few years later quite a number of pastors now tell us that they are recovering from a 'post-Toronto depression'. 'But how wonderful,' one pastor told me, 'that we now have Willowcreek. Now that really is it!' 'Wonderful?' I thought. But I forebore to tell him what I felt like saying: that I could already see the post-Willowcreek depression beginning to grip many churches.

Six easy steps to convert a blessing into a curse

Let us slip into the devil's shoes for a few seconds: is 'copyism' not a perfect trap? For many churches, everything starts so wonderfully. Someone experiences God's blessing because he has been obedient to His word and Spirit. Someone else tells the story and it appears as a testimony. A third person creates a model out of this experience, which is then copied and cloned by a fourth. A fifth one finally suggests: 'Let's create an institution around this new model!'. He goes on to start franchises all over the world. The sixth one forms all this into a new law, which judges everyone who chooses to do things differently. Here then are 'six sure and easy steps to transform a blessing into a curse'. If we put our hands to the plough and look back – or abroad? – how dare we think we are fit for the work in the Kingdom of God?

It is high time that we saw resurrected and nurtured all that good, creative and powerful potential in the body of Christ which our Creator God put into all of us long ago and which has almost suffocated under too many layers of copied blessings. That would mean that we have to constantly learn and research which ways God is using in our part of the world, in our society and culture, to win people for Himself and His church. Could it be that our addiction to models from abroad, which we then try endlessly to adapt and contextualize, in reality only reveals a deep leadership crisis and a widespread insecurity about what we should do? Even more dangerous, could this reveal a serious deafness to what the Holy Spirit is trying to say to our churches, which we need to repent and get rid of?

But let us remain realistic. Statistics reveal that 80 per cent of all pastors will simply keep on copying other models and programmes. Fifteen per cent of all pastors will take on other models and change them a little to make them fit better. Only five per cent are true inventors of their own ways and models.

The core things of Christianity defy the unredeemed brain and, like love, faith and hope, are mostly non-logic and appeal only to those who are childlike. I have therefore a very 'unrealistic' proposal to make: should we not, in the name of Jesus and in the power of the Holy Spirit, confuse all those statisticians out there and reverse these sad figures? Sould we not stop copying and start creating in the name of the Creator God, who lives in all of us, whether we are pastors or not?

Quantity

How long did it take the New Testament house-church movement to 'fill Jerusalem with the teaching' of Jesus Christ (Acts 5:28)? Maybe 2 to 3 years, maybe even less. Again, quantity started with quality, with passionate tears in the eyes of the man who cried for this city; and not much later we see the very same city filled with the teaching of the one who had His eyes filled with tears for it. What stands out in the Jerusalem experience was that the growth was like yeast or sour dough: it was infectious, like a virus spreading, transforming everything it touched with a dynamic power. It was as if Christianity had reached a critical mass, and become a self-propelling chain reaction and could not be safely contained nor controlled any longer, except by God. Each believer was a particle of yeast, carrying a core genetic code that he was able to deposit through every open door of every possible house, and transform each cell with its Kingdom-of-God genetic code into a part of the Kingdom of God, into a house church.

Spiritual DNA

Following the initial work of the Austrian monk Gregor Mendel (1822–84) it was the American biologists Francis Crick and James Watson, who discovered in 1953 the chemical structure of DNA (deoxyribonucleic acid), the basic building block of life. DNA contains sugar molecules (deoxyribose) and phosphate molecules in a regular pattern, which form the so-called DNA-spine. Attached to the sugar molecules is one of four 'bases' or 'genetic letters', called adenine, cytosine, guanine, thymine. The way those four 'letters' A, C, G and T are put together makes up the information itself contained in this ingenious pattern. This genetic letter combination makes up the chromosomes or seed-structure of life, and is responsible for the species, size, shape and quality of the organism which is created out of it.

The powerful effects of a spreading virus infection depend very much on the power of the DNA of the virus. The virus infects a perfectly normal cell, and introduces its own DNA into it, whereby the 'host' cell is transformed into the image of the virus – and becomes sick. Similarly, we are all carriers of a spiritual and heavenly DNA, the DNA of the Kingdom of God, containing the pattern of the church right within each of us. Everything we touch, therefore, will also be infected with, or at least affected by, with this wonderful disease

and transformed into the image of Christ on earth,
literally forming His body according to the genetic code
everywhere we go. The result will be growth through
infection, a true multiplication system like yeast in a
dough, almost unstoppable in terms of quantity. If the
quality of the DNA is right, all we need is to work
towards a critical mass by building up an appropriate
structure, and leave to the 'God of numbers' to what
heights He Himself wants to raise the quantity of it all.

The right prototype is more important than full warehouses

All this leads us to a painful but pressing question. If our
present-day quality of church with our present-day structures, existing types of churches and church-based methods and programmes do not necessarily lead to the
discipling of the nations, qualitatively and quantitatively,
what will?

In the world of business, research and development are
two very important areas. Most attention is given, and
most money spent, in developing the right product, a
tested and working prototype, before going into mass production. The right prototype is more important than a
warehouse full of low-quality products. The slightest
error in the original can cause catastrophic results, with
costly recalls, once the assembly lines start running. Management consultants tell us 'It is 50 times easier to start
again than to correct a problem.' I believe we do well to
spend the bulk of our time on developing an appropriate
quality prototype of church in each nation or people
group first, and only then develop strategies for church
multiplication.

This way of thinking, however, can also prove to be a
genuine trap for people who are fascinated with quality

and have a slightly perfectionist attitude. So often our greatest weakness is hiding in the shadow of our greatest strength. The danger is that we might forever work in our spiritual laboratories and never get our product out of the experimental stage, because we feel it is not yet ripe or good enough. A sure sign for a really good prototype is that it soon gets out of our hands anyway. Either it will be stolen through industrial espionage, sold by a corrupt scientist for a ridiculous sum to a fascinated sponsor, taken red-hot from the hands of the scientists straight to the sales department, or, if it is an organic thing we are working on, just stand up all by itself and walk out on us.

How big is big, and how many are many?

'But the rock that struck the statue became a huge mountain and filled the whole earth,' explains the prophet Daniel (Dan. 2:35,44), obviously referring to God's heavenly Kingdom, partly expressed by the church. It is clear that the number of the redeemed will at some point reach proportions which John, in his revelation, felt 'no one could count' (Rev. 7:9). God 'wants all men to be saved' (1 Tim. 2:4), the whole dough to be worked through by the yeast (Mt. 13:33). He will 'make the nations and the ends of the earth the inheritance and possession' of Jesus (Ps. 2:8), and 'the earth will be filled with the knowledge of the glory of the Lord as the waters cover the sea' (Hab. 2:14). The vehicle to make known 'the manifold wisdom of God', says Ephesians 3:10, is the church, obviously spread around the earth in truly global proportions.

Are we content with a relatively full hell and a relatively empty heaven?

If we are too accustomed to an only moderately effective church and mediocre missionary results in the past, it might wrongly lead us to believe that the future will also be rather like the past.

With more than 6 billion people populating the planet, then out of the possibly 20 billion humans that have lived and died since the beginning of history, more than 25 per cent of them are alive today. Jesus says that He came into the world not to judge the world, but that the world, through Him, might be saved. Many Christians, and even many of our mission strategies, seem to be overwhelmingly satisfied with scratching the surface, winning a few, not 'saving the world'. The fact is that, even if many of our contemporary strategies succeed, we would still be left with a relatively full hell and a relatively empty heaven. Can we truly say: if five per cent are saved, it is enough? If we win a handful out of each nation, is our mission really completed?

If we are too accustomed to an only moderately effective church and mediocre missionary results in the past, it might wrongly lead us to believe that the future will also be rather like the past. This would limit our expectation through the blinkers of our experience, and we would, looking back from our plough, be found unfit for the work in the Kingdom of God (Lk. 9:62). We may reluctantly accept a vision 'to win 10 or 20 per cent' of the population as 'realistic', because according to our methods and experiences this might be possible. But the real reason might be that we are not able to imagine anything beyond that, and inwardly wonder whether anything more really is God's will. Is it not up to God's election? I do not fully know, and

I am afraid of easy answers. But I know this: God has elected the elect mainly for the purposes of the non-elect.

The God who wants to be pleaded with

In Genesis 18, the first patriarch Abraham awkwardly bargains with God over the fate of Sodom and Gomorrah, God granting him enormous freedom and influence, while Abraham wonders whether God will become angry with his audacious requests. In Ezekiel 22, God is looking for an intercessor to stand in the gap, literally to stave off His divine judgement on the nation. Finding none, God goes ahead with the prophesied destruction, a case in which God implies that this clearly did not need to happen. Jesus speaks of the persistent widow, who is blessed only because of her refusal to take no for an answer (Lk. 18:1–8). Moses and Paul both went on record with God that they would personally be willing to be damned, to have their own salvation revoked, if somehow God would save their fellow countrymen.

Few Christians today would stand up to the Sovereign Almighty the way Abraham and Moses did. They virtually said, 'Not so, Lord!' They had the audacity to question the divine intention, based on their human understanding of the character, glory, power and love of God. They appealed to God on the basis of His promised mercy, on the basis of the shame that would be brought on His name throughout the nations if He finished off His own people.

If we know one thing about prayer, it is that we are supposed to pray 'according to the will of God', according to God's deepest desires. We know that God, Maker of all, desires that none should perish, that all be brought to the knowledge of the truth, that all be brought to repentance, that all be saved. Is God waiting to answer a pleading prayer from around the world that has not yet been prayed by 100 million followers of Jesus who will not take no for an answer, who will only be satisfied with a heaven that is full and a hell that is (relatively) underpopulated? What could possibly hinder this from happening?

Overcoming strongholds in our own minds

This type of intercession most certainly involves breaking down the stronghold in our own minds concerning the possibilities of God's future for earth and its peoples. Argentinian evangelist Ed Silvoso coined the following definition for a spiritual stronghold, in his book _That None Should Perish!_: 'A spiritual stronghold is a mindset, impregnated with hopelessness, which causes us to accept as unchangeable, that which we know to be contrary to the will of God.'

Contrary to popular thinking and translations, the Greek wording in Matthew 16:18 does not suggest the 'gates of hell' storming against the church, but the church storming against the gates of hell.

If we refuse, for whatever reason, to pray 'that none should perish' and all be saved, would not this very refusal be in itself a 'spiritual stronghold', a blockage, a 'hard ground' in our own head? Would we not have to develop church-planting and mission strategies only after a breakthrough in our own mind and spirit, overcoming any hopeless and limiting thoughts and reasoning in the power and Spirit of the One who came to save the world?

Satan will triumph over every unnecessary person who is in hell because of a sleeping church, a limited vision, a middle-of-the-road approach and Christians only defending themselves, instead of 'prevailing and plundering hell'. What did Jesus mean, after all, when His one definitive statement about the church was that 'the gates of hell would not prevail against it'? Contrary to popular thinking and translations, the Greek wording in Matthew 16:18 does not suggest the 'gates of hell' storming against the church, but the church storming against the gates of hell. Whatever or whoever or wherever those gates are, they will be unable to withstand.

Is it the church which will, in the end, crash the entrance of hell and somehow depopulate it, since hell, we know, was not prepared for people in the first place (Mt. 25:41)? If there was ever a time, given the present population explosion, when even the slightest adjustment to the audacity of our pleading prayer, the size of our vision and daring of our strategies would have maximum consequences, it is now.

The little flock that inherits the Kingdom

Many have said that the 'little flock' Jesus speaks of in Luke 12 means that the church will always be a small minority. Jesus actually does not say that at all. Maybe He spoke quite literally about a 'little flock', the normal small size of His church, gathering in groups of around 10 or 15 in homes. They are to be small flocks with a large inheritance: 'The Father is pleased to give them the kingdom.' The unimpressive structure of a house church should not fool anyone about its spiritual, moral, economic and even political potential: it is God's delight to turn the standards of the world on their heads and let the meek, as Jesus puts it, probably with a 'meek structure', inherit the earth.

God and His vision of what His 'small flock' can and will do is probably 'as high above the earth as the heavens', and will not only stretch us all mightily as we try to come to grips with God's global vision, but leave us completely speechless even in our abilities to 'comprehend in part'. The small flock of a large God may be bigger than the large flock of a small God.

The smaller the church, the larger its growth potential

In a worldwide research project, German church-growth researcher Christian Schwarz has studied the average number of people added to a local church, over a typical five-year period:

Size of church attendance	People added in 5 years	Growth as percentage of the whole church
1–100 (average 51)	32	63
100–200	32	23
200–300	39	17
300–400	25	7
1000+ (average 2856)	112	4

A church of up to 100 attenders (average size in his research: 51) won 32 new people over a period of five years, and grew from 51 to 84 attenders, which is a growth of 63 per cent. In contrast, a large or even megachurch of over 1000 people (average size in his research: 2856) won 112 new people in five years, which is a growth of 4 per cent.

Comparing the growth rate of a church of under 100 with that of a church of between 100 and 200 people, the difference is already very significant, the smaller church showing almost three times the growth rate of the larger. This startling research also shows that a church of 2856, which is 56 times bigger than an average 'small church' of 51, wins only little over three times more people than the small church.

In other words, if we took the megachurch and divided it into 56 churches of 51 people each, they would, statistically, win an average of 1,792 people in the same five-year period, 16 times more than if the megachurch remained as it was. From a different perspective, the average megachurch structure *prevents* 1680 people (i.e. 1792 minus 112) from being won every five years. The bottom line of this research shows that small churches are much more effective in attracting people. The relationship is as simple as a see-saw in the playground: the statistics show that in the overwhelming majority of all cases, as quantity goes up, growth potential goes down.

The quantum leap from organized to organic growth

What Schwarz does not show us, however, is what happens if you compare the growth potential of the organic house church with the organized and traditional 'small church' according to the congregational pattern. It would be like comparing mustard-seed growth with building a pile of rocks. The growing congregational model usually grows by addition; the house churches usually grow by multiplication. One system will result in linear growth, the other in exponential growth. Although we have no global empirical figures for comparison, the signs are very clear that the growth potential continues to increase as the church size continues to go down, and it seems to reach a maximum potential at the size of 10–15 people per church. All of us will have come across numbers games and strategies to save the world, and I very much agree that statistics of this sort should not be taken too literally. For us, they only serve to point out the explosive growth potential of the organic house church.

Smaller churches are usually better churches

Another factor which many have known or at least felt before, and which is now backed up by empirical data from Christian Schwarz's study, is that as the size of the church goes up, usually the quality goes down. A smaller percentage of the overall attenders are using their spiritual gifts in larger churches than in smaller churches. The smaller the church, the better the quality of fellowship. Large churches have a greater tendency to transform attenders into passive consumers of a thrilling programme than small house churches, for whom the involvement of almost everyone is absolutely vital.

A shop-window for God within walking distance of every person

If all people on earth are not only to hear and read but 'see and understand' the gospel (Rom. 15:21), and if the economic situation in the next few decades remains basically the same, meaning that a great percentage of people will not have private transport, a logical answer to this logistical problem would be that we should work, in a united effort, towards the goal of placing a church within walking distance of every person on earth.

In order to make people 'see how they love each other', we would literally have to place the church, the body of Christ, as 'a shop-window for God' in the neighbourhood of every person on the planet. More and more people are now catching hold of this type of apostolic goal as a personal vision for themselves, their movements, their cities, people groups, countries, states, regions and countries.

Chapter 10

Fathering the Next Generation

Who will do all the work?

Who will be the people to start all those necessary house-churches? Who will be carrying out the fivefold ministries? Who will do all the work? And where will all those people come from? Ultimately, we would all agree that it will have to be ordinary people made extraordinary by God – people who, as in the old days,

> *Could it be that we may actually be doing most of the training and developing of elders – and therefore church-planters – but not seeing the connection between the role of sound and healthy families and church-planting?*

may still smell of fish, perfume and revolution. If elders are to father house churches, we will simply have to spot and develop potential elders. Elders are people of wisdom and reality and, typically, fathers or mothers of families. Many 'family ministries' already exist today. Could it be that we may actually be doing most of the training and developing of elders – and therefore church-planters – but not seeing the connection between the role of sound and healthy families and church-planting?

Policemen without uniforms?

Leadership development within our traditional structures has often meant preparing people to grow up in
order to fit the existing structure and maintain it and, if
possible, extend it. Leaders have often been 'made' by pre-
scribing authority to them, 'ordaining' them. In many
countries, however, this type of authority is deeply suspect. Many have seen political or religious leaders with
honey on their lips and an iron whip in their hand. One
of these groups is what is called 'Generation X', the
bulk of the present young generation in the West. The last
type of authority which Genera-
tion X, and other groups like
post-communist Russians, will
accept, is institutionalized
authority, prescribed from
above, authority which needs a
superstructure to authorize it
with titles, badges, medals and
uniforms. Imagine a policeman who, in his spare time, is
standing at a crossroads without his uniform, trying to
direct the traffic. He will be ridiculed, ignored or even run
over by the cars, because he does not wear his uniform.
Many churches feel like this unhappy policeman, sensing
that the population does not take the religious collars,
crosses, colourful shirts, robes and headgear sufficiently
seriously. People feel that the life of the church as they
have experienced it does not match the revolutionary
message of the gospel they sometimes hear. As a result,
they take the liberty of ignoring church uniforms, and
authority prescribed and ordained from a distant superstructure. They require, in other words, leadership that is
earned amongst them, proven in gifted servanthood on a
daily basis.

> *People feel that the life of
> the church as they have
> experienced it does not
> match the revolutionary
> message of the gospel
> they sometimes hear.*

Does our leadership training truly develop leaders?

Traditionally we have been asking God to 'fling out workers into the harvest', praying for Him to provide more people. As the twelve disciples did this, they became an immediate answer to their own prayers: they got flung out themselves first (Mt. 9,10). If we truly desire to see more people involved in taking on responsibilities in the Kingdom of God, we will invariably be involved ourselves and drawn into the process. For this purpose we today arrange recruiting conferences for young people, see them dedicate themselves at 'altars', arrange mission mobilization events, beat the drum for our mission group or organization, conduct leadership and training seminars, establish and multiply Bible schools and theological training institutes, and write books and teaching materials. This is good, but is it good enough? At the heart of spiritual leadership in the New Testament is not head knowledge or special abilities or even the wish to lead, but an innocent capacity to obey God. I believe it was my friend Greg Groh from the World Leadership Council who said to me: 'I have only one problem with current Christian leadership training. It does not train leaders.'

Training leaders or raising sons?

As the ministries of Barnabas and Paul, then Paul and Timothy, or Elijah and Elisha show, apostolic and prophetic ministries produce new people, very much as fathers 'give birth' to sons and daughters. Paul writes to Galatians: 'My dear children, for whom I am again in the pains of childbirth until Christ is formed in you ... I am perplexed about you' (Gal. 4:19,20). He does not address them as his students, disciples or trainees, but as his children. This is probably one of the true

254   *Houses that Change the World*

hallmarks of New Testament and contemporary apostolic people: they are constantly in spiritual labour. It is unnatural for a man to give birth to children, since that is the gift of women. Still, people are born again by the Spirit, and, I suggest, also born into ministry by the same Spirit. As any Bible school dean will agree, the mechanical process of a student going though some teaching modules and experiencing a transfer of head knowledge will not produce strong leaders. There is much more to it, namely the fathering of spiritual sons and daughters. The core issue is this: we may want to train many new leaders, but God the Father wants us simply to raise spiritual sons. To raise a son is much more than just teaching him a few lessons or courses. As anyone with children knows, there is no pain-free parenting. It is utterly involving, frustrating and exhilarating at the same time; it brings you to your knees or drives you up the wall, makes you weep and laugh, and usually you end up perplexed, just like Paul, about your children and, often enough, about yourself. It is the most engaging task I know. This is the price we need to pay for the spiritual generations to come. Are we ready for this? Cheap training shortcuts, emergency crash-courses, relationally uninvolving seminars and purely academic efforts are as effective as quick-fix parenting and pain-free book-writing.

Church-planting starts in the kid's room

One of the qualifications of a biblical elder is that 'he must manage his own family well and see that his children obey him with proper respect. If anyone does not know how to manage his own family, how can he take care of God's church?' (1 Tim. 3:4). This first litmus test of authenticity of someone's character and personality through his very

own children is so inge-
nious and natural that I
sometimes jokingly remark
that 'church-planting starts
in the kid's room'. Healthy
children respect true
authority, but naturally
avoid empty authoritarian
behaviour and cold dicta-

> *His Holy Spirit, residing in kids who are born again, is not two, five or seven years old, but it is the age-old Holy Spirit, capable of theoretically doing anything that a mature and old disciple can do in the power of the same Spirit.*

torship without proper character. If ever a father makes
the mistake of demanding and not commanding obedience, he has lost his child right there. No amount of
stubborn threats and punishment will win back that lost
trust; only true brokenness, humble tears and asking forgiveness from your own child will get you ahead.

I strongly believe that God can use young children for
his purposes, because His Holy Spirit, residing in kids
who are born again, is not two, five or seven years old, but
it is the age-old Holy Spirit, capable of theoretically doing
anything that a mature and old disciple can do in the
power of the same Spirit. However, there is a difference. It
has become fashionable to arrange short-term evangelistic ministry and summer outreach trips for young kids
and unmarried adults, and the results of such trips for the
kids are mostly positive. Most pastors I have asked, however, agree that for the establishment of churches, evangelistic short-term ministries of young unmarried adults is
rather limited. Although Jesus himself and people like
Timothy were unmarried, God has chosen generally to
link the establishing of His church with the socially
proven lives of fathers and mothers, qualifying in real life
as capable fathers for their sons and daughters, and
reflecting the loving and passionate heartbeat of the
Father in heaven.

Master and disciples, not teacher and students

The issue of raising a new generation of spiritual sons and daughters for bringing in God's harvest is about life transfer. Life was literally breathed and rubbed into others. It was caught over a period of time, not just taught. The biblical model of doing this was through the close and natural, and even lifetime, relationship between a master and his disciples, a father and his spiritual sons who imitate him naturally and unashamedly. A professor brilliantly teaching his students, but not being much involved in their lives, is no match for the efficiency of a father and his spiritual sons. Masters and spiritual fathers do not just train their disciples in the technical sense: they give birth to them and raise them, and quite literally, as Jesus did with his disciples, inject their spirit into them and therefore reproduce themselves.

A programme can no more make a disciple than a machine can make a son. I have sat under many fascinating professors and teachers, but to be honest, I usually do not remember a word they said – but I remember the way they were, and that is what has stayed with me. As master and disciples share lives, not 45 minutes in a sterile classroom every week, they are able to love, show, coach, correct and encourage each other. They make themselves vulnerable to each other. This is what it takes to make disciples, and to make disciples is one of the core commands of Jesus. We cannot delegate this task to paper or a programme or do it by radio or from a pulpit or a director's chair. A programme can no more make a disciple than a machine can make a son. Discipleship is about people getting involved with each other. It is about masters and disciples, spiritual fathers and sons, finding each other; and then it involves a process of nurturing and release.

Sons without fathers

Sons and spiritual disciples do not really want to be part of your wonderful programme: they want you! Have you ever wondered why it is that many of today's church leaders are in their leadership position not *because of* but *in spite of* those who should be their spiritual fathers? Why is it that, unlike Jesus, many contemporary leaders not only have a history of breaking away from existing churches, denominations and organizations in order to live out their own calling, but have a sizeable track record of spiritual sons turning away from them also, often bitterly disappointed, to start their own thing? Does the trauma which goes with having to break away in order to break out affect – and in fact curse – Christian ministry much more than we ever dared to think?

The way we inherit is as important as what we inherit

It is beyond question that, for the remaining task of discipling the 230-plus nations of this world, we will need scores of bold, radical, fearless and faithful leaders, young and old. Most of the older generation of Christians are in agony about where the young and able ones are who will step into their footsteps and carry on their life's work. Could it be that this fear is related to the way the generations are currently relating to each other? Has a pattern emerged, woven through with habitual sin, which effectively makes the young and older leaders split from each other before they can become effective together? Or worse, has an unbroken curse been handed down through the generations leaving both of them trapped, hindering the effective passing of the baton from one generation to another to see God's work on earth completed?

Why is it that spiritual initiatives are still constantly being reinvented by the emerging generations, who feel they need to break away from their spiritual or physical father's beaten path and start all over again, rather than finishing an inherited course? I suspect that the way we inherit is as important as what we inherit. Many older leaders, just like some fathers, are so afraid of letting other and younger leaders take over, that they only release the steering wheel as they literally drop dead. If we inherit over a dead body, or from somebody who only grudgingly, or because of some serious sickness, gives up control, it will only be a bitter–sweet experience.

I have often wondered why Jesus could 'retire' at an age of approximately 33, and not 65. Once His redeeming work on the cross was done, He could go home because He had introduced and instated His disciples into the proper inheritance of the Father in heaven. I know that I am not much qualified to write this, since I often feel to be just a miserable father myself. But I am toying with the idea of retiring at 50, and I dream of using all the energy that God may leave me to invest in the up-and-coming generation, and be available to as many as I can as one of their spiritual fathers.

'Be a father to him'

One December evening in 1996 I was sitting with Rudi Pinke of Christliches Zentrum Frankfurt. I admire Rudi, a former journalist, since I feel he is one of those radical new church leaders, ready to go and do the unthinkable. I shared with him what I felt the Holy Sprit is doing around the world, about the reinvention of house churches, multiplying cell churches, miracles, strategic alliances and all that. Suddenly he looked at me and exclaimed: 'Wolfgang, we here are just not radical enough!' Now if it had been almost any other pastor I know, I would most likely have politely smiled and thought to myself, 'You don't know how right you are.' But this was Rudi Pinke. And there in his office it struck me. To be radical is not the point. It is not nearly enough. And I was reminded of another incident that had happened recently.

There he stood, one metre away from me, pale, stiff and seemingly unable to move. I had just preached in this radical church in Germany, a typical mission-mobilization type of a sermon: go and see your nation discipled, for God's sake think the unthinkable, do the undoable, raise the dead, and plant 50,000 churches in Germany. The pastor had made an altar call. For some reason I never like altar calls, and usually try to escape to the side. But the young man had caught me even as I was hiding behind a pillar. He came close and stood in front of me. I remembered that he was a youth leader in the church, deeply committed; he knew his stuff, was respected, and, I am sure, was at that time included in many prayers of unmarried girls in the church.

I did not know what to do, so I prayed that God could give me a hint. 'Be a father to him,' I heard God's Spirit speak to me. So I hugged this young man, and prayed like a father would pray to bless a son. I was stunned with his reaction. He melted like an block of ice in my arms, cried streams of tears, and just soaked in whatever there was to be soaked in. Later, his mother joined us, and repented of the sin of having her own plans for her son, rather than letting God take charge of him. I will never forget that incident. We just stood there; he wept, she wept, I wept. And there something dawned on me for the first time.

At first, I was just wondering whether it is of any significance that the very last word of the Old Testament is 'curse'. Malachi 4:5,6 reads: 'See, I will send you the prophet Elijah before that great and dreadful day of the LORD comes. He will turn the hearts of the fathers to their children, and the hearts of the children to their fathers; or else I will come and strike the land with a curse.' What immediately follows is a history of rebels and political factions, war and tensions, a leaderless time which the Bible prefers not to even mention. Could it be that the current unredeemed, unrestored relationships between fathers and children is not just the old generational problem we all know, circling around issues like contemporary fashions, the length of hair and the style of music, but the spiritual result of fathers withholding their hearts from their children? They do it usually by repeating an ungodly tradition, because their own fathers have done it too. As a result, we may well be handing down a curse through the generations, instead of releasing blessing.

> *Could it be that the current unredeemed, unrestored relationships between fathers and children is not just the old generational problem we all know, circling around issues like contemporary fashions, the length of hair and the style of music, but the spiritual result of fathers withholding their hearts from their children?*

The tears that break the curse

Just imagine yourself, a spiritual son, resting at the heart of a spiritual father who is expressing his unconditional love for you, who tells you that you are the jewel of his life, someone to be very proud of, a dream come true, and who leaves a fond tear of fatherly love and affirmation on your cheek as you leave him. Or imagine yourself, a spiritual father, hugged by a son, physically warming your heart, who tells you how proud he is of you, how secure he is in your presence, who openly admires your wisdom, gives you his heart on a silver platter and says: 'Tell me how I can be like you. What shall I do with my life?'

In that instant, something happens in both of you. A wholeness is restored which the devil wanted to steal. The father is enabled to stand up and be radical, forgetting what the neighbours are going to think and say, and boldly stand up for Kingdom values and visions, because something gives him almost unbearable strength and drive: a son believes in him and has given him his heart. In a similar fashion something clicks in the heart of the son. He is endowed with a sense of security and purpose. He can boldly go through closed doors, raise the dead, do what no one has ever dared to do before, because there is a father who loves him, believes in him, has said so and has proved it. In fact, in both of them a curse is broken, and a blessing is released.

Pounding on the door

I will never forget an incident which happened during a DAWN conference in Nottingham in 1995. I was in a seminar on youth-church planting. A young man in his early twenties stood up and expressed his passion and concern for his generation, and related the story of how they had started a youth church. Suddenly, he surprised everybody by taking up a chair and, starting to pray, pounding the chair violently against the floor.

The reaction of the spectators varied. Some were appalled by this obvious un-English and indisciplined behaviour: 'That chair might break!' Others were just puzzled.

As I sat there, I felt God's Spirit say to me: 'See, he is knocking at the door of the Father's heart with all his might. He had a lot of teachers, professors, directors, coaches, preachers, almost anything – except a spiritual father.'

A rebel is a radical without the father's heart

If fathers and mothers turn their hearts to their sons and
daughters, and sons and daughters turn their hearts to their
fathers and mothers – according to the biblical pattern
it should start with the fathers! – a new and healthy framework will be created, within which true, bold, radical
Christianity and leadership can and will grow. If this does
not happen, boldness will quickly turn into rebellion, and
use its strength to break and tear, rather than to build and
complete. We have many radicals today, in both generations, most of them growing into rebels. A rebel is a radical
without the father's – or the son's – heart. He is left with one
of the deepest traumas anyone can have: he is lost in the
generational stream without a secure anchor, and has
become a spiritual orphan.

When heaven opened at the time of the baptism of Jesus,
most of us remember the dove. But there was a voice
from heaven of a father who publicly declared: 'This is my
beloved Son, in whom I am well pleased!' Could it be that
this was the real start and launching pad for the ministry of
Jesus, the Son and lover of His father, the greatest secret
of His strength hidden in the statement: 'I and the Father are
one'?

Spiritual orphans

Whoever is launched into existence without having been
given a father's heart may very well end up a spiritual
orphan. A study done by Dr Pierre Rentchnick in 1975
under the title *Orphans Rule the World* has proved that
many people who made their radical mark on history
were in fact orphans. Nearly 300 of the world's most influential politicians where orphans: Alexander the Great,
Julius Caesar, Charles V and Louis XIV, George

Washington and Napoleon, as well as Lenin, Hitler, Stalin and Castro. This is similarly true for religious leaders: Moses, Buddha, Confucius and Mohammad where all orphans. The trauma of growing up fatherless bottled up enormous energy which they used to prove themselves to the world, because they had never heard a loving father say, 'Well done, son!', never rejoiced, relished and relaxed in that knowledge and security.

Many churches, denominations and organizations have unwillingly given birth to a wave of children who are spiritual orphans, fatherless leaders who had to break away in order to obey their life-calling. Many people in Europe lament that two world wars have killed our fathers; whole generations have been bombed away. When the wars started, 'all the daredevils went to the front and died. Who was clever enough to stay behind? The accountants. And today we have inherited their genes and drown in a flood of bureaucracy!' says my friend Bob Smart of Reading, UK, with that dark, spot-on English humour. He meant it as a joke, but maybe there is more truth to it than meets the eye.

Spiritual fathering is one of the greatest needs of today's Generation X, many of them unable to believe in the consistent and unfailing love of the father in heaven because of their fathers on earth. They are over entertained and underfathered. They are, in fact, spiritual orphans.

Turning hearts in order to prepare people for Jesus

In Luke 1 there is a startling verse about John the Baptist: 'He will go on before the Lord, in the spirit and power of Elijah, to turn the hearts of the fathers to their children and the disobedient to the wisdom of the righteous – to make ready a people prepared for the Lord.' In obvious fulfilment of the Old Testament prophecy of Malachi about the 'second Elijah', his ministry is to roll out the red carpet for King

Jesus. His own father Zechariah doubted: 'How can I be sure of this?', since he might have had other great plans for an eventual son. Zechariah had to undergo a radical spiritual surgery before he was to be filled with the Spirit and join his own son in prophetic ministry (Lk. 1:76). The life-message of John the Baptist was 'Repent!', turning the hearts of the fathers away from their sins and traditions and their eyes towards the coming son, Jesus: 'Look, the Lamb of God . . . This is the one!' (Jn. 1:29, 30). The turning of the hearts to the Father and His Son is in obvious relationship with 'making ready a people prepared for the Lord'. John had a prophetic ministry: turning the hearts in order to make people ready for Jesus.

Releasing nations

Brian Mills, intercessory prayer leader in England and a dear fatherly friend, is one of those men and women who still can weep unashamedly and openly; one who loves children and therefore has more spiritual children than he and his wife probably know. As we discussed this issue of parents and children he told me how England gave birth during the period of the British Empire to some 44 nations. But instead of giving her heart to those children, Britain took what was most precious, their natural and human resources and the political fame of ruling those nations. Britain robbed the children instead of fathering them, and now has a spiritual debt to repay to nations like India, which still celebrates its independence, but needs help to move on into liberty. As individual and spiritual fathers turn their hearts to their children, denominations to their unwanted offspring, organizations to their breakaways, and colonial nations to the emerging nations, and not only in symbolic or fleeting acts of political diplomacy, it will cause a release because it will be breaking a curse.

Encouraging healthy radicals

To disciple whole nations by spreading house churches into every corner until countries are full of them is a radical thought for many and requires a special

> *Yesterday's radicals are often today's trusted pillars of the church.*

kind of faith. But yesterday's radicals are often today's trusted pillars of the church. If we want to see a multitude of Christians take up their calling and inheritance in the Kingdom of God and go and see whole nations, people groups, cities and regions discipled, we need to provide for them an atmosphere and an environment where they can be growing up healthily and without the trauma of being spiritual orphans. To be radical usually means to be ready to walk on thin ice, and even if no one we respect is there to really believe in us, we would still do it.

I would like to call us all to a prophetic, concerted and systematic effort to encourage the remaining and emerging fathers among us to start this process, and give their hearts to the sons. That in turn will allow the sons also to give their hearts to their fathers.

This last prophecy of Malachi seems to me the most impossible and challenging thing of all, staunchly resisted by any devil on earth, since he knows and fears what would happen. We therefore need to call upon God and his Holy Spirit Himself to come and melt the hearts, crack the walls, bridge the gaps, break the curse, apply the redemption Jesus has accomplished at the cross in our lives and churches and organizations, and pray to God to light fires, throw bombs, thunder from heaven or do whatever it takes to make fathers and sons run into each other's arms.

Following anti-leaders

Many prophets say that the future leaders of the Kingdom of God will have no faces and no titles. They will be nobodies, anti-leaders, without impressive titles on their visiting cards; they will be frail and weak rather than powerful and overwhelming. They will clearly not be stars. They prefer to be known as a father rather than a leader, and be in broken agony about the lost rather than boasting shamelessly about their latest 'ministry victory' and about what God has achieved through them and their great programmes.

The new leaders will not be interested in control and power; they will be actively ignorant of their public image, deaf to the cheerful lures of worldly Christian fans wanting to elect their next King Saul, only to see them riding on a wave of human applause into spiritual oblivion, cashing in here on earth whatever awards God wanted to give them in heaven. But who listens to prophets? Have we not always stoned them in the name of good old tradition?

Three stages to becoming effective disciples

God's eyes are constantly searching for whom He can send. Once He finds somebody who is willing, He will guide them and gift them and bring them into relationships with the right people. I have observed the following three stages through which a person usually goes in order to become an effective disciple and then an effective discipler.

1 Spiritual spring-cleaning
People are sinners and need to repent, repent of each known sin and have a clean past. Most people have not only sinned

but have been sinned against, through wrong and ill-treatment, hate, anger, jealousy etc. Here you may need inner healing and counselling to 'forgive those who have sinned against you, and bless those who have cursed you'. Redeem your relationship with your father or children, as I have tried to explain above. Accept as a God-given fact how, when and where you were born in the natural sense of the word. It is all in God's plan that you should be fat or thin, male or female, bright or not so bright, or from a Hindu or Christian or Muslim background. Thank God in detail for all he has invested in you so far. As a clear result, you will be able to say with the Psalmist: 'I am wonderfully made.' Thank God for your natural and acquired gifts and abilities: He did not teach you to swim in order to let you drown. Be reasonable in the core disciplines of Christianity and display fruits of the Spirit in a Christian's life: prayer, joy, peace, patience etc. Once you have a redeemed past, you will start to have a redeeming future. You will not have to carry traumas, wounds, hurts and other spiritual mortgages into your ministry life and hurt others. I call this phase 'spiritual spring-cleaning', the process of accepting and appropriating personally the salvation Jesus has given us, which cleanses us, as much as possible, from sin and the consequences of sin. It is just as in real life: when we have washed and brushed, and put on clean clothes, then we can go out in public.

2 Discovering spiritual gifts – the tools of the trade

Each Christian has been given one or more spiritual gifts (1 Cor. 12–14; Rom. 12) at the time when Jesus started to live within the believer through the Holy Spirit (Rom. 8). These gifts are supernatural empowerment from God, the tools of the trade for Christians, necessary to be a useful team member with a master-builder. A certain number of Christians are then gifted and called in a special way and

develop into one of the five equipping ministries mentioned in Ephesians 4:11. They stop just having a gift, and
start becoming one. There are three ways to discover
spirituals gifts:

a. *'By their fruits will you know them'*: in the context of
   ministry and church life, believers can help each other
   identify their area of spiritual giftedness by tasting and
   telling about each other's fruits.
b. *Spiritual gift analysis*: appropriate tools and tests such
   as spiritual gift tests are available in most nations.
c. *Prophetic ministry*: prophetic people often can 'see' the
   area of people's giftedness. In this case, associate yourself with a person who is years and miles ahead within
   the ministry area in which God has gifted you. Carry
   their bags, learn from them; if possible live with this
   person, and rub off as much as you can, by asking
   question after question. Be their disciple.

3 *Spritual apprenticeship: practical, specialized training*
Be trained for a few days, months or years in relationship
with and under the supervision of someone more experienced than yourself, preferably someone in the very area
of your own ministry calling. In this way, prophets would
train junior prophets, apostles junior apostles, mature
evangelists junior evangelists and so on. The apprentices
would carry the bags for their masters, pour water over
their hands, live with them, see how they function.
Instead of idol-worshipping 'a holy man' at a distance,
they would get to know a person of God and learn from
them in real life. Spiritual superstars and unapproachable
giants in 'a class of their own' have done more to prevent
others discovering their own giftings and callings than
many may realise. If you learn from a person who has the
same gifting and a similar calling to your own, your

learning curve will be phenomenal: you will learn in the very area of your giftedness, which will be exciting, and you will also dictate the speed of learning – your learning curve will be as steep and as fast as you come up with really good questions.

This should all be carried out in the natural and healthy context of house churches. Training should not necessarily be an 'out-of-body experience'. As house-church planting establishes and multiplies new groups of believers in homes, the best way to be trained to do this is to see it working at first hand, to get infected with the pattern, so we can reproduce it wherever we go.

Time and finances

Many people ask when they should 'come forward for ministry', as we say in Asia, and who will pay the bills. I have room here only to answer briefly: you come when you know you are called, and what God orders, He pays for.

The problems often begin with a nation's whole educational system. It is usually geared towards preparing a person for a place in the economic work structure of

> *God is able to provide for those who serve Him wholeheartedly.*

the world, from which, in more ways than one, God wants to save us. One pastor recently put it like this: the most crucial years of youth are spent – or shall we say sacrificed? – on the altar of education, with the parents pouring the fuel on the fire. As a result, many people only think of being discipled in their late twenties, and then think back to the many 'lost years' earning degrees they never needed anyway. God is able to provide for those who serve Him wholeheartedly. Those to whom you minister will be empowered by God to empower you, including financially. One or two house churches of 15 people each can easily finance one full-time Christian in the West, and between five and ten house churches can finance a full-time prophet, evangelist, apostle or pastor in the rest of the world. You will experience the promise contained in Matthew 6:33 first hand as you go in faith and make your first steps.

Chapter 11

Models of Church Multiplication

How to plant churches without manufacturing them

If you want to multiply churches, stop 'planting churches'!

Jesus never gave an express command to go and plant churches. Many church-planting movements have struggled in vain to show biblical evidence that the New Testament actually commands church-planting. The whole core of the message of Jesus revolves around three very basic commands:

⟨ 'Repent of your sins.'
⟨ 'Love your neighbour.'
⟨ 'Go and make disciples.'

This is our part. God's part is: 'I will forgive; I will accept your neighbour also; I will build my church.'

If we assume God's own part for ourselves, trying to build His church, we will in a way usurp a responsibility that we do not have, taking the reins out of God's hand and assuming we can still go and build the 'temple of God' any time of the day. This is not only a solemn action, but a usurpation of what is God's prerogative, an intrusion into an area of responsibility which God has kept for Himself. If we do not stop, we may find ourselves manufacturing churches, creating assembly lines for them, franchising churches, experimenting with churches, building what look like churches: but we might simply be like Saul, starting to usurp a ministry which was not his, sacrificing on the altar which only the prophet was supposed to do.

If we do what we are supposed to do, God will do what He promised to do, and build His church.

As we allow ourselves to become part of God's plan by accepting our very own responsibility to repent, love and disciple, He will use us accordingly in multiplying house churches. If we do what we are supposed to do, God will do what He promised to do, and build His church. In this sense, true church-planting starts when we stop trying to manufacture them. Discipling is at the very core of God's message, and is a simple and effective way of multiplying ourselves. As we multiply ourselves, Jesus will be able to multiply churches, made up of multiplied disciples.

Five organic stages

The church should be where the people are, in order to saturate society with the glory of God (Mt. 13:33, Rom. 15:18–21). Each church should therefore be a 'shop-window for God', where people can see God and exclaim: 'See how they love each other.' This needs to happen repeatedly, locally, convincingly, in order to allow neighbours of the churches to become and remain disciples of Jesus Christ.

Most churches go through five organic stages in their developing process and lifespan, which can be compared with the development of a human being:

1 *Conception*: the spiritual seed of a new church is conceived by someone, either individual or corporate. The person(s) is (are) now 'pregnant with an invisible church'. It can be a direct word of the Lord, a vision, a calling, a growing conviction, or just being part of a church-planting movement.

2 *Pre-natal phase*: during this planning time, the church of the future is being discussed (who, where, when, how, why) and everything is prepared for the birth. This is a good time for inspired dreaming about the future, just as parents do when they know a child is on the way.

3 *Delivery*: the time of actually planting the church, when it begins to function as an organic entity.

4 *Visible growth phase*: the church grows and matures by addition and, as with any adult person, finally reaches the time when the organic growth reaches its maximum point.

5 *Multiplication*: this is the time when the church multiplies itself, or, if it fails to do so during the appropriate time-span, usually enters a spiritual menopause and starts to die. During the healthy multiplication process, the fivefold ministry develops, and starts to ensure quality development and continuing multiplication.

Practical models of church-planting

Since there are many cultures, languages, ministries and circumstances, there are probably countless ways to plant churches. Again, we should be creative, and not blindly copy other people's models, looking for recipes for success and failing to listen to God individually. This is why God chooses the apostolic and prophetic ministries to 'lay the foundations', to do the founding and planting work, because of their in-built ability to initiate and invent, to be uniquely pro-active and prophetic.

However, I want to list some models which seem to repeat themselves around the globe as general or generic models of church-planting. They can serve as initial guidelines and provide insight into some principles, but should not be taken as a blueprint for sure success. We always need to be aware of God's creativity and His probably unique way of starting His church in a specific place and time.

1 The 'House of Peace' model

The goal is to plant a multiplying house-church movement in an area. A New Testament model for this is Luke 10, where disciples go two by two and stay in the house of 'a man of peace', a person who is not necessarily a Christian but is ready to open his house and his family for the message and presence of ambassadors of the Prince of peace.

A typical process of planting such a house-church often has seven steps:

a. *Christians start sharing their own life* with its inbuilt gospel message for a period of a few days or some weeks with a 'man of peace', who could be a Christian or a God-fearer. They literally live with the family that has opened its door. These not-yet Christians may have become interested after an event such as a public or publicized healing or exorcism, or a conversion, or they may be seekers asking for a church to be established in their own home or the home of a neighbour or friend.
b. *Model a house church* with them and for them, eating, praying, sharing together, teaching each other how to live according to the word of God.

c. *Establish local elders* right from week one by talent-spotting the future elders and spending significant and special time discipling this person or persons. At this stage, not only can the gift of prophecy or spiritual discernment be very helpful, but we can simply observe to whom people 'naturally' look for leadership.

d. Insist on developing *local and not foreign patterns* of church.

e. *Build organically* and ensure church multiplication as, or before, the house church reaches its organic optimum, the border-line where it still is organic, but in danger of becoming organized. This needs to be built into the thinking of the new Christians from the beginning.

f. *Establish a local model of celebration,* if possible, with a number of house churches meeting together, or with other churches in the same area linked through the existing or emerging fivefold ministries.

g. Ensure that *apostolic and prophetic mentoring* is established and the house church pattern is able to reproduce itself.

As I said before, many house churches today have between 8 and 15 members, and typically multiply every six to nine months. Many of them are fathered by an unpaid elder, usually working together with elders of other house churches for contact, teaching and planning. Sizes and forms of house churches vary greatly. In former communist Bulgaria, some house churches even met in houses for celebrations, gathering up to 250 people quietly in order not to attract attention from neighbours. In some house churches in China, during such celebrations in the home, sometimes more than 1000 people were baptized.

Some house churches meet at the same home, others in

four or six different places during the week, in order not to attract too much attention and allow for a number of hosts to be involved. There are 'house' churches which meet on occasion in caves, or sometimes simply rent a bus to show a few visitors around and have a teach-in in the process, or meet in a hotel room every now and then, under a tree, in an office at night-time, in a restaurant family room, on a boat or ship, or many other places. But the main heartbeat of the house church happens in the very houses of the members.

2 The family approach to church-planting

This church-planting method does not build by winning only individuals for Christ, but a whole family unit. It seeks to start a new house-church with a whole, newly converted family, which is then linked with other families into multiplying house churches. This is geared to seeing household conversions occur, as in the case of Cornelius (Acts 10) or Lydia (Acts 16), and then forming house churches in the homes of the converted family.

This is a three-step model which was developed in a predominantly Muslim context, but should be considered as only one of many ways to do it:

a. Pass out the word that you are ready to pray, free of charge, in the name of Jesus for anyone with problems.
b. If someone requests your ministry, ask in a friendly way for two conditions to be met: (1) I am ready to come only if the whole family is present, because I do not want to do anything behind your back and I do want you to feel safe on your own ground. (2) If I come, I want you to give me permission to explain what I am going to do when I pray in the name of Jesus, so that you can be sure I am not practising magic. If invited,

the church-planter can share the gospel of the Kingdom with the whole family present. No one will inter-
rupt, because they want him to pray. After his
presentation of the gospel, he may go and pray for the
sick or demon-possessed person. He prays aloud, and
usually leaves straight after his prayer. If something
happens and people are healed or delivered, it is much
better to respect the dignity of the family and let them
think over what they have heard and seen in the
privacy of their own home. Otherwise they could feel
'a religious defeat' in the presence of someone from
another faith.

c. If the family has decided, after a period of reflection,
that they want to know more about Christ, they will
usually ask the church-planter to come again. This
time, he again has one condition: the whole family
should be present, like last time. If they agree, he goes
with the firm intention of calling the whole family to
faith in Christ and leading them into a family-based
conversion, starting a church with them that very day.

3 Radio church-planting

This strategy uses the existing medium of radio in an
apostolic way to plant
churches. Rather than evangelizing the many in order to
get the response of the few,

> *The traditional evangelis-
> tic radio programme usu-
> ally produces the SRC, the
> Single Radio-Christian.*

and build them up into follow-up programmes, this strategy is geared to building a movement, which is specially
suitable for geographically disparate nations, or where
there is a severe limitation on Christians meeting together.
It could happen in four phases, similar to a model practised by FEBC in China or IBRA Radio in the Middle East.

Phase 1

This phase usually already exists. It is the traditional evangelistic radio programme usually producing the SRC, the Single Radio-Christian, who has decided to follow Christ through the messages heard on the radio, but, as in the case of the estimated 3–5 million SRCs in the Middle East, may never see another Christian in their entire lifetime. They miss out on the community and fellowship aspect of Christianity, and often remain lonely, weak, and sad. Traditional follow-up patterns like Bible correspondence courses do not significantly change the SRC pattern, and have only a very limited potential to reach the millions of listeners.

Phase 2

An additional programme like 'How to be a better Christian', 'How to interpret dreams', or 'How to raise Children', is introduced by the radio station, geared to breaking the individual listening patterns. The SRCs are to invite trusted friends or neighbours and listen to these programmes *together*, with an emphasis on group discussions and studies.

Phase 3

The next step is the introduction of the 'radio church', the 'Church in your house' or any other programme with a culturally appropriate title like 'God in the house'. Its intention is to coach people into becoming a church. Usually this programme consists of a taped house church meeting in the local language and manners of the target group, where the listeners are encouraged to meet and participate according to the house church pattern which is broadcast. The radio takes the place of the apostle or elder for a while. After modelling the house church pattern, the participants can be trained and taught how to plant and form house churches by a short teaching programme on the same radio station. This could happen 30 minutes or an hour after the radio house-church meeting was broadcast, so there is time for a corporate meal, as a part of the house-church experience. After some weeks or months, those who want to continue the new house-church pattern they have observed, practised and been taught, constitute themselves as a new 'radio church'. They then write to the radio station, which in turn informs a local house-church network which can follow up and incorporate the new church into their network.

Phase 4
The emerging house churches are connected to an existing network of churches in their areas to ensure their proper care and further apostolic oversight. FEBC has seen thousands of churches planted that way, and even runs a programme called 'China Dawn' with the goal of planting one million new house churches.

4 *Partnership between crusade evangelism and church-planting*

One of the biggest losses in the concept of 'Crusade evangelism plus follow-up plus integration into local churches' is during step 2, follow-up, and step 3, integration into local churches. Research shows that on average only one per cent of so-called 'new converts', those who have actually prayed to 'receive Christ' at a rally, will actually become members of local churches and go through steps 2 and 3. The rest are not only lost, but often even vaccinated against the gospel, because they say with all seriousness 'I tried it, and it did not work.'

Realistically, rally evangelism will not cease to happen in the foreseeable future, and so we need to look for ways in which this can contribute to church-planting. Two things are required: firstly, an openness and willingness on the part of the evangelist and his team to actually serve and help the local church leadership and their vision in their long-term work of multiplying churches; and secondly, a readiness to combine the evangelistic ministry with local apostolic ministries and develop local patterns of church-planting.

As a result, instead of trying to incorporate seekers into existing churches, losing most of the seekers in the process, the goal is to plant new house churches during the evangelistic event itself. Local or, if necessary, imported apostolic ministries will train existing Christians locally to start house churches several months before the actual rally. Then, up to ten seekers can be directed at the rally itself to register their names with a local house-church elder from their area, who will then invite the seekers within 24–48 hours to a first house-church meeting in their very own neighbourhood, either in the home of one of the seekers, or in the house of the house-church elder. From there it is the responsibility of the house-church leaders to develop this initial meeting into house churches. This should by no means be a follow-up meeting, but the real thing, the house church itself. A religious follow-up meeting is much less attractive than a house-church meeting with a meal: seekers are looking for spiritual parenting more than Bible teaching, and they need to be taught how to live naturally in a Christian way rather than the doctrines of a particular church just yet.

If this is done strategically, out of 10,000 seekers at a large rally, where with the traditional follow-up and incorporation strategy usually about 100 will end up incorporated into churches and 9,900 will not, the retention rate of seekers incorporated into house churches will typically be much higher. Some experiences indicate that retention rates of 10 or even 15 per cent will be possible, and in some extraordinary circumstances even up to 25 or 30 per cent. The fact is, however, that the existing model of evangelism-cum-follow-up is so deeply rooted in our thinking and evangelistic tradition that there are painfully few evangelists today who see the connection between church-planting and evangelism; and given the constant stream of new invitations for them to preach, very few are even considering a change in their model.

A similar approach to house-church planting through the proclamation type of evangelism can be used for showings of the *Jesus* film. Instead of linking this evangelistic tool with the traditional follow-up-cum-incorporation strategy, on that same day or evening of the screening, new churches can be formed with the new seekers. A church-planting team from a local or nearby church can accompany the film team and stay behind after the show for two or three weeks to model house churches and celebrations, praying to detect and train future elders etc. In many countries where the *Jesus* film is shown, between 20 and 50 per cent of those who see the film indicate they would like to follow Christ. This could be a permanent opportunity to start church movements amongst such a high number of seekers in close co-operation with the film teams.

5 *Planting churches by giving others a vision*

Planting churches is a work of the Holy Spirit. Some people, especially apostolic and prophetic people, are uniquely gifted for this and can simply catalyze and enhance the work of the Holy Spirit through other

There are many undiscovered, uninspired and therefore spiritually unemployed church-planters in the world. They need to be strategically recruited to use their gift.

individuals. They inspire and release a vision and new
action in people. They 'make others spiritually pregnant', as
David Yonggi Cho once put it, and new churches can be
planted by inspiring others and giving them a vision to do
so. There are many undiscovered, uninspired and therefore
spiritually unemployed church-planters in the world. They
need to be strategically recruited to use their gift, usually following a three-part strategy: seek and find those who have
church-planting potential; nurture them; release them.

6 *Church-planting in co-operation with the work of the Holy Spirit*

This strategy works by prophetically alerting and mobilizing the churches and movements of God in a given area
to be open to respond to and co-operate quickly with a
special work of the Holy Spirit, 'following up' one of His
sovereign acts of grace. It requires:

a. asking God to extend His hand to do mighty things in
    the name of Jesus (Acts 4:28–32), or recognizing that
    He has already done so and
b. getting the churches ready to respond quickly to
    an 'open door' and a 'white harvest field' by
    planting multitudes of churches quickly through the
    reorganization of resources and people.

There are many examples of this kind of church-planting:
supernaturally prepared revival, national or local crises
leading to a new spiritual hunger amongst people, well-
known power encounters, healings and exorcisms, or a
significant number of people with visions and dreams and
other supernatural experiences which beg for an explanation. Amongst the Turkish Muslims in southern Bulgaria
in the early 1990s a number of churches sprang up

amongst former Muslims due to many unusual healings and exorcisms. Many more churches could have been planted during that period, however, but not many were ready or flexible enough for this window of opportunity.

Chapter 12

Building National Momentum

How to develop a critical mass, and leave the outcome to God

As we lost our goal, we doubled our speed.

Mark Twain

Church history has seen many movements without real momentum. What we really need is momentum, and the movement, I am sure, will follow. A big avalanche starts with a small snowball starting to roll. Then it picks up speed, incorporates more snow and other materials, and builds up momentum, reaches a critical mass, and becomes unstoppable. Webster's dictionary defines momentum as 'a quantity expressing the motion of a body or system, equal to the product of the mass of a body and its speed'.

The house church has a revolutionary and flexible ability to contain and build momentum. It has a huge potential for multiplication, it is flexible, and can adapt quickly to a changing situation. But the main reason why I prefer house churches rather than a movement to build up momentum is that, with momentum built up, only God truly controls the outcome. Should God wish to see 80 or 90 per cent of the world's population saved and incorporated in the church, a movement, no matter how visionary and daring, will most probably simply not have room to accommodate the sheer magnitude of this type of vision. I am quite comfortable with the thought that God can very well accommodate it; and as we do our business of repenting, loving our neighbours and making disciples, He will do His business and build His church.

That does not mean that we should not work towards goals. Goals are manifestations of our vision, statements of faith; they express today what we believe about tomorrow, and they release motivation and focus energy. Goals have an important mobilizing effect and can solve problems which arise if we only stare passively the status quo. Some of the most beautiful developments take place when the body of Christ in a region or nation adopts a collective goal, a corporate mission statement of what the Christians intend to do together about the future.

Imagine a small boy who shoots at a barn door with his bow and arrow. After he shoots, he goes to the door and draws a target around the arrow with a piece of chalk that he takes from his pocket. He then takes a few steps back, puts his hands proudly on his hips and says 'Bull's-eye, right in the middle!' Such behaviour is all right for a small boy, but not for the church. Hebrews 11:1 speaks of a future-oriented faith, a 'certainty of what we do not see'. Is that our real target, or do we, at the end of each year, get out the piece of chalk from our pocket?

Who really rules nations?

In many nations which are caught up between political and religious ideologies, personality cults, moral decay, growing organized crime, ecological and economic developments which seem to have run out of control, one question appears on more and more people's lips: Who really rules nations? And in this regard, an age-old prophecy comes back to many with critical importance: 'Ask of me, and I will make the nations your inheritance, the ends of the earth your possession. Therefore, you kings, be wise and be warned: serve the Lord with fear and rejoice with trembling. Kiss the Son' (Ps. 2). The Lord Jesus Christ is the one of whom this prophecy speaks; He is the very one who said 'Go and make disciples of all nations.' Only a master of nations can speak this type of language unashamedly. Many heads of states, presidents, chancellors, dictators, kings and generals as well as their staff know deep inside themselves, like Pilate of old, that they have no real power 'if it were not given to them from above' (Jn. 19:11).

Since the days of Moses and Aaron, God has raised prophets in every generation to speak into the lives and circumstances of nations. Even today God raises people like Paul Cain (USA), Bernard Ancoma (UK), Jeremy Sunderraj (India) or Erich Reber (Switzerland), who have spoken or will speak regularly into the lives of presidents and other heads of states on God's behalf.

In the very near future many national governments will have to make a tremendous choice, as Jesus fulfils his promise: 'The meek shall inherit the earth.' This God-given inheritance begins with prayer, is received in prayer, and ends with prayer. And only the meek are meek enough to truly believe that; that is why they will experience it.

Discipling nations

It is part of the God-given task of the local church to 'disciple the nations'. Many of us are familiar with discipling one or two people; but how do you disciple a village, a street, a city, a region, a people group or a nation?

How did Jesus disciple people? He invited everyone, and chose some to be His special apostles. Then He shared His life with them, literally showed them how to live, how to die, and how to do the 'works of God'. The result was a mixed people movement: some followed Him, some rejected Him, and all knew about Him.

A disciple of Jesus follows his master in community with other disciples. Jesus never identified Himself fully with any one Christian, but He identifies Himself with 'the church', His body on earth. An individual Christian cannot therefore bring 'the full gospel'; the local church can. The individual Christian 'knows in part', is a member but not a representation of the full body. An individual Christian may act on behalf of Jesus as an 'ambassador of Christ' in a special mission or task. But every believer is ultimately 'dead to himself and alive in Christ'. The new life in the spirit is corporate, not individual. This is important, because it means that the place to disciple people is the local church.

This then has a further important consequence: the way to disciple the nations is through multiplying churches until we have enough of them. No evangelism nor Bible study nor discipleship programme, no matter how excellent and sound, will ever achieve what only the local body of believers can do: to disciple each other and their neighbourhood in real life, teach each other how to live in spirit and truth, change each other's values and lifestyles, offer accountability, correction, love, grace and forgiveness, and be an ongoing mutual encouragement to each other. Only this will make Jesus transparent to each other and the world around us, so that people will not only hear and read about, but truly 'see and understand' (Rom. 15:21) the gospel, so that all may know and see what there is to know and see about Jesus.

A church within walking distance of every person

As long as the church relies on methods and strategies leading to addition and not multiplication, the Great Commission to disciple whole nations will simply never be accomplished.

For each human being to 'see and understand' the gospel of the Kingdom, expressed through the local body of Christ, there needs to be a vibrant fellowship – a shop-window for God – within walking distance of every person in each nation. The yeast of the Kingdom must work 'all through the dough' (Mt. 13:33). No person should be out of earshot of the life of the local church. There should be no 'neutral territory' where people simply do not know about Christ. The church needs to be God's outstation on earth, and needs to be found in every village, community, kraal, neighbourhood, barrio, high-rise building and apartment block of a given nation. These churches need not be perfect, nor will they ever be; but they need to strive as much as they can to be of New Testament quality and calibre, so they will not only fill, but truly 'disciple' a nation. If we need to work at the quality of our churches, then this is the place to begin. If we find we do not have enough churches within our nation, then we have to plant whatever number is necessary. In short, we need the right quality of churches in the right structures in sufficient quantity in all the right places. Most populations multiply because families as their basic unit multiply. As long as the church relies on methods and strategies leading to addition and not multiplication, the Great Commission to disciple whole nations will simply never be accomplished.

Objectives before methods

Since David Barrett published his booklet on 700 global plans to evangelize the world, even more plans and initiatives have developed which all ultimately want to see one or another methodology reach global proportions. Every Chris-

> *We are all in danger of falling in love with methods and starting to believe that the evangelization of the world has to do with spreading this or that method across the globe. This is far from the truth.*

tian, says Pastor Bill Hybels of Willowcreek Community Church, Chicago, should answer three basic questions: What? Why? and How?

1 What do you ultimately want to achieve (and how do you measure it)?
2 Why do you want to achieve this goal and not another?
3 How, i.e. by what means and methods, do you intend to achieve your goal?

The problem is, he says, that many Christians start the wrong way round, with the methods first. Then they find some reasons for keeping on doing what they are doing, and often enough they do not end up getting done what they originally wanted to achieve. The methods have become the goals, and are now an end in themselves. We are all in danger of falling in love with methods and starting to believe that the evangelization of the world has to do with spreading this or that method across the globe. This is far from the truth.

The whole soup is better than just the garnish

One of the excellent slogans of the evangelical Lausanne Movement for World Evangelization calls for 'the whole church to take the whole gospel into the whole world'. The church itself, as we have seen in church history, has been the biggest part of the problem. As God is making the church 'whole' again by allowing it to return to its relational, organic and truly holistic life, a missing piece is restored to the equation: the wholesome nature of the church. In many nations Christians know that 'God seems to be up to something': a 'new apostolic reformation', as C. Peter Wagner calls it in his book *Churchquake*. To illustrate it with a picture: it is as if God is bringing about a new wholeness of the original church, with all necessary elements and ingredients, according to an apostolic and prophetic pattern. If it were a soup which God were brewing, he would be adding spice after spice, ingredient after ingredient, patiently waiting for the whole dish to be balanced and cooked to perfection, before going to feed the world. Many of us humans may not have His heavenly patience, and stand close by the pot, excitedly snatching away a pinch of salt and this or that ingredient, whether it is a new ministry sensation or spiritual wave, creating ministries and organizations around each ingredient and covering the globe with them. But one part is not the whole piece, the ingredient is not the soup, and the effects of even a right and vital ingredient alone will not satisfy for long. Let God finish cooking His soup! God seems to be rebuilding the quality of church first, and if that quality reaches its right proportions, it will find and develop its own structures everywhere, and spread itself globally, propelled by God's means, infecting everything it touches like a heavenly virus, transforming society and all people groups with its God-given spiritual DNA according to the law of critical mass.

Discipling nations, not just filling churches

Being brought up in Germany where there are places today of 20,000 or more people without a single evangelical church, I felt I had entered pure heaven when I arrived in Florida, USA, for the first time. In a superficial research I once did in Sarasota, Florida, I found to my astonishment that in that town there is one evangelical church for about every 650 inhabitants, about 30 times the saturation level of some areas in Europe. However, and I hope my American friends will forgive me for saying so, in everyday life I had to reluctantly admit that I did not feel much difference between the two worlds. 'Some contend that many nations are evangelized – yet they remain significantly undiscipled,' says James Engel. 'A power-driven, top-down style leadership built large churches but tragically fell short in discipling people. As one Christian leader in central Africa said: "The missionaries brought us salvation but never taught us how to live." '

Discipling speaks about introducing a new quality of life first, and then addressing the issue of quantity. Christians in a number of nations have told me something along the following lines: 'If the quality of the present-day church does not drastically improve, we might very well fill our whole country with churches of the prevailing kind, but we will not truly disciple it.'

Jim Montgomery of Dawn Ministries contends that we need to work towards the goal of having one church for every 500 to 1000 inhabitants in each nation. However, this calculation is based on a typical traditional church with an average of between 50 to 100 people. Each person, sociologists say, can effectively influence only a limited number of other people with his or her ideas and values. As there will be many more house churches in the future in each nation, two things may happen. Firstly, the average church may become smaller and sociologically reach fewer people, compared to the traditional 'small church' of 50 to 100 attenders. Secondly, it may simultaneously become more powerful in its witness, because it regains its organic dimension, is placed in real life, and develops a huge multiplication potential. I still believe, therefore, that it is a good strategy for the body of Christ in any given nation, region or city to work towards an initial goal of seeing one church planted for every 500 to 1000 people. Because this process will be geared to reaching a certain kind of saturation level, where a natural limit is reached, this type of process is called saturation church-planting – planting as many churches as are needed to fill the land with the presence of God.

Saturation church-planting, if it is carried out by a significant minority or even the majority of evangelical churches in a nation, creates several important dynamics. It creates a goal-oriented unity based on strategic vision; it reduces competition, and it focuses all our energy in a common direction. We can express these dynamics by means of some graphic illustrations.

How to eat an elephant

The missionary task which Jesus left us is an undertaking of mammoth proportions – as big as an elephant. Its size alone is sometimes depressing and disabling. In Africa, there is a proverb for such cases: 'How do you eat an elephant? Simple: cut it into small pieces!'

In our situation, the incredible responsibility and task of saturating nations with the gospel must be distributed equally on many shoulders all over the world. Each person, each church, each group is to work in their locality doing what only they can do towards the common aim. The individual pieces of the work are ideally just the right size that they can be achieved in a given time-span; the pieces are neither so large that they destroy or discourage us, nor so small that anyone starts to believe that they can do it all alone.

The process is like that of Nehemiah in motivating the people of God to rebuild the walls of Jerusalem together. After sharing the vision with them, he distributed the work towards a common goal, giving each family a piece of work appropriate to them. As a result, they were not just piling up an ungainly heap of rocks, but were truly building a wall.

The rabbit hunt

In a traditional rabbit hunt, hunters hunt a rabbit with dogs. Before the hunt begins, the hunters wait at the starting point with their dogs. It is interesting to look closely at these dogs. Before the race starts, they are all nervous, bark, bite each other, mark some territories, and generally make a din. That all changes, the moment the horn sounds and the rabbit is released. In an instant, these dogs are transformed. They suddenly have a powerful common goal: to get the rabbit! Shoulder to shoulder they chase the rabbit until they catch it. If a dog is more interested in biting other dogs, marking trees or just barking, it does so of its own volition. It opts out of the chase, because it has other priorities.

A rather rough interpretation of this comes from South Africa. Many evangelistic and missionary projects today, and many of our groups, movements, churches and fellowships, can be compared to the dogs in the illustration, often enough as they are before the start! What they truly need is a 'rabbit', a common, concrete aim for working together; a goal which is large enough to challenge each of the participants thoroughly and to motivate them to join

in a common strategic process with a clear focus. Or, as
Paul puts it: 'If the trumpet does not sound a clear call,
who will get ready for battle?' (1 Cor. 14:8).

The competing ants

Picture two ants standing in front of an elephant. They are
arguing over which of them will eat the elephant. The
average evangelical church today has around 100 members. Given certain sociological factors, a local church has,
typically, an evangelistic potential of a factor 10, i.e. it can
effectively touch the lives of about ten times as many people as it has active members. A church of 100, then, can
'reach' around 1000 people in their basic cultural, ethnic
and social layer with the gospel. That means that in a city
of 15,000 inhabitants, we realistically need about 15
churches – one for each 1000 inhabitants. That does not
mean each church will have to grow to 1000 members; it
means that each church has a task – their own piece of the
elephant – of reaching the lives of 1000 people.

Many churches are likely to speak in terms of competition
if a second active church is founded in a small town with
15,000 inhabitants. Not only are both these churches necessary, but another 13 are probably needed as well. There is, in
other words, no need to fight over which ant will eat the
elephant. The only solution is to call for more ants. If the
magnitude of the goal is realistically clear to all churches in
an area, competition is reduced, and erstwhile competitors
can become colleagues and then, hopefully, friends.

PIPS

Where to start and how to arrive at such a nationwide
process? Jim Montgomery has written two books on
this very subject, so I can be very brief in this regard. For

our purposes here, I want to highlight four strategic keys: people, information, prayer and strategy.

People first
'God's method is a man.' Like John Knox of old in Scotland, who prayed, 'God give me Scotland or I die', there are men and women of God who, more than others, know and carry a special agony and burden, a true pain for their nation, city, region or people group. Often they are apostolic or prophetic people, carrying a heavy load on their shoulders which others rarely understand. They are often tearful and broken; in essence they are modern apostolic fathers and mothers, pregnant with God's dreams, ready to give birth to a nationwide vision. Often you will find them ready to carry the last responsibility, go any distance, sell their house, car and spiritual birthright, do anything, walk on water and go through fire if necessary, to see their nation saved.

Historic movements of God never started with committees. They always started with visionary individuals. That is why such people need to come first in priority. They are the ones anointed for leadership and servanthood, and around them a national movement can emerge.

Information
'The truth shall set you free.' The devil likes the Christian endeavour to be clouded in a mist of confusion, where we do not know whether we are marching backwards or forwards, where we do not understand the status quo or the direction we should take from here. That is why we need information. The way to get that information is twofold: we pray, and we ask questions. Prayer will supernaturally reveal things which God wants us to know. Systematically asking questions is what we call research.

Like Joshua and Caleb, as they spied out the promised land, we need Spirit-directed research on the 'harvest force' (the church) and the 'harvest field' (the world). We need to pray about the mismatch between having a church within walking distance of every individual and the situation today. We need to observe the signs of the time; we need to read and interpret the newspapers, statistics, trend analysis and whatever helps us to understand the nature and magnitude of the unfinished task in a nation.

Since we cannot really love what we do not know well, knowing our country better allows us to love it better. Love is one of the strongest motivators on earth. If some people, for example, can read that their own country, district or city really needs 10,000 more churches; and that if the present-day church continues the way it does things today, it will not change the spiritual state of the nation significantly in the next 200 years; and if they then continue reading the newspaper without becoming deeply stirred and restless, then those people might have counted themselves out from the spiritual leadership of a process to change their own country for the time being. They might change their mind later, but those with a passion, on whom God has placed a true spiritual calling and a responsibility, will react differently to figures and facts, because they know these numbers represent a profound challenge: real people with real names, faces, addresses, pains and problems, and with eternal souls at stake, should the church continue on its merry way. And such motivation will mobilize the right people to mobilize others.

Prayer

When a person kneels, God deals. Prayer pleads with God for a nation, and fuels vision and passion. Prayer moves mountains, raises the dead, heals the sick, restores the wounded, blesses those who curse, asks forgiveness for sins and therefore heals the land, and touches the Father's heart. Our strengths sometimes separate us; but prayer humbles us all again, and therefore it unites us. Prayer is not only a means to do better spiritual work, it is spiritual work itself.

Since prayer is essentially communication with God, and good communication goes two ways, prayer also involves God speaking back to us in one way or another. As we pray for the discipling of nations through the mass multiplication of the presence of Christ in house churches, alone and together, God will begin to speak to us. Whether we are praying in small groups or triplets, or as a house church, in traditional churches or in 'houses of prayer for all nations' – places of permanent 24-hour prayer; whether we are praying in our huts or houses, cars or buses, celebrations or networks, God starts speaking to us. He usually alerts the prophets amongst us first (Amos 3:7,8), then unites the church through spiritual vision, combining the fivefold ministries in strategic synergy, prompting us to see in His word revelations which we overlooked for far too long, awakening more and more people in the night to intercede, giving dreams and visions, and ultimately pouring out His Holy Spirit on all flesh to shake us all awake to the redemptive purposes of God in our time.

This type of prayer goes far beyond the 'God-my-name-is-Jimmy, gimme-gimme-gimme' type of prayers, which my friend Dr Victor Choudhrie calls 'goat-prayers', because from the distance you only hear the real key word, 'meee, meee, meee'. True prayer pleads with God about the very destiny of nations. The very people who start to pray these kind of prayers, will be drawn irresistibly into becoming part of the solution to their own prayers. Jesus told his disciples to 'ask the Lord of the harvest to fling out workers into His harvest' – and the next moment they found themselves among those being sent out.

Strategy

Strategy is how we use our limited resources towards a specific goal in the most economic and efficient manner. Strategy focuses energy. As good stewards of God's talents, we will need to work profitably; unlike giving gifts, the right hand here does need to know what the left hand is doing. For national momentum to emerge and grow, we need to search and find those called and gifted by God for that very purpose. We will recognize them working at their special spiritual task. Then we need to find and release God's prayer leaders to initiate and develop prayer momentum, and start a process of research and prayerful analysis to get our facts right. As we pray about this, God may then choose to speak to us about the specific way forward.

As this prophetic message, a spiritual battle-cry that immediately resounds in the hearts of other Christians, is picked up in the house churches through conferences, celebrations or from house to house by word of mouth, God's people will be mobilized towards a common goal and objective. Then they will need a strategic framework for their activities, very much like a river needs a valley or a dam to guide the flood in the right direction. Within this strategic framework, the apostolic and prophetic ministries will be able to function freely, and the churches in each locality, city, region or nation will be able to move as one. 'Find purpose, the means will follow,' says a billboard across my street in Madras. As the body of Christ in a nation finds its redemptive purpose, the means – spiritual generals, equippers, house-church elders, money, plans, methods etc. – will follow.

The carpet

God does not require any of us to understand all this in full. In fact, it might be dangerous and corrupting to know and understand too much. It is simply those who trust God for the ultimate oversight and control in this supernatural partnership between God and humans called house-church planting, who will be able to trust Him also for the very next step. Then we can joyfully do our piece of the work and let Him link it with the rest of the picture; we can carry our cross and leave the fame and glory to be His.

Maybe God is weaving a carpet, where one thread comes together with other threads, until it forms the final product. I think there will be some cries of surprise when we realize that, as we were linking up with people and movements across the world, and doing things which sometimes made no sense whatsoever from a human perspective, God was, in fact, creating a carpet and letting us only see the 'wrong' side of it. Then, at a particular point in history, He will turn the carpet over for everyone to see – and we will be stunned by the genius of the design. And we might be even more stunned when we realize that all of this is part of that red carpet, welcoming back Jesus Christ the Messiah to the earth He created, to take back what is rightfully His. What greater joy for any of us than to have Him come past our group, our town, our city, our country, stop for a moment, smile at us and say: 'well done, you faithful servants!'

Suggested Materials

General reading

Donald McGavran, *Founders of the Indian Church*, CGAI, POB 512, 13/2 Aravamuthan Garden Street, Egmore, Chennai 600 008, India

Christian A. Schwarz, *Natural Church Growth*, Diedersbüllerstr. 6, 25924 Emmelsbüll, Germany. Fax (+49) 4665–252

Watchman Nee, *The Orthodoxy of the Church*, The Gospel Book Room, T.C. 2/1444, Pattom, Trivandrum 4, Kerala, India

Barney Coombs, *Apostles Today*, Sovereign World Ltd, PO Box 77, Tonbridge, Kent TN11 9XT, England

Kari Törmä, *Whole Marriage Ministry*, Keinutie 8.i.54, 00940 Helsinki, Finland. E-mail: kari.trorma@ymca.inet.fi

Roger Ellis and Chris Seaton, *New Celts*, Kingsway Publications, PO Box 827, Eastbourne, BN21 3YJ, England

Larry Crabb, *Connecting*, Word Publishing, Nashville, USA

Literature on house churches

Bob Fitts, *The Church in the House*, 5851 Kuakini Hwy. #107, Kaulua-Kona, HI 96740, USA. Fax (+1) 808–334–9673. E-mail BobFitts@compuserve.com

Dr Met Castillo, *The Church in Thy House*, Alliance Publishers, 13 West Capitol Drive, Pasig, Metro Manila, Philippines

Material on and from DAWN

DAWN Fridayfax: Great stories about the Great Commission, weekly one-page up-to-date information written by Wolfgang Simson about what God is doing around the world. Available on subscription by fax, post and e-mail from Dawn International Network, PF 212, 8212 Neuhausen 2, Switzerland. Fax: (+49) 7745–919531, tel. (+49) 7745–919528. E-mail: 100337.2106@compuserve.com
DAWN web pages: www.Dawn.ch; www.dawneurope.net; www.dawnministries.org; www.wolfgangsimson.de
Jim Montgomery, *DAWN 2000: 7 Million Churches to Go*
Jim Montgomery, *Then the End Will Come* [Sequel to *Dawn 2000*]
Roy Wingerd, *DAWN Research Handbook*
Brian Mills, *Developing a Prayer Strategy*
Cathy Schaller, *DAWN Intercession Handbook*
All these titles are available through Dawn Ministries, 5775 N. Union Blvd, Colorado Springs, CO 85918, USA. Fax (+1) 719–548–7475; tel. 719–548–7460

Literature on cell churches

Ralph W. Neighbour, Jr, *Where Do We Go From Here?*, Touch Publications, PO Box 19888, Houston, TX 77224, USA
Larry Kreider, *House to House*, House to House Publications, 1924 West Main Street, Ephrata, PA 17522, USA
William A. Beckham, *The Second Reformation*, Touch Publications, PO Box 19888, Houston, TX 77224, USA
William A. Beckham, *Church Growth and the Home Cell System*, Church Growth International, Yoido PO Box 7, Seoul 150–600, S. Korea
Howard Astin, *Body and Cell. Making the Transition to Cell Church: A First-Hand Account*, Monarch Books, Broadway House, The Broadway, Crowborough, East Sussex, TB6 1HQ, England
Larry Stockstill, *The Cell Church*, Regal, USA

About the author

Wolfgang Simson works as a strategy consultant, researcher and journalist within the DAWN International Network (see below). After working as a social worker and taxi-driver in Stuttgart, Germany, he studied theology and missions in Switzerland, Belgium and the USA, and travelled extensively to research growing churches and church-planting movements. He is a board member of both the British and the German Church Growth Associations, and editor of the *DAWN Fridayfax*. He is of Hungarian, German and Jewish descent, and has an Indian wife, Mercy. They have three sons, and have recently moved from Madras, South India, to live in Germany.

DAWN International Network

The DAWN International Network is a vision- and friendship-based global strategy network, not an organization with headquarters or members or staff. The goal is to facilitate, be available to and cheerlead national and regional movements for saturation church-planting led by those individuals, groups or movements which God calls and gifts from within each nation or people group or area for that express purpose.

1 The network welcomes those people, movements, organizations, churches and denominations to participate as long as they share a vision and a practical conviction for saturation church-planting. It appreciates and blends itself with other and similar networks, such as the World Evangelical Fellowship, AD2000, the Lausanne Movement etc.

2 Within the network, participants are encouraged to relate to each other as friends, not just formal colleagues. The core vision is to see the Kingdom of God extended through the multiplication of New Testament churches leading to the 'discipling of nations' (Mt. 28:18–20), not to see individual or organizational or denominational goals reached. There is no membership, rather a dynamic link system, within which every group or person defines the amount and quality of relationship or input he or she wants to give or receive.

3 Every participant brings a certain core competence to bear upon the task of saturation church-planting on a national or regional scale. This can be moral support, research, writing, intercessory, financial or administrative abilities, or any one of the fivefold ministries. Everyone is therefore encouraged to function within his or her God-given gifting and speciality to blend into an informal strategic partnership towards the spiritual transformation of a nation.